WHAT IS THE PRESENT?

What Is the Present?

MICHAEL NORTH

PRINCETON UNIVERSITY PRESS

PRINCETON & OXFORD

Copyright © 2018 by Princeton University Press

Published by Princeton University Press,
41 William Street, Princeton, New Jersey 08540

In the United Kingdom: Princeton University Press,
6 Oxford Street, Woodstock, Oxfordshire OX20 1TR

press.princeton.edu

Jacket design by Karl Spurzem

Images on pages 171 and 173: From *Here* by Richard McGuire, copyright © 2014
by Richard McGuire. Used by permission of Pantheon Books, an imprint of the
Knopf Doubleday Publishing Group, a division of Penguin Random House LLC,
and The Wylie Agency. All rights reserved. Any third party use of this material,
outside of this publication, is prohibited. Interested parties must apply directly
to Penguin Random House LLC and The Wylie Agency for permission.

All Rights Reserved

ISBN 978-0-691-17969-8

Library of Congress Control Number 2018935461

British Library Cataloging-in-Publication Data is available

This book has been composed in Arno Pro

Printed on acid-free paper ∞

Printed in the United States of America

10 9 8 7 6 5 4 3 2 1

CONTENTS

WHAT IS THE PRESENT?

Introduction

FOR MUCH OF the summer of 2014, a long stretch of Sunset Boulevard was lined with banners bearing the slogan "New.Art.Now" punched out in screaming red letters. These banners were advertising the second Biennial of the Hammer Museum, the actual title of which was the much less arresting phrase "Made in L.A." In fact, the punchy three-word come-on appearing so prominently on the banners was relatively absent from the catalog and other promotional materials surrounding the Biennial, as if the museum was a little embarrassed by its own boldness. But it is not hard to see why these three words would have appealed in the first place as the slogan for an exhibition of recent art. For "New Art Now" distills into three cheeky syllables what seems to be the easiest and most natural definition of contemporary art. *New* and *now* seem to be virtual synonyms, so closely are novelty and the present associated in any modern conception of time, and together they serve as a double synonym for the contemporary. All the art in any museum might be said to exist in the present, but only contemporary art is new right now.

However, the slogan is so obvious, its presentation so exaggerated, that it begins to seem less like a description and more like an ironic comment. For the word *now* has become so ubiquitous in the titles and slogans of recent art exhibitions that it threatens to displace the contemporary itself. Also in the summer of 2014, Prospect New Orleans, another contemporary biennial, chose for its third iteration the title *Notes for Now*; the Art Now Fair in Miami Beach announced its new season; and Galerie Perrotin in Paris showed the works of Daniel Arsham under the title *The Future Is Always Now*. Toward the end of the year, the Museum of Modern Art opened a new exhibition of contemporary painting under the title *The Forever Now*. In fact, such exhibitions have become so ubiquitous that Helen Molesworth has given them the general title "the 'what's new now' show."[1] Perhaps the Hammer Museum was hoping to wield its slogan as an ironic talisman against such criticism.

In any case, these exhibitions are vivid examples of a development Richard Meyer recently decried as "the rise of what might be called now-ism in art history."[2] Meyer is not just worried about titles or even exhibitions but about a general temporal myopia in the art world at large, what Pamela Lee has called, with similar anxiety, "creeping presentism."[3] The term *presentism* as Lee uses it no longer has its former technical meaning of judging the past by standards formed in the present, because it seems the past is not considered at all. According to Meyer, Lee, and many others, the contemporary, until fairly recently ignored by serious scholars of art, has grown in influence until it threatens to displace interest in all previous periods. Academic concentration on contemporary art is such that students planning dissertations no longer look very far even into the 20th century for their topics.[4]

Art critics and scholars are hardly alone in this anxious sense of a certain temporal narcissism. For quite some time now, it has been an article of faith that modern society in general is far too concentrated on the particular moment it happens to occupy. Modernity, by any definition, values the present over the past, and modernism is often taken to stand for "the autonomy of the present from the past and future."[5] Thus it is a commonplace that modern writers and thinkers, and perhaps modern people in general, have a concern for the immediate, for the now, that is different in kind from the version of that concern that may have prevailed in earlier times. It has also been suggested that in addition to thinking differently about the present, perhaps as a result of thinking about it so much, modern people have actually come to experience it in a new way. Beginning with Stephen Kern, who argues that there was a kind of "thickened present" prevalent at the turn of the 20th century, critics and scholars of modernism have identified in it a protracted or intensified version of the moment happening now.[6]

This same concentration on the present has been consistently identified as one of the hallmarks of the postmodern, despite its other differences from the period before. According to David Harvey, the postmodern lies at the end of a long process of acceleration and compression that has continued until "the present is all there is."[7] For Fredric Jameson as well, one of the classic features of the postmodern is "a dramatic and alarming shrinkage of existential time and the reduction to a present that hardly qualifies as such any longer."[8] For Jameson, the present defined by modernity still had a measure of value because it retained a certain content, but the present characteristic of the postmodern period no longer qualifies as such because it is empty and anonymous.

Whether the postmodern period is over or not, this version of the present still seems to subsist, for more recent criticism continues to echo these claims. Paul Virilio says almost exactly the same thing as Harvey, only twenty years later: "Past, present, and future contract in the omnipresent instant, just as the expanse of the terrestrial globe does these days in the excessive speed of the constant acceleration of our travels and our telecommunications."[9] Or, as Bernard Stiegler puts it, there is now "a permanent *present* at the core of the temporal flux."[10] For Stiegler, as for Virilio, this is a horrific situation, though the political import of a permanent present is not at all clear. Virilio's position, at least, is frankly reactionary, filled as it is with nostalgia for the *grands recits* of the past, the long lost "depth of time of the past and of long durations."[11] François Hartog also laments the way that "this present daily fabricates the past and future it requires, while privileging the immediate," and he finds symptoms of this temporal myopia everywhere, from "real time" technologies to the "Californian jogger."[12] One can only imagine what Hartog might have thought if he had followed one of these joggers down to Sunset Boulevard and found it lined with banners celebrating the now.

The present, by these accounts, is too much with us, and its ubiquity is not limited to the world of contemporary art shows but extends to encompass everything we do, all of it balanced on the head of the same pin. For all these vivid denunciations of the temporal domination of the present over other periods of time, however, it is not clear exactly how the present is supposed to have changed. In the years since Kern's influential study was published, it has become easy to assume that the present has been "thickened," which is apparently to say that it has become longer, annexing bits of the past and future around it. This would certainly seem to be the case in literary works like Virginia Woolf's *To the Lighthouse*, in which a relatively brief moment just before sundown of a particular day turns out to have in it vast tracts of narrated time. But Harvey and Jameson speak in terms of shrinkage and reduction, as if the ubiquity of the present were all the worse because it has become too brief. This is the condition also identified some time ago by Martin Heidegger, who famously complained about the loss of the present that occurs when people are pushed around by the demands of modern life.[13] In this analysis, the present has shrunk to the vanishing point, so that it seems even shorter than the instant ticked off by the clock. This theory could find abundant support in the literary and artistic awareness of the sudden that has come to be called the shock of the new.[14]

Thus the consensus that *something* has happened to the present is complicated by the lack of consensus about the nature of the change. Did the moment get longer and fuller, so that modern minds were seduced into a permanent present, or was it shortened and impoverished, so that people were ultimately banished from the present altogether? In either case, it makes sense to wonder what this new present is being compared to when it is said to have been lengthened or shrunk. Long or short in comparison to *what*? Locke once observed with some sadness that "since no two Portions of Succession can be brought together, it is impossible ever to know their Equality."[15] Leibniz, in his response to Locke's *Essay*, added the notion that "our measurement of time would be more accurate it we could keep a past day for comparison with days to come, as we keep measures of space."[16] Since we can't keep past presents around for comparison, though, it is hard to see how we might say with any certainty that the present has changed.

Literalizing the issue in this way raises other questions as well. Is the purported change in the present physiological in nature, or is it phenomenological, or perhaps sociological? Is it, as most recent theorists seem to say, a cultural change that comes to have intimately personal effects? For many recent critics, technology and the senses form a kind of feedback loop in which the speed and sensationalism of one excites an increased demand for rapid response in the other.[17] The present acquires a nervous shudder as it rushes past itself. For others, the technological need for speed actually provokes something like the opposite response, an attentive stillness in which the present comes to be fixed in time.[18] And other critics wonder, with some justice, if something like the human sensorium can actually change on such short notice.[19] A purely physiological change seems out of the question due to the disproportion between the time schemes of technological development, the human lifespan, and evolution. But even a general behavioral shift would seem to require more time than is available, unless the beginning of the transformation is dated back to something like the Renaissance.

It would be easier, then, to say, as many seem to do, that the change is really one of attitude, not physiology or phenomenology. People of the present, in this analysis, simply care too much about it, turning away from the past and the future. Some critics, like Richard Meyer, are more concerned that we have forgotten the past, others, like Marc Augé, that we no longer anticipate the future.[20] Both would agree, though, with Peter Osborne, who insists that the present has somehow lost its inherently threefold nature, deprived as it now is of past and future.[21] Arguments of this kind are frankly normative. A descriptive claim, that people in other times have cared more about the past and/or the future, becomes the normative demand that people in all times should care similarly for those periods of time. Even if the descriptive claim is true, though, it does not justify the normative demand, which does seem in some cases like an automatic conservatism.

In any case, the descriptive claim is not necessarily true. Recent discussions of the present seem to have forgotten the advice of Marcus Aurelius, perhaps the best-selling self-help author of all time, which is to "throw everything else aside, and hold on to these few things only and keep in mind that each of us only lives in the present, this brief moment of time."[22] This advice is echoed by fellow Stoics such as Seneca, who maintained that "the sage enjoys the present without depending on the future."[23] It might be fair to say, in fact, that this purposeful ignorance of past and future has been far more consistently influential than the threefold present that is sometimes assumed to be essential to human experience. The classic attitude itself, the calm self-sufficiency that the modern world found so intriguing in the ancient, is nothing more than this Stoic belief in the sufficiency of the moment. For Goethe, in fact, the sickness of modernity began when it lost "that splendid feeling of the present."[24] That feeling of happiness and freedom is achieved when the present is liberated from past and future and experience becomes unified in the moment. By many accounts, including that of Georg Lukács, loss of this unity is the tragic fate of a modern world cut off from its ancient happiness.

Often, though, when the current concentration on the present is discussed, the term is used in a more expansive sense to mean something more than the present moment, something like the present year or the general period of time in which we now live. When people are said to care too much about the present, their attention span is sometimes measured in months, not milliseconds. The time frame under discussion might be called the historical present, no matter how much that might seem a contradiction in terms. But the issues raised at this higher and more general level of time, the historical present, are not really much different from those that occur at the level of the experiential present, for the simple reason that the former is usually understood in terms of the latter. Here Osborne follows a common trajectory, taking the "phenomenological present" as a basic structure that the "historical present generalizes and complicates."[25] In fact, normative judgments about the historical present often rely for their authority on assumptions about human nature and its ostensibly inherent ways of processing time. What Paul Ricoeur has called the "living present" is often used as a standard of judgment at all timescales, despite Ricoeur's own doubt that it can serve as a model for any more general synchronizations of time.[26]

In any case, the essential unanswered questions are the same whether the present is measured in nanoseconds or years. What is this period in which we must center our experience and our lives? Does it have some necessary length or an optimal duration? If it is distinct in some inevitable way from the past and the future, how does it then come to be connected to them? In the presentation of its second Biennial, the Hammer Museum came up with some fairly terrifying answers to these questions. The website for the Biennial, for instance, featured a calendar in the form of a time-line. On this, the current date was marked by a fine ruled line as "Now," and everything below that line was designated "The Past," while everything above it was "The Future." Helpful sliding links were provided that allowed the time-traveler to "Scroll Up for the Future" and then quickly jump "Back to Now." According to this somewhat satirical device, the present is infinitely small, as fine as a geometric line, but also as long as a day. It is connected to past and future, but also ruled off from them by its very nature as a division in time. "Now" always means the same thing, but also always means something different, as those who tried to go back to the website later found out, when the now of the second Hammer Biennial had become the past.

Arguments about the present may therefore have had good reason to skip the fundamental step in which the term under discussion is defined, for it is not by any means easy to nail it down, and some of the very longest and most sophisticated analyses, including those of Edmund Husserl and Paul Ricoeur, have ended in deep skepticism. The most frequently quoted of all statements on time is also one of the oldest, Saint Augustine's hand-wringing confession that "I know well enough what it is, provided that nobody asks me," and this also turns out to be true of his long, fraught attempt to determine the nature of the present.[27] At the far end of history and in the opposite corner in intellectual sophistication is the insight of Mason Evans Jr., who decides after smoking dope at the end of Richard Linklater's *Boyhood*: "It's, like, it's always right now." And yet this simple stoned revelation is really no less mysterious or puzzling than Augustine's long disquisition. Critical commentary on the issues surrounding the present is inevitably hampered by the fact that experts from Augustine on have been far more impressed by the elusiveness of the term than by any of the definitions available.

It is tempting at this point to appeal to the sciences. Unfortunately, post-Newtonian physics has tended to undermine the very notion of a specially privileged slice of time called the present. Even before Einstein, Henri Poincaré had noted the apparent absurdity that occurs when an observer on Earth registers a burst of light from a distant star that had flamed into being many centuries before. Does it make sense, he wondered, to think of these two events, the birth of the star and the awareness of the observer, as simultaneous?[28] Einstein then made it clear that simultaneity, and therefore the present, is relative, so that the present is really a subjective concept, tied to a particular point of view. He once confessed to Rudolf Carnap that "the problem of the Now worried him seriously."[29] In this, he confessed his discomfort at having demolished a concept so fundamental to ordinary common sense. More recent developments in physics, however, have posed even more serious challenges to what seems commonsensical. In the quantum world, according to the physicist John G. Cramer, "the freezing of possibility into reality as the future becomes the present is not a plane at all, but a fractal-like surface that stitches back and forth between past and present, between present and future."[30] A present that is not really present at one point in time but at many, that does not make different points in space simultaneous but rather separates them, hardly deserves the name of present at all.

Even if modern physics has made it harder to rely on the idea of an objective present, it does seem to have left in place the subjective present, at least as the center of experiential time. As far back as Aristotle, the simultaneity of the senses, the fact that we can sense at once that an apple is both red and hard, sweet and fragrant, has been a basic physiological warrant for the integrity of the experiential present. In a way, it is a little too weak to say that the present is the time frame in which this happens, for Aristotle implies that the fact that it happens is our best evidence for the existence of the present itself. The present, in this analysis, is constituted by the synchronizing of our five senses into single experiences.[31] Aristotle is thus the first to discuss what has become notorious in philosophy and psychology as the "binding problem." Scientists in many fields would like to know just exactly how milk comes to be both white and sweet simultaneously and without division, though the two kinds of sense data are received by different sensors and carried via different pathways to different parts of the brain. All of this is complicated by the fact that even in the case of purely visual stimulus, different aspects of the input, such as shape and color, are processed at different rates.[32]

In fact, the convergence of all this data on a single point in time seems so fantastically difficult that a more parsimonious explanation has occurred to many scientists: it does not happen at all. Thus the editors of a recent collection of articles on this issue sum up the findings of several of their contributors by saying, "Just as there is no one place where 'it all comes together,' there is no one time where cotemporal events are simultaneously represented."[33] The present, in other words, is not the effect of a basic sensory simultaneity but just an experiential assumption by which we compensate for the essential asynchronicity of our sense data. So much of the phenomenological research on temporal experience depends on the idea that sense data do come to be synchronized that doubts about this basic fact of experience might threaten the whole project. As Ian Phillips puts it, "extant theories of temporal consciousness take the principle of simultaneous awareness as their point of departure. If we discard it, it is unclear why we need a philosophical theory of time consciousness at all."[34] By the same token, if simultaneous awareness is not a basic principle of human consciousness, it is hard to see how to sustain our commonsensical belief in the present as an inevitable subjective state.

The scientific evidence suggests, then, that "the present" is not a physical or physiological datum, to which our explanations and descriptions will become progressively more adequate as our investigations progress, but rather that it is a convention, imposed on a physical and physiological reality that is far more fluid. Kant maintains that the various parts of time, presumably including the present, are not empirical concepts derived from experience. Time itself is the precondition of experience, not something we think about but something we think with. This would explain why it is so hard to think about time, since doing so would be a little like trying to drive a nail with another nail. Therefore, when we try to think about time, Kant says, we inevitably resort to analogies.[35] The time-line is his example, and this would also suggest that the points on that line, the various presents it implies, are also analogies. Time is not a line, and it is not composed of points, but the inevitable limitations of empirical thought require that it rely on some such approximation.

Whether time is or is not an a priori condition of experience, Kant's sense that our thinking about time is inevitably analogical certainly seems to be borne out by the history of philosophy. The whole lifework of Henri Bergson was based on a conviction similar to Kant's, that whenever we try to think about time, we inevitably end up thinking in terms of space. More recently, the analytic philosopher David Cockburn has lamented the fact that whenever anyone tries to say anything serious about time, they end up "suggesting that it is really, at bottom, something else."[36] As far apart as they are in time and philosophical orientation, Bergson and Cockburn agree that this resort to "something else" is a mistake that prevents us from appreciating time as such.

If modern physics and biology are to be believed, however, there may be no "as such" about it, at least where the present is concerned. The present, that is to say, may just *be* an analogy, a figure by which we focus our understanding on the otherwise amorphous stuff of time.

At least this would help to explain why the history of thinking about the present is so liberally studded with vivid metaphors. One of the most famous of these comes from Husserl, who says there is "a comet's tail that attaches itself to the perception of the moment."[37] This is a powerfully subtle metaphor, insofar as the comet's literal tail seems to resemble the visual afterimage of a moving light source. Husserl thus uses the metaphor to argue that experience of the present spreads out in time, incorporating parts of the past and the future. William James's metaphor for the same phenomenon was the halo or fringe. The present, in other words, is imagined in visual terms, with a "vaguely vanishing backward and forward fringe."[38] James also had a jaunty Western metaphor for the same interdependence of past, present, and future: "a saddle-back, with a certain breadth of its own on which we sit perched, and from which we look in two directions into time."[39] This last may be a merely illustrative metaphor, but the comet and the glowing spark are much more, since the visual afterimage, which is itself a physiological phenomenon, serves as an example of a psychological process of retention otherwise buried too deep in the brain for direct inspection.

For the same reason, works of art have always had a privileged role in discussions of the present. This tradition starts with Augustine, when he puzzles over the psalm "Deus Creator omnium." Though he understands that some of the syllables of the psalm are long and some are short, he cannot fully understand how he can compare them if only one syllable can ever occur at any one time.[40] Thus the psalm exemplifies one of the basic problems posed by the very notion of the present: if moments come to us one by one, then how do we understand as wholes such things as musical phrases or sentences? Surely we feel that we sense these things *as wholes*, though they must inevitably stretch well beyond the bounds of any particular present. More recently, this issue is explored by means of an analogy between temporal consciousness and film. Cinema, according to Hollis Frampton, embodies "a philosophical fiction . . . that it is possible to view the indivisible flow of time as if it were composed of an infinite succession of discrete and perfectly static instants." As such, it mimics the "kineses and stases . . . of consciousness," the moment of perception, distinct from those around it and the larger arc of time always implied by such moments.[41] The fact that we see in film a whole arc of motion as a unit, despite the fact that it is actually nothing more than a series of individual still frames, serves as a powerful argument for the notion that consciousness does something similar with actual experience.

As Frampton says, though, this is a philosophical fiction, akin to metaphors like Augustine's psalm, Husserl's comet, or James's glowworm spark. As solutions to the puzzles of the present, though, they bear a heavy responsibility, for they may, in fact, exacerbate the very problems they were supposed to solve. These figures are supposed to resolve the basic conundrums of the present: how long is it; how can it be connected to the parts of time around it? Thus they tend to start with the assumption that the present must *be* connected because it is inherently solitary and separate. But if modern physics is correct, there is no real "now" in objective reality, and if current neural science is on the right track, then there may not be any reason to believe in a subjective present. Thus the very arguments that are meant to resolve these issues may keep them in play by offering new and more elaborate metaphors for something that is itself already a metaphor.

Some of the most basic assumptions that underpin current concern about the present—that it is too long or too short; that it must or should be connected to other discrete times around it—are therefore functions of a long history of metaphorical thinking about the nature of time. To find a way through these debates, then, it would first be necessary, before any empirical investigation, to understand the analogies on which the arguments have been modeled. The time-line so fundamental to pre-relativistic science, the three-part experiential present, and the historical period in which disparate events are felt to be simultaneous are all metaphorical structures that have determined what can be thought when the present is under consideration. The arts in particular must play a very important role, since thinkers so frequently call on songs, photographs, or other pictures to guide them through the present. Understanding the frameworks offered or imposed by these models is a first step toward judging where we really stand in relation to the time zone called the present.

Such an understanding would have implications well beyond the problem of "presentism" in art history or even in contemporary society at large. For example, the question of human identity has always depended on the extent to which human experience seems to be continuous. From Augustine on, this issue has been most consistently raised in discussions of memory. Without memory to link disparate experiences together, he is one of the first to argue, there would be no self-consciousness, and therefore mind and memory "are one and the same."[42] British empiricism, continental phenomenology, and contemporary analytic philosophy have largely agreed.[43] But it is fairly easy to see that the continuity of human experience depends primarily on the present, on the question that is frequently raised about the way in which we manage to perceive an extended sequence of moments as a single whole. How could we hope to understand the way in which a whole life is unified if we cannot understand the way in which a few moments come to be perceived as one? Whether this process involves memory or not, and what the implications are if it does, are among the most basic questions addressed by theorists of the present.

By the same token, the common post-structuralist argument against identity, based on the idea that the self is never coincident with itself, begins with a dispute about the present. As Maurice Merleau-Ponty puts it, "a thickness of duration already intervenes between myself who has just had this thought and myself who thinks that I have just had this thought, and I can always doubt whether that thought, which has already gone by, was really as I currently see it."[44] If experience is always spaced out in this way, then the self is continuously invaded by something else, and the sense of identity is nothing more than a salve against dispersal and confusion. Jacques Derrida based his career as an influential critic and philosopher on a similar conviction, phrased first as a critique of what he saw as Husserl's residual dependence on a punctual concept of the now. Resisting this version of the present is the first step for Derrida in questioning the crucial myth of the self-identical and with it the rest of western metaphysics: "We cannot raise suspicion about it [the now] without beginning to enucleate consciousness itself from an elsewhere of philosophy which takes away from discourse all possible security and every possible foundation."[45] Thus the twin notions of difference and deferral that were to be so influential in the last decades of the 20th century had their own beginnings, insofar as origin can be found for a refutation of the origin, in a philosophical and phenomenological argument about the present.

Because the present often seems so private, there wherever and whenever we are, as all else changes around us, it has a difficult involvement in theories of the social. Belief in what Robin Le Poidevin calls "the essential egocentricity of time" has run deep in the English tradition especially, where the fundamental presence of tenses in language seems to evince a basic human predilection for marking all time in relation to one solitary moment of it.[46] Fashioning some means of escape from the confines of egocentric time is therefore a major preoccupation of a large part of the contemporary literature on the problem of the present. For some philosophers in the continental tradition, though, the fundamental noncoincidence of the present with itself forms the basis of the relation with others. If, as Emmanuel Levinas puts it, the present is "a rip in the infinite beginningless and endless fabric of existing," then it is also, by definition, "departure from the self."[47] Displacing and expanding the present is therefore an essential part of Levinas's attempt to show that "time is not the achievement of an isolated and lone subject, but that it is the very relationship of the subject with the Other."[48] Levinas's ideas have such resonance because they confront a long tradition of empiricist philosophy in which the isolated moment and the isolated consciousness mutually define one another.

Some of the most fundamental ideas in aesthetic theory also depend on assumptions about the present. Well before G. E. Lessing made it formulaic in his essay on the *Laocoön*, the distinction between time arts, such as literature and music, and space arts, such as painting and sculpture, depended on the commonplace idea that any visual representation is confined to an instant. As E. H. Gombrich explained in a classic article first published in 1964, this meant that the entire set of options for understanding the present was rehearsed again within the context of aesthetic theory. Enlightenment art theorists such as James Harris and Anthony, Earl of Shaftesbury, insisted that painting always had to work within the experiential limit of a punctual instant, so that the clever painter had to exert all his talents to pack as much implication as possible into that unaccommodating sliver of time. But the conviction that, as Gombrich paraphrases it, "static signs . . . can only represent static moments"[49] leads not just to the endless frustration of painters, but also to logical and experiential absurdities. "As soon as we assume that there is a fraction of time in which there is no movement, movement as such becomes inexplicable."[50] This is just another way of registering one of the oldest objections to the mathematical instant, that time sliced into segments that contain no time has lost all its temporal qualities. In fact, Gombrich implies that photography originally came into being because of artistic frustration with the confines of the present, though of course the camera was, in the beginning, even more temporally confined than the eye. Whatever its merits as technological history, Gombrich's essay makes it clear that the representability of the present is a crucial issue for the traditional arts and their successors.

What is certain, in any case, is that the problems in defining the present are implicated in a great many other puzzles that preoccupy contemporary philosophy, neuroscience, psychology, history, and aesthetic theory. Thus it is necessary, in approaching the present, to take a very broad approach, including as many of the relevant disciplines as possible. The following chapters therefore touch on philosophy, historiography, the history of science, physio-logical psychology, aesthetics, narratology, film history, and film theory. There are bound to be gaps and thin spots in a survey so broad, but it is also possible that the interdisciplinary approach will yield results that could not have been achieved otherwise. In any case, one of the central ideas to emerge from this analysis is that theories of the present in science and philosophy have often relied on figurative models rather than empirical facts, so that to ignore the way the present has been imagined in art and literature would leave the story partial and incomplete.

The chapters to follow are grouped in two parts. The first of these considers models of the present as such, arranged by size. Thus the analysis starts in the first chapter with the very basic idea that the present is a point in time. One of the more influential and ubiquitous of all the models of the present, the point seems both intellectually inevitable and deeply counterintuitive. Attempts to define and explain the point-like present thus bring into the finest focus some of the most nagging questions about the present in general. Is it a part of time or a division in time? If it is a part, how much time does it contain? If it is a division, then how can it contain anything, even consciousness? The answers to these questions are surprisingly varied, and their differences are historically significant, since the point occupied by the present expands dramatically in the modern period, but without ceasing to be a point.

The notion that the present might be but a point was vigorously rejected by psychologists and phenomenologists, once these disciplines began to cohere in the 19th century, on the grounds that a dimensionless instant could not accommodate what we think of as temporal experience. The second chapter considers their alternative, which might be called the experiential present, an exceedingly brief stretch of time that coheres within itself while also constantly serving as a bridge between past and future. This version of the present is assumed to be an empirical fact and not just an intellectual idealization, like the point. But scientific attempts to determine the extent of this present ran into difficulties that were both practical and theoretical. Being able to measure it by way of scientific instrumentation seemed to substantiate its existence, and yet the measurements were distressingly variable, and there were serious questions about what exactly was being measured. All of this mattered because the present has always been placed at the center of consciousness in more ways than one. The coherence of different sensations in a particular moment has been the primary instance of the coherence of consciousness in general. To find this center of coherence, at least in temporal terms, was to find the mind itself, and by the same token, to bring the existence of the experiential present under suspicion was to cast doubt on the mind, at least in its role as general superintendent of sensation. The stakes are thus quite high in the researches that culminate in the theories of James and Husserl, though the explicit issue may only be the exact length of the present.

For many, though, the term *present* means something much longer than the eye-blink or the moment of reaction time, something like the contemporary period, the time zone in which we live. This temporal unit, which is sometimes called the historical present, is the subject of the third chapter. This version of the present is not only the longest but also the most purely normative. The very term implies that a certain version of the present, one including past and future in a historical configuration, has been a historical constant. Though this is also the norm on which so many criticisms of the contemporary present have been based, the actual evidence for it seems to be quite slim. In fact, a look at the history of timekeeping and calendars suggests that the ability of a society of any size to synchronize itself around a common time is a quite recent accomplishment. Perhaps, then, it is not so much changes in the present that provoke contemporary critics but the present itself, which may not be a primordial fact of human existence but a relatively recent development, the precondition for and also one of the self-reinforcing effects of a highly organized society.

If the theoretical basis and empirical evidence for these versions of the present—ideal, experiential, and social—is so questionable, then how has it become solidly lodged in our ideas about time? If the present is more a metaphor than a cosmological or experiential fact, then perhaps the answer is to be found in the arts. That, at any rate, is the starting point for the second part of this study, which is devoted to the role of the present in aesthetic theory and practice. The fourth chapter therefore starts with the idea that the present is actually to be found in pictures, or at least in the language conventionally applied to pictures of a certain kind. History painting, in particular, poses the problem of the present in graphic terms. How to tell a story within the temporal limits of a visual artform? The conventional answer to this question, that moments have in them references to before and after, was put under severe pressure by the invention of photography, especially instantaneous photography, which showed a great many moments that had no such references, that seemed illegible in their brevity. In any case, history painting is not to be thought of as the whole of painting, a more expansive examination of which will show the presence of presents that systematically violate the temporal standards of beauty set up by neoclassical aesthetic theory.

The questions raised by history painting, though, also recur in narrative theory, which is the subject of the fifth chapter. The present is both necessary to narrative, as the causal link between past and future, but also inimical to it, as the stillness that drags narrative to a halt. Thus the present has always been an irritant to narrative theory, and the present tense has been relegated to very specialized duties in narrative itself. Narrative also plays an important role in normative discussions outside literary criticism, since so many disciplines seem to think of human beings as necessarily narrative creatures. But the evidence for this, too, seems to be quite thin, and the testimony of at least some philosophers and linguists suggests that the tenses themselves are ex post facto constructions and not basic facts of human experience. Contemporary fiction written in the present thus poses a very complicated threat to narrative. By collapsing the apparently necessary difference between the time of the story and the time of its narration, such fiction exposes the inherently fictive nature of the temporal distinctions on which most narrative theory has been based.

The same issues can be looked at from the other side, as it were, in the case of film narrative, since film advertised itself from the first as taking place in the present. The sixth chapter takes up this claim and considers it in relation to still photography. But it also examines the tension that arises when the power of film to place its audience in the present is modified by the imposition of narrative constructions of the kind pioneered by D. W. Griffith. How is the simple now that Griffith celebrated as the particular tense of film modified when he starts to cut back and forth between different phases of the same action? The practice of cutting between parallel actions seems to send the film on a zigzag course through time, and the convention that successive actions are to be understood as happening simultaneously sets up an odd form of the present that can stretch and double back on itself. Finally, in films like *Intolerance*, the question of the present is raised in almost cosmic terms, as the film places before its audience a simultaneity that crosses over thousands of years. For Griffith, the basis of this simultaneity is religious, while for Christopher Nolan, whose time-traveling films strongly resemble *Intolerance*, the justification for the dislocations in narrative time finally comes down to the scientific theory of relativity, which now provides the intimations of eternity once found in God.

Though conclusions will be drawn throughout the discussion, a conclusion will also follow the six chapters, not a summary of the arguments but rather a kind of inventory of what remains after the dismissal of so much of what has passed for the present. What remains, in fact, does not seem particularly constrained or impoverished. In several of the preceding chapters, contemporary examples will have suggested that the present as it is now conceived is not shorter or narrower than it has been but rather much larger and more comprehensive. A brilliant example of this tendency in the present is to be found in Richard McGuire's graphic novel *Here*, which is also about now, the temporal counterpart of here. The present that emerges from McGuire's book is so vast and so intriguing in its complexities that it seems quite sufficient, even if it is the only part of time we have.

Taken together, these chapters might be considered an extensive answer to a question posed toward the end of his life by Michel Foucault. Teaching a course at the Collège de France on Kant's "Answering the Question: What Is Enlightenment?," Foucault began with an idiosyncratic take on this famous essay, rereading it as if it were not so much about autonomy as about the present. The "new question" that Kant introduces, Foucault says, "is the question of the present, of the contemporary moment. What is happening today? What is happening now? And what is this 'now' which we all inhabit, and which defines the moment in which I am writing?"[51] Foucault returned to "the question of the present" in an even later analysis of Kant's essay, one that he did not live to deliver. In both of these pieces, he defines modernity as a certain complex relation to the present. But it is also obvious to him that before that relationship can be understood, the present itself must be defined: "What is my present? What is the meaning of this present? And what am I doing when I speak of this present? Such is, it seems to me, the substance of this new interrogation on modernity."[52]

On one hand, then, Foucault seems to be asking for something like a history of the present, an account of how attitudes toward it have changed over time, and how those attitudes sharpened in some way around the time of Kant. On the other hand, though, he ends his essay by asking for an "ontology of the present, an ontology of ourselves," and he puts this question at the center of "a form of philosophy which, from Hegel to the Frankfurt School by way of Nietzsche and Max Weber, has founded a form of reflection within which I have tried to work."[53] As Vincent Descombes points out, it is not at all clear why Foucault insists on calling this project an ontology, when everything he says about it seems historical in nature.[54] But the difference between the historical and the properly philosophical seems to be marked for Foucault by the necessarily critical nature of the latter. Talking about the present in a merely descriptive way means accepting what people have had to say about it, while a more fundamental account of the present would have to take a step away to some critical distance from existing ideas about it. And this does imply having some idea of what the present is, as such, apart from any particular opinion about it.

The book to follow is in some sense a history of the present. It aims to survey as much as possible of what has been said and thought about this particular aspect of time. One of the things this history will establish is that the question of the present is a perennial one and not something that European philosophy woke up and discovered one day. This account in itself must tend to have a critical effect, since so many different things have been thought about the present in the course of human history. For all the time we have had to study this subject, which is never unavailable to us, it would seem we should have made more progress. But the analysis to follow also means to be critical in a sharper sense in that it finds most notions of the present to be fundamentally metaphorical. It ends, then, not as an ontology of the present but rather as the opposite. *Now*, it seems, is one of the words that fools us into believing it represents something real. The puzzles that have accumulated around it over the centuries are, therefore, not problems to be resolved but rather signals that the term itself might be dissolved.

At the same time, though, it is hardly possible to ignore so much history, so many generations in which the present has been taken for granted as the very bedrock of experience. Something must be there when we point with the word *now*. And it does turn out that in a number of unconventional ways, writers and artists have established their own practical ontology of the present. As forms of art, painting, narrative fiction, and film have to contend with the question of the present, since they have to represent it in some way. Thus the arts often make it hard to take the present for granted and in so doing establish a critical relation to it. The second part of this book will be an account of how this happens, how the arts necessarily contend with narrow conventions of the present and, in some cases, replace these with their own working definitions of that term. The second part of the book will therefore have a somewhat uncommon relation to the first part, since the arts will not be called upon to illustrate the ideas proposed by science and philosophy but rather to critique them.

The reason for doing all this has been explained quite effectively by Foucault. The questions he ventriloquized in the 1980s—What is happening today? What is happening now?—are even more insistently asked right now, as the issue of the contemporary comes to dominate conversations about art and politics. However, what might seem the necessary next question—What is this "now"?—does not seem to follow. A recent anthology on the problem of the contemporary promises what it calls "a vocabulary of the present," but the vocabulary it offers is almost all modifiers.[55] The present itself is apparently too fundamental to be included in the lexicon. To be sure, the editors of this collection are certainly right to assert that temporality as we now experience it is multiple and even contradictory. Wouldn't it be useful then to square this assertion with the otherwise unexamined notion that there is something called "the present"? All our conversations about the present seem so constrained because they are caught within the straitjacket of the concept itself. Perhaps the only way to step beyond the contemporary as a historical conundrum is to step outside the conceptual boundaries that convention has erected around the now.

Part One

1

This Point in Time

I

What is the present? The most obvious and natural answer to that question may be provided by a simple graphical representation: a point on a line. Time-lines like that used by the Hammer Museum for its second Biennial are common enough to suggest that they involve an inevitable metaphor, time as a linear progression from point to point. In principle, a point denotes position without regard to size, and therefore the increments into which a line is divided may stand for days, months, years, or even centuries. Though it is not uncommon to use the term *present* even for the very largest of these units, it is probably most natural to think of points as designating the smallest parts of time. The very concept of *punctuality* suggests that we think of temporal precision in terms of such points, measured as finely as possible. An aural equivalent is provided by the ticking of a clock, which can sound, under certain circumstances, like time itself steadily dripping away, bit by bit.

Expressing time in terms of such bits is a convenience and maybe even a necessity whenever it comes to synchronizing things. It is a habit that has also acquired a certain authority over the years. Kant, for one, thought that our inner sense of time itself has no shape, and thus we must resort to analogies, the most basic of which is the line, along which points would represent the fundamental relation of successiveness.[1] Aristotle, whose analysis of time in the *Physics* is the basis of most discussions to follow, frequently uses the phrase "point of time" when he means to speak of the smallest division of it.[2] The representation of time in terms of two-dimensional geometry is a feature of some of the most basic tools of modern science, including the Cartesian coordinate system, whenever time serves as one of the axes. In Newton's physics, time is divided into "temporal places," indivisible moments that correspond to geometric points, except that they are spatially invariable, as spatial points are temporally invariable.[3]

While geometric points might be useful in the representation of time in the abstract, they pose certain problems when it comes to time as it is experienced by human beings. In its purest form, the temporal point is a time period without any time in it, and this does not seem to afford much scope for experience. Even in Newton's day, philosophers differed as to whether time could be sensibly divided into moments without any extension.[4] Locke divided time into discrete, uniform instants arrayed, at least in principle, along a single line.[5] These instants were thus points in every respect except that they could be understood to have some dimension. Hume, however, argued that in space and time the least possible increments have no magnitude, so that the briefest moments of time are point-like in being unextended and nondimensional. These are recognized in experience by their successive relation to one another, not by virtue of their own temporal breadth.[6] This argument about points and time-lines has never really died down. In the 20th century, Henri Bergson argued on one side that the geometric metaphor is fatal to any real understanding of time, while Gaston Bachelard argued on the other that "duration is made up of durationless instants, just as a straight line is made up of dimensionless points."[7]

The notion of "durationless instants" does have a few logical arguments in its favor. Hume's contention that the smallest imaginable increments of anything cannot possibly have any magnitude is one of these. Aristotle used another such argument when he pointed out that a now with some dimension to it will be divisible into parts, some of which will be past in relation to others, so that the present will turn out to have another time-line within it and not be the present at all.[8] One of the oldest and still most influential definitions of the present, that of Saint Augustine, begins with this inevitable and yet counterintuitive idea of a moment in time that takes up no time: "In fact, the only time that can be called present is an instant, if we can conceive of such, that cannot be divided into even the most minute fractions, and a point of time as small as this passes so rapidly from the future to the past that its duration is without length."[9] By Augustine's reasoning, the present moment must be indivisible and dimensionless, since if it had dimension it would then contain within it past and future and no longer remain simply the present.

Though Augustine's reasoning seems sound, it has left behind it a number of logical problems. Kant was to insist rather stoutly that "any part of time is a time," and thus it would seem that any moment must itself occupy some time.[10] There is an elementary inconsistency, in other words, in dividing time up into instants that themselves take up no time. How could any series of such temporal zeroes add up to a positive amount? In any case, how could anything happen in a dimensionless instant? What sort of experience could exist in a temporal space so small it can include no change? As Aristotle had insisted long before, "if there is in the time-continuum a time so small as to be absolutely imperceptible, then it is clear that a person would, during such a time, be unaware of his own existence, as well as of his seeing and perceiving."[11]

Aristotle put a great deal of effort into redefining the now so as to avoid these logical absurdities. He notes that a line is not really made up of points but rather is infinitely divisible by them. Points, that is to say, are not uniform stations situated along a line, like beads on a string. Between any two points on a line there are as many more points as anyone might care to mark. The line, in other words, is a continuum and, as such, is infinitely divisible.[12] The point on the time-line we call the present is, therefore, not a part of time but a limit to it, more like a cut or division than a discrete bit. As such, it is itself indivisible and dimensionless, and so it does not contain any time within it.[13] An important benefit of this redefinition for Aristotle is that it helps to refute the reasoning behind the famous paradoxes of Zeno, some of which derive their power from a conception of time as composed of indivisible parts. Zeno contends that a flying arrow must always be in one of these parts and, while in it, must be at rest. Therefore, the arrow can never hit its target, since it must always be in one of these parts. Aristotle responds that "time is not composed of indivisible nows any more than any other magnitude is composed of indivisibles."[14] Time is not composed of nows but is a continuous magnitude divided in two by a particular now.

Though this solution may have dispelled some of the intellectual tension that had built up around the paradoxes of Zeno, it also created some problems of its own. If we agree with Aristotle that time is not composed of nows, we may then wonder exactly what it *is* composed of. And if we agree that the now is not a part of time, we may rightly wonder what, if anything, it *is* a part of.[15] Does it make sense to think of the present as radically distinct from the time around it, from which it seems to emerge and into which it seems to blend? Aristotle frequently speaks of nows in the plural. In fact, all the comparative measurement that goes on in this section of the *Physics*, all the reasoning about time AB as opposed to time CD, depends on the possibility of simultaneous yet different nows, for that is what a division in time is by definition.[16] The now could hardly be used to count up time if it were unique and singular. In the midst of one of these discussions, Aristotle remarks that "the nows are infinite in number," but here he must be speaking about potential nows because otherwise this would seem to contradict the dictum that time is not composed of nows.[17] But this passing comment threatens to expose some unresolved issues in Aristotle's account of the present. Is the now singular and in contrast to the rest of time in its indivisibility and lack of dimension, or is it multiple and therefore somehow part of the continuous time it delimits?

Everything Aristotle says about the now suggests that he would not answer but reject these questions. For him, the now is the sort of limit that is both a division and a connection at once. As a divisor, it is unique and "always different," as he puts it.[18] This seems to mean that it is always different from itself, as each now is a new now, and also always different from the time it delimits, which is continuous. As a connector, though, the now is "always the same," by which he seems to mean that it is always the same now but also always a part of the time it connects.[19] As Wolfgang von Leyden puts it, the now is presented as if it were a sort of unit and also the repetition of that unit in a series.[20] One way of bridging this gap between the unit and its repetition in a series would be to imagine the now as constantly and steadily in motion. Though Aristotle quite clearly insists that there can be no motion *within* the present, since there is no dimension there for motion to occupy, he is less clear about the possibility that the now may itself be *in* motion. Thus Richard Sorabji complains that Aristotle speaks indistinctly of two different nows, one that moves and one that stays put.[21] The one that stays put might be compared to a geometrical point, which stays in the place it denotes because it is identical to it, while the moving now is always shifting to a different place in time.

In fact, Aristotle's comments on the now are inconsistent enough to raise the suspicion that he actually has two different nows between which he finds it impossible to decide. One of these, which might be called the instant, is fundamental to his basic association of time with number. When he defines time as "the number of motion in respect of 'before' and 'after,'" Aristotle makes counting essential to any sense of time. Counting, in turn, depends on the sort of distinction marked by a static now.[22] For this reason, the present is very much more than a part of time. It is, in a sense, the very basis of time, not just the standpoint from which we perceive it but also the fixed point that allows us to count and thus to establish its very existence.[23] For this purpose, though, the now must be instantaneous, without any temporal dimension of its own. If a point in time is to serve as a limit to some interval, it can hardly be an interval itself.[24] By the same token, the position of the now is arbitrary. It might be situated at any place along the time-line. As Paul Ricoeur puts it, "this break can be made anywhere. Any instant at all is equally worthy of being the present."[25] All the infinite instants arrayed along the time-line are identical, at least in the purely negative sense that they have no characteristics, as they have no dimension. Though Aristotle identifies time with number, his time-line is a bit like a ruler from which all the numbers have been erased.

The problem with the instant, then, is not just that it is short but, more importantly, that it is not unique. What we ordinarily think of as the present is not just *a* point in time but *this* point in time. The relations of before and after might obtain between any two points on a time-line, but the relations of past and future only make sense in relation to the point occupied right *now*. Of course, a great many arguments have grown up over the ages about these issues. J. E. McTaggart argued, for example, that the relations of before and after are fundamental and unchangeable, since Caesar's birth will always come before his death, for all eternity, while the relations of past, present, and future are but stages that any moment can occupy only temporarily.[26] One problem with this solution is that it does without the present altogether and thus asks us to give up the idea that there is something particular about the part of time we currently occupy. That sense of the particularity and uniqueness of the present has been very hard to relinquish.

This tension between the arbitrary instant and the unique present has sometimes been described as a contest between cosmological and experiential time, between objective and subjective definitions of it.[27] But Aristotle makes it quite clear that the sort of reckoning on which he rests his definition of time can only occur within some human consciousness. Counting, he says, cannot exist without someone to do the counting.[28] The instant, in other words, is a mental construction. If so, though, it is a particularly ideal mental construction, unlike anything found in nature or, for that matter, in ordinary human experience. As Aristotle says himself, a part of time with no time in it affords no scope for experience or even for self-awareness.[29] The tension, then, is between two different human conceptions: an ideal instant, postulated but not actually experienced, and the sort of present that is more or less identical to human experience itself. The instant is a device that allows Aristotle to resolve many of the logical problems that had vitiated previous thought about the present, but in the process, it removes much of what made the present worth thinking about in the first place.

II

Aristotle defines time as that which can be counted, but this is certainly not the only way in which the ancients imagined time, nor is counting the only kind of measure. In the *Statesman*, Plato divides the art of measurement into two parts, "positing as one part all those sorts of expertise that measure the number, lengths, depths, breadths, and speeds of things in relation to what is opposed to them, and as the other, all those that measure in relation to what is in due measure, what is fitting, the right moment, what is as it ought to be—everything that removes itself from the extremes to the middle."[30] Here Plato seems to be establishing a distinction between quantity and quality, measure by the reckoning of sums and differences and measure by comparison to a norm.[31] It is the difference between having *an* amount of something and having the *right* amount, the difference between any random moment in time and the *right* moment.

The word translated here as "the right moment" is *kairos*, a term that has had a significant influence in discussions of the present. Plato's discussion makes clear the original meaning of *kairos*, which is something like "due measure."[32] Originally, it had no particular temporal connotations but meant "the right amount" in general. By Plato's time, it had acquired a temporal meaning among its others, and Aristotle also uses it in the same sense, though it is significantly absent from the discussion of time in the *Physics*.[33] Gradually it came to mean not just the right time but also a very short time, and in that form, it offered a very powerful antidote to Aristotle's instantaneous now.

Kairos, in its adjectival form, was first used to denote a very small space, particularly a flaw in a piece of armor, a usage unique to Homer.[34] Gradually, it comes to be used in a figurative sense to denote any small but crucial amount, rather like the straw that breaks the camel's back.[35] When it came to be applied to time, therefore, it tended to mean a very short but crucial amount of time. An ancient statue of *Kairos*, attributed to Lyssipus, holds a knife to show how he cuts time into brief but potent slices.[36] Almost inevitably, this short but crucial moment in time came to be identified with the present, though this was a present considerably different from the one defined in Aristotle's *Physics*.

In Thucydides and the Greek tragedians, *kairos* could have negative or positive connotations, as a moment of crisis or of opportunity.[37] It is the turning point or moment of decision. So *kairos* is not just the right or appropriate time but also the time at which the protagonist must act correctly, *be* right.

In *Oedipus Tyrannus*, the protagonist challenges his daughters "always to live at the point of *kairos*," which is to say at that point of moderation between extremes that he had failed to attain himself.[38] The implication here is that living at the point of *kairos* is a constant balancing act, a constant striving to avoid extremes and live in the right way. In fact, it does not seem that the right is a way at all but a point, so fine is the balance between alternatives. The right, then, is not so much a particular value as a recipe, a formal description of what the right must look like. It looks a lot like the instant, since it is clearly a temporal point of very limited extent, but it differs from the instant in crucial respects. For it is unique, even if it happens more than once, and it is important, as full of significance as it is of value.

Kairos also escapes from the temporal limitations of the instant, perhaps because it is associated with value, which, for the Greeks at least, was timeless. In the *Philebus*, the *kairos* is bestowed by "eternal nature" on humankind so that it might be able to distinguish between the temporary and the lasting.[39] To make this kind of discrimination is, in the tragedies at least, the work of a moment, but making the decision correctly involves ignoring the temporary and local in favor of the eternal and universal. Perhaps for this reason, *kairos* came to be associated with *aion*, or eternity.[40] This is not as impossible as it might sound, for *aion* is a kind of time that is not measured because it is present all at once.[41] In this sense, it converges on *kairos*, concentrating its eternal nature on a single point as *kairos* expands its minimal extent to touch on the eternal. Without too much trouble, then, *kairos* might be seen as eternity itself compacted into an instant.

It has been common for some time, therefore, to juxtapose *kairos* to *chronos* as if these two different Greek words exemplified two different understandings of time, the first an eternity compacted into a certain crucial moment, the second the dull, stately plodding of ordinary linear time. Frank Kermode's *The Sense of an Ending* is an especially influential example, in which *kairos* comes to designate virtually any kind of narrative emphasis, as opposed to the flat uniformity of chronicle.[42] Kermode admits that James Barr had already exploded the notion that these two words were used as precise alternatives and with that analysis had undermined the idea that they somehow stand for rival conceptions of time.[43] But it is not necessary to hypostasize these words to see that *kairos* offers a distinct alternative to Aristotle's definition of the present. Plato, it will be remembered, uses *kairos* in precisely this way, in contrast to the kind of measuring that is fundamental to chronological time. This is a habit that grew ever stronger in the Christian era.

It was already common for Latin writers to draw a distinction between *tempus generale*, a dated and measured time, akin to *chronos*, and *tempus speciale*, an unpredictable but auspicious time, akin to *kairos*.[44] Augustine and Jerome both refer to this distinction, using the Greek terms.[45] But it is the New Testament, as Kermode says, that is responsible for the sense in later ages that there is a kind of time, an auspicious moment, apart from the ordinary course of everyday time. The prototype for this moment is perhaps the conversion of Saint Paul, which occurs when a light appears "suddenly" on the road to Damascus and then "immediately" when the scales are made to fall from his eyes.[46] Thus the Pauline epistles are full of references to auspicious, fruitful, or appropriate moments, at which everything promises to change, as at II Corinthians 6:2: "Behold, now is the acceptable time (*nun kairos euprosdektos*); now is the day of salvation."[47] Though it might be said that *kairos* has come to mean *time* in a very general sense, so that it needs the modifying adjective in order to keep the normative sense that was implicit in prior times, the constant use of *kairos* in such contexts helps to give the sudden and unexpected moment a strong normative charge. The New Testament constantly testifies to a sense of the present as the unexpected moment in which the chance to be right will be presented to one and all.

By the time of the New Testament, then, Aristotle's instant had been supplemented by an entirely different model of the present, one that not only preserved but accentuated its significance as a unique point in time. Though the Christian *kairos* was a normative measure, as the ancient *kairos* had been, it was normative in an entirely different way. For the ancient *kairos* denoted a norm currently in existence, while the Christian *kairos* pointed to a norm not of this time. This is true not just because the Christianity of Paul's time was an insurgent movement but also because its ultimate standards were referred to a day of judgment promised for the future. In its very structure, the *kairos* that Plato describes is a conservative measure, finding its very existence in the avoidance of extremes. Though the Christian *kairos* is more or less the same shape and size, it is more like a point of leverage than a point of balance, and thus the emphasis in its usage is always on the possibility of change, not stasis. The Christian *kairos*, then, is revolutionary and not conservative. What this means in terms of time is that the Christian *kairos* is a time out of time, a prefiguration of a time to come. This present is a sort of door always standing open, waiting for us to step through, into eternity. As such, this model of the present was readily available to later ages when they needed to express their impatience with the ordinary accounting of time.

III

Though the difference between the instant, as explained by Aristotle, and the unique and significant present of the New Testament is a historical and cultural difference, it might also seem to have a certain formal necessity. For Aristotle's instant is basic to quantification and as such can have no dimension, indeed no characteristics, of its own, except uniformity. Like other uniform units of measure, it exists only so that we can estimate other things. It has no intrinsic value and is indifferent to the quality of what it measures. The present proclaimed in the New Testament, on the other hand, is unique and thus is useless to any kind of counting, any quantification. The difference it enjoys is thus qualitative. The instant, though brief, is at least multiple, while the present, equally brief, is solitary but deep.

In the end, the difference between these two models may involve nothing more than a necessary choice between incompatible characteristics. The now seems both unique and multiple. It is always with us and also always gone. There is too little time within it for anything to happen, and yet if this is true, then it would seem that nothing can ever happen. Aristotle makes a particularly Aristotelian choice from among these unhappy alternatives, in favor of a now that is uniform, multiple, dimensionless, and thus conducive to measurement. Saint Paul, for instance, makes another choice, opting for a now that is unique and full of significance. Obviously, there are all sorts of empirical reasons for such choices, but they are not made from an infinite array of possibilities. This is why the same models tend to recur across the centuries, although it is also certainly the case that the prestige of Aristotle or Saint Paul helps to ensure the survival of their models. In fact, given enough time, these models cease to be mere alternatives and come to be active antagonists.

Kermode may be wrong to suggest that the words *chronos* and *kairos* represent alternative Greek conceptions of time, but if so, he is merely reading back into history an opposition that is fundamental to modernity. On one hand, modernity means science as opposed to superstition, and science is inconceivable without abstract standards of measurement. On the other hand, modernity means, more or less literally, the new, the unexpected, the unprecedented. Modern time is uniformly measured time, the same everywhere, as the abstract uniformity of Newtonian space-time is brought down to earth and made practical. But modern time is also the time of revolutions, of moments wrenched out of continuity at which everything changes. Perhaps this is true of all ages, for the choice between continuity and change must always be inevitable and difficult, but if so, the modern period seems to have made a particular issue of its inability to choose.

Early on in the modern period, then, the question of the present becomes a contest, fought out in the form of an opposition between the calculated, uniform instant and the unique, significant now. As before, these are both points in time, but beyond that they are in utter opposition. A pertinent example is offered by Kierkegaard, who devotes a lengthy footnote in *The Concept of Anxiety* to the instant, as it is described in Plato's *Parmenides*. The problem for Kierkegaard is that the instant "remains a silent atomistic abstraction."[48] Its lack of temporal dimension means that it is featureless and empty, good only for delimiting one time from another. As for an alternative, Kierkegaard maintains that "it is only with Christianity that sensuousness, temporality, and the instant are to be understood, because only here does eternity become essential."[49] With Christianity, in other words, the present enjoys a qualitative existence, full of meaning and thus potentially eternal. Here Kierkegaard's philosophical quarrel is with the Greeks, but his practical quarrel is with the temporal organization of his own time: "Life has at present more than ever the appearance of a transitory and fleeting moment. But instead of learning from this how to grasp the eternal, in chasing the moment one learns only how to pester oneself, one's neighbors, and the moment too, to death."[50] Kierkegaard thus offers one of the earliest and most influential versions of the argument that has become so familiar, to the effect that something has gone wrong with the present.

Just a few years after *The Concept of Anxiety* was published in 1844, Marx made the same point in a more practical way. Under the conditions of modern industrial capitalism, he says, "men are effaced by their labour; . . . the pendulum of the clock has become as accurate a measure of the relative activity of two workers as it is of the speed of two locomotives. . . . Time is everything, man is nothing; he is at the most, time's carcase. Quality no longer matters. Quantity alone decides everything; hour for hour, day for day . . ."[51] Decades later, this would become a key passage for Georg Lukács, who rails against the way in which industry transforms time into "abstract, exactly measurable physical space" and thus robs it of its "qualitative, variable, flowing nature."[52] Though Marx's analysis is more pointed that Kierkegaard's, they seem to agree that the conditions of modernized life have brought about an atomization of time into meaningless, uniform units that have none of the actual qualities for which time is valued. The alternative to this meaningless instant is an alternative form of the present, the moment of religious revelation and catharsis for Kierkegaard, the moment of revolution for Marx.

Kierkegaard was particularly devoted to another model of this present, syn-onymous with *kairos* and derived from the same parts of the New Testament. As he puts it in *The Concept of Anxiety*: "The New Testament has a poetic para-phrase of the instant. Paul says that the world will perish [in a moment and the twinkling of an eye]" (I Corinthians 15:52).[53] Kierkegaard was particularly taken with this metaphor, which seemed to give a kind of homely reality to the tempo-ral paradox of the *kairos*: "Nothing is as swift as a twinkling of the eye, and yet it is commensurate with the content of the eternal."[54] The *øjeblik*, or eye-blink, is itself paradoxical, since it suggests a type of experience that cannot be expe-rienced, a kind of time that seems instantaneous because it passes only when our eyes are closed. The eye-blink takes up no time because we are insensible to time for the instant of its occurrence, but for that very reason it can contain any amount of time at all. Thus it represents an ever-present possibility of transcen-dence, a door to eternity that might open unexpectedly at any moment.

For Kierkegaard, this transcendence gives the eye-blink the normative force that *kairos* had had from ancient times. Late in his life, he published a journal called *Øjeblik*, in which the eye-blink was celebrated as a moment of ethical choice.[55] If this journal was written in favor of one version of the present, it was also vehemently against another, what Kierkegaard called the "God-forsaken moment," in which most people seemed to spend their time. It was a polemic against the mere instant, quantitative, repetitive, without character. To live in this moment, he made it clear, was not just mistaken but sinful. "Just as the road to hell is paved with good intentions," he warns, "so is eternity destroyed by sheer moments." And he concludes, "that person sins who lives only in the instant as abstracted from the eternal."[56] Just as the *kairos* is the right moment, commitment to it makes one right, as a lazy repose in the repetitive world of instants makes one wrong.

European philosophy after Kierkegaard repeatedly confronts this choice between the good and the bad present. This choice is fundamental to the work of Heidegger, for example. In *The Basic Problems of Phenomenology*, he replays in great detail Aristotle's analysis of the now in the *Physics*, concluding that "Aristotle's definition of time is only the *initial approach* to the interpreta-tion of time."[57] The problem with Aristotle's definition, which for Heidegger is also the common definition, is that it makes time into a mere sequence of nows, multiplying the present and thus depriving it of its most essential characteristics. Among these, Heidegger puts particular emphasis on "signifi-cance and datability," or, in other words, on the meaningful uniqueness of the present.[58] The argument is rehearsed as well in *Being and Time*, where "the vulgar understanding of time" is said to limit itself to "the sheer now, cut off in its complete structure, that is called the 'present.'" What this vulgar understanding cuts itself off from is the authentic temporality of "*this now*."[59] Thus Heidegger draws his own distinction between the multiple, countable nows fundamental to Aristotle's definition of time and the single, significant now in which human experience seems to reside.

Like Kierkegaard, Heidegger identifies this second now with an instant of ethical choice. In *The Basic Problems of Phenomenology*, he expressly names the *kairos* as the principle missing from Aristotle's account of the now.[60] What Heidegger particularly values in the ancient concept of *kairos* is its bias, as a moment of decision, toward the future, because this, for him, is what makes the dull conventional now into a real present. Where Kierkegaard finds an opening to the eternal, Heidegger finds an intimation of the future and with it a tendency that takes the isolated present out of itself and gives it meaning.[61] In its own way, then, Heidegger's version of the authentic present is just as normative as Kierkegaard's, though it has lost most of its Christian vestments. Those who live in the vulgar time of successive nows lapse into repetition, while those, probably few, who respond to the challenge of the authentic present will lead us into the future.[62]

These distinctions reappear in Walter Benjamin's theses "On the Philosophy of History," for which he adapts a term, *Jetztzeit*, to designate the authentic present. *Jetztzeit*, which could be rendered in English as "now-time," is opposed in Benjamin's theses to the "empty, homogeneous time" of ordinary life. As such an alternative, it has all the characteristics of *kairos*: it is a decisive break in the continuity of time, one that rescues the present from its own redundancy and makes it unique.[63] Blasting the present free of the continuity of time, as Benjamin puts it, also gives it a significance it cannot have as one moment among many others. To some extent, this significance is historical and political, and to some extent it is religious. Benjamin maintains that the *Jetztzeit* contains "splinters of messianic time." Whether this is to be understood in a purely theological context or not is hotly debated,[64] but, in any case, it is clear that this privileged version of the present carries with it the same sort of normative force that had attached to the *kairos* from ancient times.

M. H. Abrams made it clear some years ago that versions of this moment blasted out of the continuum around it are a constant feature of Romantic and post-Romantic philosophy and literature. His examples extend back to early German Romantics such as Schelling, who identified a moment that "sets absolute eternity into the middle of time," and Hölderlin, who celebrated particular moments "in which the imperishable is present in us."[65] Abrams also lays out the literary heritage that follows this philosophy. Wordsworth is his primary example, with his "spots of time," but also Blake and Shelley.[66] He even continues this story as far as the Beats.[67] A key figure in the transition from the Romantics to the 20th century is Walter Pater, who has such a pathetic consciousness of the impossibly point-like nature of the present, "a single moment, gone while we try to apprehend it, of which it may ever more truly be said that it has ceased to be than that it is."[68] Pater's response to the awful flight of time, of course, is to seize the moment and by sheer concentration make it yield in intensity what it lacks in extent. In this, he seems a perfect example of the Romantic tendency, as visible in Marx as in himself, that Isaiah Berlin once called "this violent revolt of, as we might put it, quality against quantity."[69] In terms of time, this means a revulsion from repetition and regularity, from the dullness of clock-time, even a deliberate sacrifice of temporal breadth, in favor of the singular present, which we know is genuine because it is unique.

Perhaps the best and most commonly cited example of this tendency in the modern period is Virginia Woolf. At the beginning of her essay "The Moment: Summer's Night," Woolf asks, "Yet what composed the present moment? If you are young, the future lies upon the present, like a piece of glass, making it tremble and quiver. If you are old, the past lies upon the present, like a thick glass, making it waver, distorting it. All the same, everybody believes that the present is something, seeks out the different elements in this situation in order to compose the truth of it, the whole of it."[70] The implication here is that the present is never seen for what it is, for itself without the interposition of past or future, and thus the whole of it never appears. At the end of the essay, this almost happens as the pace quickens and a moment of "terror," of "exultation," almost occurs. But the reality of the quotidian reasserts itself, and the essay ends with the closure of routine, as the garden party and the essay both pack up their belongings and go inside.[71]

The result is different in the famous essay by Woolf called "A Sketch of the Past." Here, too, most days are said to consist primarily of "non-being," in which life is wrapped in "a kind of nondescript cotton wool." On a few occasions, though, there is "a sudden violent shock," a moment in which the ordinary continuity of time fails and one cannot progress but must hang, suspended. For the most part, these are horrible moments for Woolf, who is recounting her own experiences in the essay, but in one case, this shock is not "simply a blow from an enemy hidden behind the cotton wool of daily life; it is or will become a revelation of some order." At such times, the conviction arises that there is "some real thing behind appearances," that behind the cotton wool is "hidden a pattern." In other words, such moments provide access to the real itself, which is stable and orderly, unlike the moiling obscure nonsense of the everyday. This seems to be the whole truth where the present is concerned, that it is a point of access to something beyond it, something that is also present but in a different sense in that it is timeless. That eternal present is always there, only obscured by the false, repetitive present that stands in the way of our enlightenment.[72] Who would not willingly sacrifice any stretch of false presents for sight of the true one in its vivid singularity?

For this is one of the basic truths about the kairotic present that exerts such an influence in the modern period, that it does not actually stand on its own but exists only in contradistinction to that other present, the repeated, nondescript instant that Aristotle thought was the necessary vantage point on time. The fact that the authentic present is rarely defined except in opposition to its quotidian counterpart raises the further suspicion that it is nothing but an inversion, its characteristics point-for-point reversals of the troubling, illogical features that have always, almost from the beginning, made the present impossible to fathom. Thus the common but somewhat odd rhetorical habit of defining the full, significant present only in negative terms, as the opposite of its counterpart. For example, Kierkegaard says, "the instant is not properly an atom of time but an atom of eternity."[73] Karl Jaspers uses a similar formula: "The atom of time is of course nothing, but the instant is everything."[74] Thus the unique present somehow comes to depend for its existence on the multitude of false instants around it. We come to sense its fullness only within the prevailing emptiness, as Woolf comes to sense her moments of being as openings in the dullness of the cotton wool. But there is more at work here than a definition by contrast, for the very same attributes that make the instant nugatory also give the present its positive force. The fact that the present is infinitesimal, virtually nothing, for example, is the inverted evidence for its plenitude, its eternity. This is the structure of paradox, of course, and time is nothing if not paradoxical, but this itself raises the possibility that the modern present is not an alternative to the instant but simply a restatement of it in more palatable terms.

IV

On the surface, Aristotle's instant and the present deified by modern writers and philosophers seem to share only one quality: their point-like size. The Aristotelian time-point is multiple, quantitative, and repetitive, while the alternative is unique, qualitative, and singular. The first is merely descriptive, and the second is prescriptive or normative. The first is actual, as it serves to count out time in useful ways, while the second is authentic, which is to say that even if it does not occur, it has a certain force and presence as a value. Life in a time measured by instants is essentially passive, since there is nothing we can do to change the way they march on, whereas the authentic present requires active commitment from us if it is to happen at all. Change in a time of instants is incremental, piecemeal, while the change particular to *kairos* is total and thus potentially violent. Considered more closely, though, these apparent opposites start to look like twins.[75]

One of the ancient, abiding choices where time is concerned is between continuity and discontinuity. Aristotle arrives at his definition of the now by starting from the assumption that time is continuous. A few modern philosophers, among them Bachelard and George Herbert Mead, have suggested the exact opposite, that time is radically discontinuous, so that it is renewed at every tick of the clock. For the most part, though, philosophers following from Kierkegaard and writers such as Woolf seem to imagine a time that is mostly continuous but with random episodes of breakage. The suddenness and abruptness that characterize *kairos* could hardly be sustained if very many moments were to have these characteristics.

For Kierkegaard, though, this break in continuity is actually the occasion for another kind of continuity, that which is accomplished by a leap: "Between these two moments lies the leap, which no science has explained and which no science can explain."[76] In other words, the cut is also a join, and anyone asking how this happens is simply wasting their breath. Jaspers and Heidegger also speak of this leap across the empty space opened up in time.[77] For Benjamin, it is "the dialectical leap Marx understood as revolution."[78] One of the negative moments of being in Woolf's essay is an episode in which she found it impossible to step past an apple tree that was somehow associated with the suicide of a neighbor.[79] But Woolf does not transform this hiatus into a leap, and thus it leaves her stranded in despair. For Kierkegaard, on the other hand, the hiatus is an opportunity because it signifies a lapse in logic as well as a gap in time. Without logic clogging its heels, faith takes wings and leaps across the gap. The leap, then, is a sort of figure for itself, for the way in which figurative thinking takes him over the steps missing in logic. This otherwise unfortunate lapse in time is also a happy fault, a fortunate fall, because it offers the occasion for a continuity much more significant than that postulated as a constant condition of temporality. The very fact that the continuity achieved by the leap is less common, since it is somewhat episodic, means that it is of a higher and purer kind.

From Zeno's paradoxes on, the issue of temporal continuity has also been associated with the problem of change. Aristotle thought that by making time continuous he had protected it from Zeno's mischief, which was aimed at showing that change is illusory and nothing really happens. Bachelard, for one, insisted on the exact opposite, that all change depends on a discontinuity in time.[80] Kierkegaard and Heidegger apparently felt much the same way, so that they saw ordinary, incremental change as no change at all, leaving seismic stresses to build up over time until they rupture. Then the change is total.[81] In one sense, then, the difference between stasis and change is absolute, as the transition between them is instantaneous. In another sense, though, that caesura between times, that pause, is indispensable to the totality it promises. Only when time stops is it free to change utterly. Thus, in a way, the stoppage of time, or stasis, is itself the total change that might seem its opposite.

One of the most constant criticisms of the Aristotelian instant is that it is empty, without content because it is without character.[82] But the authentic present that is supposed to be its alternative is also empty, except that this emptiness is also the precondition for its fullness. The prototype for this kind of fullness is the *pleroma*, the fullness brought to the moment by the Incarnation.[83] That fullness, the fullness of time mentioned so often by Saint Paul, stands opposed to the waste stretches of empty time before it. Over and over in later philosophy, however, this auspicious moment is described as empty and full at the same time. For Jaspers, repeating Kierkegaard, the emptiness of ordinary time is a necessary condition for the appearance of time's fullness.[84] For Benjamin as well, the exceptional moment is "filled full." It "comprises the entire history of mankind in a tremendous abbreviation."[85] Only in the temporal clearing opened by a crisis is the true condition of time apparent. For Heidegger and Ernst Bloch as well, the empty pause of the critical moment is but the flip side of the fullness it can lead to.[86]

What the critical moment is full of, in these cases, is time, which is to say that, though it is infinitesimal in extent, the present comes to contain eternity. Kierkegaard puts it bluntly: "The present is the eternal, or rather, the eternal is the present and the present is fullness."[87] Heidegger says much the same, especially in the long analysis of boredom in *The Fundamental Concepts of Metaphysics*. As he sees it, when the present is pulled out of shape by experiences such as boredom, it comes to contain the full extent of time: "Neither merely the present nor merely the past nor merely the future, nor indeed all these reckoned together but rather their *unarticulated unity* in the simplicity of the unity of their horizon all at once."[88] Thus one of the most basic puzzles of time, how we manage to have connected experiences from one instant to another, is solved in an almost literal flash of lightning. Paradoxically, though, the solution comes only when the ordinary passage of time is frustrated and the present is concentrated within itself. Only when the present becomes as dimensionless as possible is the infinite opened to it.

In short, the present that is preferred by these modern writers and philosophers is a figurative inversion of Aristotle's model of the present and a figurative solution to the riddles about the present that he approached logically. To a great extent, the figurative nature of this present is overtly acknowledged and even celebrated by its proponents. In *The Concept of Anxiety*, Kierkegaard says that the instant "is a metaphor and therefore not so good to deal with. But it is a beautiful word to take heed of."[89] Jaspers says that the eye-blink is a "cipher" whose power is dispersed by scientific speculation.[90] For Benjamin, the relation of "what has been to the now" is "not temporal in nature but imagistic."[91] Taken in one way, this preference for the figurative might seem to put this model at a disadvantage in comparison to Aristotle's, reasoned out as it is, step by step. Taken in another way, however, it might be taken to highlight the inevitably ideal nature of Aristotle's model itself.[92] What is a point, after all, but a figure for a temporal datum that we know is not really point-like at all? When Aristotle replaces the point with something like a cut, he simply substitutes another metaphor, one that forcibly combines at least some of the incompatible characteristics that feature in the discussions of Kierkegaard and Heidegger, particularly continuity and discontinuity. Perhaps the openness of such later philosophers to the figurative simply exposes the fact that the present just *is* a metaphor, not a datum that we approach only haltingly by way of some figure but a figure itself.

The difference between Aristotle's model of the instant and the alternative present that comes to be so important in the modern period is not, therefore, the difference between the cosmological and the experiential, the objective and the subjective, but between two different figures, and the two can only be compared in reference to the effects they might have. One of the defects of Aristotle's instant is supposed to be the way it evens out all the moments of time, so that the present loses its privilege as the singular moment in which we live. On the other hand, the most peculiar feature of the kairotic present is that it is so rare it may never come. The authentic present is not just different from the actual one but in some sense its opposite. It is the exception that, as Carl Schmitt has it, makes the real: "In the exception the power of real life breaks through the crust of a mechanism that has become torpid by repetition."[93] Surely we have the right to ask, though, what kind of "real life" is available only in rare moments, moments that are so few and far between that Woolf can count them on the fingers of one hand. In its own way, then, the model based on the ancient *kairos* evacuates the present just as surely as does Aristotle's instant, perhaps even more so, since this kind of present is one that we somehow have to earn, as if we did not come to deserve it just by living.

Indeed, it is an explicit part of the various explanations of this exceptional present that it is experienced only by exceptional people. As Kierkegaard puts it, "the crowd . . . is untruth."[94] Heidegger is also overt in his disdain for the routine existence of human beings in the mass, and Woolf implies as much in the very organization of a novel like *To the Lighthouse*. The three sections of this novel are unevenly populated: the first and last involve the Ramsays and their guests, on isolated days of particular significance; the middle section is called "Time Passes" and is inhabited only by two chars, who have no more interiority than the furniture they tend to. The Ramsays live in a present that is brief but also full of meaning, while the chars toil away in an extended time that is empty because it is repetitive.

Quantifiable time is also characterized by incremental changes, so small at each step as to be apparent only in the aggregate. The change brought by the *kairos*, however, is not just sudden and unexpected but total. Everything changes all at once. One baleful implication of this is that these changes will also be violent. As Fredric Jameson puts it, there is "an intimate relation between violence as content and the 'moment' as form."[95] Violence, then, is not just an incidental attribute of the moment, a side effect of its suddenness, but in some sense its purpose. As Benjamin puts it, apparently without flinching, "the Messiah comes not only as a redeemer; he comes as a victor over the Antichrist."[96]

What appears in Benjamin's formula is the essential normativity inherent in the *kairos* from ancient times. The kairotic moment is the time to make the right choice, to be right, at least in part by rejecting what is wrong. Unfortunately, over time, the classic norm that had attached to *kairos*, the avoidance of extremes, had not only leached out of it but had gradually turned into its opposite. Originally, *kairos* had stood for a full and complete integration into society as it existed. Proper observance of it meant submission to the conservative notion that what is is right. For Kierkegaard, for Heidegger, for the Romantics, for many modern artists and writers, what is is wrong, and the function of the exceptional moment is to call us to another standard. But that standard, by its very nature, has no actuality and thus no content. In modern times, the *kairos* is normativity without a norm. It is pure, unadulterated longing for a moral standard without particulars. If the classic *kairos* meant submission to what is, the modern version means submission to what might be, whatever fullness may lie beyond the emptiness of the present.

Finally, the kairotic present remains tethered to the abstract instant because it has no other definition of ordinary time. The moment celebrated by modern philosophers and writers is not a redefinition of the ordinary, repetitive present but an exception to it. Since it comes at rare moments, perhaps only once, it leaves the vast majority of time untouched. In fact, much of the glamor of the exceptional moment would evaporate if it were not an alternative to its fallen, degraded counterpart. In its way, then, the kairotic present is just as false to experience as the abstract instant. If one is too short to allow for actual experience, the other is too vast to be comprehended by it. If one robs the experiential present of its significance, the other gives it a significance so far above and beyond the everyday as to annihilate it. Of course, this is not by any means an unintended effect. It was the purpose of philosophers like Kierkegaard and Heidegger, writers like Woolf, to describe a moment in which one would transcend everyday time. But this left everyday time exactly where it was before. If the repetitive present of standard time were to be reimagined, it would have to be done by others.

2

The Search for the
Experiential Present

I

The way we ordinarily speak of the present has little to do with abstract instants or with ecstatic leaps into the infinite. When we say *now,* we may have all sorts of time spans in mind, stretching some distance into the past and the future. Even Aristotle admits as much. In the *Physics,* he describes a version of the present in which *now* simply means something near in time. When we say he will come now, to take Aristotle's example, we may simply mean that he will come sometime today. Perhaps we have been waiting for this visit, or perhaps it has been put off several times, so that we are relieved it will finally happen *now.* The time span so designated might include some considerable extent of time, stretching off indefinitely into the future. Of course, the way in which Aristotle puts this still implies that there is a *real* present, what he calls "the indivisible present 'now,'" that anchors this larger time span loosely referred to as if it were present.[1] In fact, this is what the very concept of "near in time" refers to, the punctual instant from which all accounting of time must proceed. The very way in which Aristotle concedes that the common now may contain some bits of the past and the future depends on a prior division of time accomplished by the indivisible, instantaneous present.

Apparently, Aristotle doesn't wonder why our linguistic ways of representing the present differ so much from the strict truth of the matter. But he had suggested one explanation himself in *Sense and Sensibilia,* his treatment of sense perception. There he maintains that "no portion of time is imperceptible."[2] Indeed, he states as a basic principle that "it is possible to perceive every instant of time."[3] This must be so, because otherwise there would be gaps not just in our perception of the outer world but in our inner sense of our own existence. But the "indivisible present 'now'" referred to in the *Physics* has no magnitude, since it is not a part of time but an infinitesimal division in it, which is why it can be considered indivisible. Since it is not a magnitude, it does not fall under Aristotle's generalization in *Sense and Sensibilia* that "all magnitudes are perceptible."[4] If Aristotle is not just contradicting himself, then, he must be using a different model of the "instant of time" when he explains sense perception, one that has some temporal magnitude. If the account in the *Physics* is to be credited, though, this long instant must have inside it another, the truly instantaneous instant itself, just as the loose *now* of ordinary parlance has within it the actual present.

This odd hybrid, this compromise between Aristotle's accounts of time and experience, is, in fact, one of the oldest and most durable models of the present. The ancient Stoics also insisted that, though the division of time marked by the now is actually point-like, the present is often spoken of as "the least perceptible time surrounding the actual division."[5] The common linguistic habit of using *now* to refer to some elastic stretch of time, lazy as it may be, is founded on an experiential fact, that the smallest part of time we can process is still a part and not a dimensionless division. And yet that present must still contain at its center "the actual division," the actual present, which must be without extension. A similar formula appears as well among the Epicureans. Thus Lucretius claims that "in a single time during which we have perception, there are hidden many times whose existence is discovered by reason."[6] In this, he too suggests that there is a present within the present, a present of which we are unaware, though it is intellectually more defensible than the one we can notice. There is, in other words, a present available to the intellect, which can postulate an infinitely small division, and another available to experience, which is incapable of processing anything below a certain threshold. In Aristotle, these two different models of the present are, for the most part, handled in different parts of the corpus, and thus they don't necessarily collide, but in the Stoic and Epicurean accounts they are spoken of in the same breath, as if on the same level, and this is a habit that was to cause confusion for centuries to come.

The mischief that can arise from a mixture of these two models is apparent in the most influential account of experiential time ever offered, that in Saint Augustine's *Confessions*. Augustine begins by whittling the present down to no size at all. It is, he says, an instant that "has no duration."[7] Nonetheless, he affirms the fact that we are aware of periods of time, and this is puzzling, because a durationless present offers no scope for such awareness. The solution is to superimpose some parts of the past and the future on the punctual present: "It might be correct to say that there are three times, a present of past things, a present of present things, and a present of future things."[8] Insofar as the present involves remembrance and anticipation, it includes past and future, though it has no duration and "exists only for the instant of its passage."[9] Augustine's explanation of this threefold present is not very specific, and it is also somewhat asymmetrical in that it offers a mechanism for the effect of the past that cannot be used also for the future. This explanation depends on "impressions," which Augustine seems to understand in a fairly literal way, left by past experiences on the mind.[10] Since these persist, inflecting the time to follow, successive presents are already marked by the past before they occur. The process of expectation is supposed to function in a similar way in respect to the future. In fact, Augustine describes a metaphorical conveyer belt whereby expectation is steadily converted into remembrance. This conveyer belt is called "attention," and within it the future passes through the present into the past.[11]

Though this has been an immensely influential description of the way that the mind may process time, it does raise a number of questions. For one thing, the present seems to occur twice and in two different forms. In describing his temporal conveyer belt, Augustine says that "the faculty of attention is present all the while," implying that attention unifies past, present, and future into a larger present of some indeterminate extent.[12] If it does so, though, it must still contain within it a more basic present, the dimensionless instant, the existence of which is fundamental to the very definition of past and future. What exactly is the relation between this present and the threefold present of which it is a part? If the dimensionless instant still exists within the threefold present, perhaps as the "present of present things," then it seems we have hardly solved the problems presented by its punctuality, particularly its resistance to experience. Worse yet, in a way, is the possibility that the process of expansion that results in the threefold present could continue indefinitely, so that the "present of present things" in its center would become another threefold present, and so on, ad infinitum. In any case, what Augustine seems to have demonstrated, despite himself, is the radical incompatibility of the dimensionless instant, which is, after all, a purely intellectual construct, and the experiential present that must take up some time.

This conflict persists even as philosophy concentrates more exclusively on human experience for its ideas about time. For an empiricist like Locke, the smallest unit of time in principle is the smallest part of it that can be experienced. He calls this unit a "moment" and says it corresponds to "the time of one *Idea* in our minds."[13] This is a very neat and sensible division, and Locke does not complicate it with any metaphysical speculations about time periods shorter than the ones we can notice, though it would seem obvious that there must be some. In his account of perception, however, Locke marvels at "how very *quick* the *actions of the Mind* are performed."[14] These are so quick, in fact, that we are often unaware of them. In this sense, then, the actions of the mind sometimes "seem to require no time, but many of them seem to be crowded into an Instant."[15] Locke is careful to present this idea as a speculation, qualified by phrases like "as it were," but he is also powerfully impressed by the fact that we frequently seem to comprehend a complex argument or a complicated scene all at once. He also mentions the eye-blink, so dear to Kierkegaard and Heidegger, to show that we habitually perform actions that happen too quickly for us to notice.

It turns out, then, that experiential time is not so neatly divisible as it might have seemed, since the mind and the senses work at different rates. This is why Locke argues that we cannot derive our notions of duration and succession from experience alone, because the senses give us such confused and unreliable examples to work with. To illustrate this problem, he introduces the vivid example of a cannonball striking through a roomful of soldiers. Though the cannonball must, by reason, be deemed to have hit first one wall and then the other, to have touched "one part of the Flesh first, and another after," all this happens too fast for anyone to notice, and it all seems over in a flash. This flash is what Locke calls "an *instant*," which he defines as "*that which takes up the time of only one Idea* in our Minds, without the succession of another."[16] This is actually a rather curious example, since it uses our knowledge of succession to call our experience of succession into doubt. Within the slow time zone of the senses, he implies, there is another, within which the cannonball strikes one wall and then the other. Our knowledge of cannonballs tells us this must be so, though we cannot vouch for it from immediate experience.

The anecdote implies, then, that the experiential present is a constant summing up of much finer gradations in time. Cannonballs fly along this faster time-line, and so perhaps does the mind. This at least would explain why the mind can surprise us with its quickness, why it sometimes seems to work in no time at all. In other words, there is another present, or a series of them, within the experiential present. The latter is a kind of sampling algorithm that converts the rapid, continuous time of things like cannonballs into units that are large enough for us to use. Locke's metaphor for this process is the magic lantern, the kind in which a series of still poses is arranged on a translucent drum and spun around a candle.[17] He introduces this metaphor to illustrate the claim that the succession of ideas can only proceed at a certain pace, using units of a certain size. But the metaphor also implies that there are unnoticed times between the units, as there are undepicted poses between each of those on the drum. The difference between the drum as still and the drum in motion is parallel to the difference between the slow, unitary time of sensory experience and the fluid, infinitely divisible time that is the source of experience. Somehow, that finer and more rapid time must register on the slower time scheme of experience, as the original movement of the images is registered in the stills, but how and in what way it is reproduced again is a mystery.[18]

One of the most tantalizing notions that Locke left to his successors was the somewhat counterintuitive idea that the mind might work at a faster pace than the senses could realize. As Dugald Stewart put it toward the end of the 18th century, "the mind is so formed, as to be able to carry on certain intellectual processes, in intervals of time too short to be estimated by our faculties."[19] If so, then a definition of the present in terms of mere experience would be far too crude, as there would always be another, finer, and more accurate version of the present within the one available to notice. Stewart also suggests that the acuity of sensory experience is not necessarily fixed. For one thing, the discovery and widespread use of the microscope convinced him that temporal experience might be extended as the microscope had extended experience in space. "Why then should it be considered unphilosophical," he asks, "after having demonstrated the existence of various intellectual processes which escape our attention in consequence of their rapidity, to carry the supposition a little farther, in order to bring under known laws of the human constitution a class of mental operations, which must otherwise remain perfectly inexplicable?"[20] Some version of the microscope, he suggests, "would enlarge our views with respect to the intellectual world, no less than that instrument has with respect to the material."[21]

What exactly is Stewart hoping to find with his time microscope? He cannot be hoping to sense the infinitesimal instant itself, the absolute zero of time measurement, because that is inaccessible in principle and not just in practice. He must, therefore, be intending to register finer increments of experiential time, the various stages of Locke's cannonball, perhaps, as it strikes its way through the soldiers in the room. There must be such increments, of course, since experiential time has some magnitude. But these increments are ordinarily unavailable to experience unaided by artificial means. What is the status of experiential moments that cannot be experienced? Does it make sense to say that there is a true present in actual time but that it is too brief for anyone to notice? It might be said, then, that the concept of a time microscope does not actually open up the present, as Stewart seems to hope, taking us farther into time, but rather puts it one step farther from our grasp. The project following from Stewart's early hint was a long one, and in the end, it seems safe to say, it succeeded in making the experiential present more of a mystery than ever.

II

When Stewart proposed his time microscope, accounts of the experiential present were still complicated by the rather confusing model of the sensory process that had been left by Descartes. For him, the mind was immaterial and without extension in space, while the body was a purely physical entity constructed and motivated like a machine. Thus the mind confronted the body across an impossible interface. Descartes does not seem to have been particularly interested in the philosophical problems associated with time, and he does not put much effort into speculating about whether the mind is or is not as inextensive in time as it is in space. But he is fairly clear about the fact that sensory evidence must move across the mind-body barrier immediately.[22] However, it does seem to take some time to get that far, as the nerves are rather like cables that "pull on inner parts of the brain to which they are attached, and produce a certain motion in them."[23] Thus a mechanical system, one that actually sounds rather ponderous and difficult, confronts an immaterial entity, to which it is somehow immediate.

To account for the processing that must occur in the brain, Descartes borrowed from Aristotle the idea of a common sense. In *Sense and Sensibilia*, Aristotle gives close consideration to a problem posed by the five senses, the problem of coordination. How do we come to know that milk is both white *and* sweet, when the whiteness and the sweetness come to us through entirely different senses? Aristotle felt that to be sensed together, these different qualities must be sensed at the same time, by some single entity.[24] He called this entity the common sense, and he identified it with the experiential present. This version of the present is not just a concomitant of the senses in coordination but is, in fact, the very ground that makes their coordination possible. Daniel Heller-Roazen calls it "a present coextensive with perception as such," and he maintains that "this 'now' is the sole element in which the different sensible qualities perceived by the soul may meet."[25] Perceptions must take place in time, and for different perceptions to achieve a unity, they must have available a time that is unified and complete. For Descartes, this happened in the pineal gland, which had the task of converting motion transmitted from the nerves into the immaterial stuff of the mind and vice versa.[26] The pineal gland appealed to Descartes because it seemed to be unique in a brain otherwise mirrored into hemispheres and because he believed that it was not present in animals. As a unique entity, it constituted the point of contact between mind and body and accounted for the transformation of time-extensive sense data into the atemporal stuff of the immaterial mind.

Even as knowledge of human physiology increased, Descartes's model tended to affect accounts of temporal experience. In the 18th century, Thomas Reid, who was actually quite hostile to Aristotle in general, influentially reformulated his notion of the common sense by separating sensation from what he called perception. Sensation comes by way of the various senses to the brain, leaving an impression there that Reid called perception.[27] Perception involves concatenation and coordination of sensations, and as the proper heir of Aristotle's common sense, it takes place entirely in the present. As Reid puts it, "the object of perception and of consciousness must be something which is present: what now is, cannot be an object of memory; neither can that which is past and gone be an object of perception or of consciousness."[28] As for the present itself, Reid agreed with the traditional wisdom that it is but "a point of time," and since points are dimensionless, there is no room within one for the experiences of succession or duration.[29] But he also concedes that though "philosophers give the name of the present to that indivisible point of time, which divides the future from the past, . . . the vulgar find it more convenient in the affairs of life, to give the name of present to a portion of time, which extends more or less, according to circumstances, into the past or the future."[30] Reid was interested enough in this other, slower present to perform some simple experiments apparently meant to determine the shortest discernible span of time, a concept that actually makes no sense if perception is to be restricted to a dimensionless present.[31]

Reid was thus the first to attempt to craft a time microscope of the kind imagined by Stewart, who was a close friend of his. A vast summary article by Herbert Nichols, published in 1891, names Reid as the first to undertake an empirical observation of the sense of time, and it dates experimental psychology itself from Reid's conclusion that a human being can discern "the sixtieth part of a second."[32] It then goes on to summarize the conclusions of at least two dozen different scientists, mostly in Germany and the United States, who had been doing empirical research on the human experience of time. These scientists were part of a vast effort, extending over the century between Reid and William James, that ran in parallel to the philosophical and literary obsession with the moment that began with early Romanticism and extended into the 20th century. Not only were these two efforts separate and almost entirely unconnected, but they were also working on the present to different ends. If the purpose of Kierkegaard was in some sense to liberate the present from practical tracts of time around it, the purpose of the scientists listed by Nichols was to anchor the present firmly in a physiological understanding of everyday temporal experience.

One of the most fundamental issues to be addressed was the relation between sensation and perception. Among the two dozen or so experimental psychologists named in Nichols's 1891 survey there was certainly some variation on this issue, but it was fundamental to the discipline that sensation and perception were to be understood as different processes working in tandem. In 1896, G. E. Müller expressed what seemed the settled consensus in axiomatic form. The first of these axioms is that "every state of consciousness is based upon a material event." Changes in and relations between sensations correspond isomorphically to changes in and relations between psychic processes, and the direction of such changes must be the same in both cases. Qualitative changes, as of greater or lesser intensity, also appear symmetrically on both sides.[33] In their strictest form, these axioms established a linear, one-to-one relation between the two sides of this parallel system.

For most of the scientists working in this tradition, establishing these parallels did not imply an investment in the sort of substance dualism that had previously made the relation of mind to body such a classic problem. Even Gustave Fechner, who has often been dismissed by later history as a mystical crank, was a monist who believed that anything in this universe must have specific material conditions. Mind and body were for him different aspects of this single thing, epistemological vantage points on it.[34] The scientists influenced by Fechner, including Wilhelm Wundt and Ernst Mach, may have loosened the connection between the two sides, so as to allow for a more independent consciousness, or tightened it, so that the relation appeared more symmetrical and causal than Fechner had believed, but they made this sort of psychophysical parallelism into a set of working standards that dominated experimental psychology by the end of the 19th century.[35]

For the guidance of the many scientists who trained with him, Wundt laid down a schema listing the steps in any psychophysiological process. Sensation, the first of these, and response movement, the last, he thought of as entirely physiological, with perception, apperception, and will installed as psycho-physical steps in the middle.[36] But the separation of the steps did not nec-essarily indicate any more fundamental ontological distinction. For Wundt, the physical and the psychic were simply two different ways of looking at the same phenomena, one from the outside, the other from the inside.[37] Sensation tended to be privileged because it was accessible, but it was valuable mainly because it offered access to psychic phenomena that would otherwise recede before the approaches of science.

Most particularly, sensation could be measured in time. The realization that nerve impulses were motivated by electricity and not by the vague ani-mal spirits postulated by Descartes had at first convinced scientists that their propagation could be essentially instantaneous.[38] In the 1840s, Hermann von Helmholtz decided to see if the speed of nerve impulses could be measured. To do this, he developed what he called "my frog-tracing machine," isolating the large thigh muscle of a frog, which also had a nicely accessible nerve, and wiring it through a galvanometer to a needle that would record the opening and closing of the circuit. Comparing the readings given at different points along the muscle allowed him to calculate the speed at which the impulse was propagated along the nerve.[39]

Helmholtz's "frog-tracing machine" later became well-known under a more dignified name as the myograph. He and other scientists used this device on humans as well as frogs, placing electrodes at various points on the human body and then measuring and comparing the speeds at which the subjects would notice a light electric shock. Attaching a rotating drum and a stylus made it pos-sible to automatically and graphically record the infinitesimally short elapsed times of the nerve responses.[40] Thus, as the Dutch scientist F. C. Donders tri-umphantly put it, the old-fashioned notion that the nervous system works at light speed was refuted, and a standard propagation speed was established at about thirty-three meters per second.[41] Switching from frogs to human beings represented both an advance and a complication, however, not least because the propagation times did not seem to be nearly as consistent as Donders claimed. The human subjects added to the bare frog leg a layer of consciousness, which presented another, perhaps quite different, problem of timing.

While working as an assistant for Helmholtz in the early 1860s, Wundt pro-posed a set of experiments to isolate and measure the psychological part of the process that came to be known as reaction time.[42] Wundt established early on that the time needed for the propagation of nerve impulses could account for only a part of the total reaction time, so that the remainder must have to be taken up somewhere in the brain.[43] Thus it seemed possible, indeed quite easy, to arrive by subtraction at the time necessary for that part of the reaction that might be considered mental.[44] Reaction-time experiments helped to establish and then were based on Wundt's five-stage schema, in which the first and last stages, involving sensation and reaction, were automatic, and the middle three, perception, apperception, and will, were conscious.[45] Presenting the subject with more or less complicated sensations and then subtracting would in theory allow for the precise timing of each stage.[46]

Wundt was not the only scientist of the time who zeroed in on the experiential present in this way. In the 1860s, Donders carried out a series of experiments in which the subjects were asked to react to stimuli that had to be processed mentally—different colors of light, for example. By subtraction, Donders arrived at what he felt was a consistent 1/15th of a second necessary to make the mental discrimination. This he called the speed of thought.[47] The machines that made these measurements were, in fact, fairly similar to the chronoscope/tachistoscope as used in Wundt's lab, though Donders chose much more scintillating names: he called them the noematachograph and the noematachometer.[48] The former was fitted out with a kymograph, which allowed the results to be transcribed onto a drum. With this device, Donders felt he had inaugurated a new technical practice, noematachography, or the writing of the speed of thought.[49] In fact, the machine did not write but simply transcribed measurements, and the mental process being measured was only determined by the subtraction of determinable physiological time spans.

As alluring as it might have been to study the speed of thought at a time when even the speed of light was not precisely known, what Wundt called "psychophysical time," the time taken by perception, apperception, and will, could not be measured in isolation.[50] In fact, the whole relation of time to the "psychophysical" was skewed. Instead of isolating the phenomenon and then measuring it, scientists used measurements and inference to establish a phenomenon that couldn't otherwise be represented at all. As Donders put it, "we know no unit by which to express sensation, reason, and will in figures."[51] To establish that mental processes took a measurable amount of time was, therefore, tantamount to establishing for science the independent existence of those processes. According to Ruth Benschop and Douwe Draaisma, the idea that "time opens up the human mind for measurement became something of a topos in psychological literature."[52] But the metaphor of "opening up" is really too weak, since it was temporal measurement that allowed scientists to represent the mind at all.

What this means, then, is that the instruments used in the psychological laboratory were not just prosthetic extensions of the human sensorium but surrogates for it, and surrogates that managed to vouch for the existence of what they ostensibly replaced. In her history of the tachistoscope, Ruth Benschop maintains that it "does not simply improve the researcher's perception of nature, it allows a clear perception of perception."[53] To perceive perception, however, is the traditional role of the mind, which had long been imagined as a common sense, collecting all the others, or as a kind of homunculus receiving impressions from the senses. The instruments in the psychology lab seemed to make the mind accessible for the first time by offering an externalized model of its temporal processes. In doing so, though, they also vouched for the very existence of the common gathering point that Aristotle and Descartes had imagined at the end of the sensory chain.

The notion of mental time that was established by the end of the 19th century was, therefore, inseparable from the instruments that measured it. As Helmholtz put it, "our senses are not capable of directly perceiving an individual moment of time with such a small duration." Therefore, "we must apply artificial methods to its observation and measurement."[54] In order to make it apprehensible, these artificial methods amplified the instant, sometimes quite literally. The first scratchings recorded by Helmholtz's myograph were themselves too tiny to yield much information, so he had to look at them under a microscope. This necessity certainly raises a question about the psychophysical status of the data under inspection. What sort of "moment of time" was Helmholtz actually inspecting under his time microscope? It could hardly be identified with an experiential present, since it was too brief to be experienced unaided, even by the most acute introspection. But it could not be the absolute present, the instant acknowledged by all philosophers from Aristotle to Reid, because that has no measurable extent. What Helmholtz and his colleagues seem to zeroing in on is a hybrid present, beyond the range of ordinary experience and yet still physical in extent. When this moment is identified with purely physical processes going on in the nervous system, it does not necessarily represent a contradiction, because there must certainly be measurable actions at that level that are too quick for us to notice. But when these same moments are identified with the conscious parts of the sensory chain, then they represent the very difficult concept of a mental present that the mind itself cannot access.

It might be said, in fact, that this is the experiential present not of people but rather of machines. It is a present that takes up some increment of actual time because machines exist in the physical world just as much as human beings do. But it converges on the absolute zero of the abstract instant in part because machine tolerances can be made so much finer than those of the human senses. Additionally, though, the psychophysical instruments of the 19th-century laboratories established the abstract instant as a standard simply by submitting mental processes to measurement. With the numbered time-line as a tool, the goal of more accurate measurement would always tend to converge on the smallest increment of a line: the point. The goal of measuring the experiential present to finer and finer tolerances implicitly established the nondimensional temporal point as the abstract ideal that human performance approximated. Though these psychophysical researchers established that the last phase of human perception must take some time, they also reestablished their own version of the common sense, sitting at the vanishing point of temporal perception.

Finally, this inconsistency about experiential time is subtended by a deeper philosophical confusion about the status of what Reid had called perception, the mental end of the sensory process. An essential and yet unexamined tension exists in the experimental psychology of this period between a residual belief in an immaterial mind and the technological models that made that mind apparent. The result with respect to time was a hybrid concept like "the speed of thought," which assumes that there is such a thing as thought, distinct from merely physiological processes, but also that it is subject to the same rules and measurements as material phenomena. This must have made sense to a science founded on the idea that the mental runs in parallel with the physical and is conditioned but not determined by it. But that science did not explain why the mind, if it exists at all, should not be free of physical limitations or, on the other hand, why the mind is not a superfluous concept if it simply runs along in perfect parallel to the nervous system. For some time to come, this inconsistency was to haunt the search for the experiential present.

III

The effects of this psychophysical research are readily apparent in William James, who did some timing experiments of his own, using a contraption triggered by a telegraph key, with the results recorded by a kymograph.[55] James traveled and studied in Germany, and he came to know many of the principals in German experimental psychology, including Mach and Wundt.[56] It is fairly obvious, from many references in *The Principles of Psychology*, that the measurements arrived at by Helmholtz and Wundt were critical in James's conception of the specious present.[57] At the same time, however, James was consistently and tartly critical of what he called the "chronograph philosophers."[58] In part, this disdain rested on a temperamental difference, one he expressed in a famous quip that experimental psychology could never have arisen in a country whose inhabitants could be bored.[59] James also felt that the conditions in the early psychology labs were artificial, and he was skeptical, as other critics were, about the notion that human consciousness could be quantified. He had a particular esteem for Fechner because he, alone among the pioneers of experimental psychology, was also a speculative philosopher.[60]

James was also influenced by a line of empiricist philosophers following from Reid who were apparently quite unconnected to the psychophysical research going on in continental laboratories. Reid apparently passed on to his friend Dugald Stewart an interest in the problem of the present and a dissatisfaction with the standard empiricist accounts of the continuity of time that Stewart then communicated to his student Thomas Brown and his associate William Hamilton, who edited the published works of both Reid and Stewart. Hamilton's ideas about the present then inspired the even more obscure reflections of the amateur philosophers Shadworth Hodgson and E. Robert Kelly, neither of whom would be remembered today if they had not been friends of James. A very thin line of concern thus connects Reid to James, which represents a slowly growing sense of tension between the strictly separated dimensionless instants of the empiricists and the apparent experience of the present.

In Brown's version of Reid's ideas, for example, experience of the present must include a "rapid retrospect," a particular kind of memory.[61] Like ordinary memory, this rapid retrospect is a present experience of something actually in the past, but it differs from conventional remembrance and recall in that it is not aware of itself *as* memory. Duration in the present and succession between presents is therefore guaranteed by a peculiar experiential hybrid, a perception that is actually a memory. Though there are a number of obvious objections to the hybridization of perception and memory, it does make it possible for present consciousness to hold more than one instant at a time. And if this is possible, then it might seem a little less unpleasant to accept the vulgar notion that Hodgson calls, with less disdain than Reid, the "empirical present." What everybody loosely calls the present is not, of course, the present *as such*, which for Hodgson is actually the "instant of change" *within* the longer, easier span of time that we seem to experience.[62] But even calling this the "empirical present" is to suggest that it is the product of actual experience and not a simple mistake in logic, which is the unfortunate implication of the more famous name first suggested by Kelly, writing as E. R. Clay, who handed these ideas on to James under the rubric of the "specious present."[63]

Though it clearly follows from the puzzlements of Locke and Reid about the relation between the empirical present and its abstract counterpart, this line of reasoning does represent a change. When Kelly took up his study of the specious present, he thought of his work in this area as essentially unprecedented. "The relation of experience to time," he says, "has not been profoundly studied."[64] How far wrong this is depends on what he means by *profoundly*, but no matter what, it correctly registers a significant shift in interest. Conventionally, that shift has been understood as the displacement of physics by psychology as the privileged science in the investigation of time, and the basic truth of this is hard to deny.[65] But psychology as practiced in the 19th century had a strong dose of physics in it, and growing awareness of the physical basis of experience had a profound effect. Thus Hamilton observes in his *Discussions* of 1856: "In the internal perception of a series of mental operations, a certain time, a certain duration, is necessary for the smallest section of continuous energy to which consciousness is competent. Some minimum of time must be admitted as the minimum of consciousness."[66]

Whatever Hamilton means by *energy*, his terminology locates human consciousness within a physical order, the limits of which are defined by the laws of physics. Since energy cannot be transmitted through matter instantaneously, consciousness must take some time. According to Edwin Boring's classic account of 19th-century experimental psychology, this idea became much more common once the first two laws of thermodynamics were proposed in 1851, at which point "it became impossible to think of the transmission of activity without a transfer of energy."[67] Since most of the physiological psychologists of this time believed in a meaningful parallelism between the nervous system and an immaterial mind, this set up a fateful conflict between physiological time and a mental construct that could still occur instantaneously.

Thus the feature of James's *Principles of Psychology* that makes it seem so utterly different from the speculations before it is the relation between brain and mind. At the end of the first volume, turning to metaphysical questions, he exclaims, "That brains should give rise to a knowing consciousness at all, this is the one mystery which returns, no matter of what sort the consciousness or what sort the knowledge may be."[68] Here he sets aside all those questions raised by the idea of a knowing consciousness as too abstruse for science; later he would renounce the idea of consciousness altogether.[69] In the second volume of *The Principles of Psychology*, he ties emotion directly to "organic changes," each of which is "the reflex effect of the exciting object," and yet he stoutly insists that emotion still has an "inward" meaning that preserves all the value traditionally attached to it.[70] In *The Principles of Psychology*, at any rate, James manages to insist that all of what is ordinarily thought of as consciousness is completely and causally dependent on the brain and nervous system but without taking what would seem the ultimately necessary step of collapsing the mental into the physical.[71]

Limited though it may have been, James's insistence on the physical had a significant effect on his ideas about the temporal status of consciousness. Since elementary physics dictates that any material effect must take time, there can be no instantaneous changes in a physical system like the brain. Therefore, "no state of the brain can be supposed instantly to die away."[72] In fact, it might be said that consciousness just *is* this constant delay, since it is "a certain slowness in the cortical cells" that allows the brain to combine sensations and ideas.[73] If it were not for the inevitable latency of mental response, then, one bit of sensory input would disappear before the next could arrive, just as the empiricists thought it did, but as it is, every input is retained just for a bit, so that it can be overlaid on and linked to the next and the whole of consciousness poured out ultimately as a single stream.

Thus it might be said that when James comes to consider the present in particular, he turns the traditional discussion of it upside down. He admits the authority of the "strict present," the dimensionless instant that is conventionally associated with abstract time, but it is not really an objective fact for him since it is a purely logical construction, "an altogether ideal abstraction."[74] The only "fact" of immediate experience is what "Clay" calls the "specious present," a "duration-block," as James puts it himself, a single, unified expanse of time that looks both forward and back.[75] Because the present has duration, we are able to experience the passage of time directly, and because it refers to past and future, we are able to experience succession directly. As part of his argument, James quotes Reid's paraphrase of Aristotle to the effect that every elementary part of duration must have some duration itself.[76] And he sums up "by saying that we are constantly conscious of a certain duration—the specious present—varying in length from a few seconds to probably not more than a minute, and that this duration (with its content perceived as having one part earlier and the other part later) is the original intuition of time."[77]

In the course of his discussion, James employs a number of subtly different metaphors for the specious present, all of which have the significant advantage of not seeming to disparage it. One of these is the saddle-back, "with a certain breadth of its own on which we sit perched, and from which we look in two directions into time."[78] Another is the boat with its bow and stern pointing up and down the stream of consciousness.[79] In the discussion of the stream of consciousness itself, James asserts that "objects fade out of consciousness slowly," and the imagery here picks up that used a page or so before, when he disputes the notion that consciousness may be compared to a mere spark of light.[80] The specious present, in other words, is imagined in visual terms, with a "vaguely vanishing backward and forward fringe."[81] This constant illumination and slow dimming out of little light bulbs in the mind does seem to have a literal basis for James. He relies for support on the experiments of Sigmund Exner, who demonstrated that separate sparks seen less than 0.044 seconds apart are seen as a single spark moving.[82] And he explicitly cites ocular after-images as psychological proof "that each stimulus leaves some latent activity behind it which only gradually passes away."[83] In other words, the fringe that James imagines surrounding the strict present is part metaphor and part fact, and its justification rests on a combination of introspective reasoning and experimental evidence.[84]

Like Hodgson before him, though, James still thinks of the "strict present" as a solid kernel of some sort at the very center of the fringed present we actually experience. Thus he speaks of "the 'present' spot of time," and though he puts strategic scare quotes around the word *present*, as if he were aware of stepping into contradiction, he does seem to think of the spot itself as some sort of nondimensional point.[85] For successive ideas to occur to us *as* successive, then, they must be presented to the mind simultaneously: "If we are to think *of* them as one after the other, we must *think* them both at once."[86] Having readily dispatched the instant as an ideal abstraction, incompatible with the workings of a physical brain, James then reimports it into his discussion with the words *at once*. Thus it might seem as though the whole discussion of the specious present has accomplished nothing. For James still believes, as though he were Locke or even Aristotle, that individual temporal moments must *be* combined, which assumes that they occur originally as distinct from one another, no strings attached.

Elsewhere in *The Principles of Psychology*, James insists that the notes of a chord, for example, are not perceived as the notes themselves and then over again as a combination, but simply *as* a chord, and he seems to lay this down, over and over, as a general law of human psychology.[87] In the case of succession, though, he accepts the old-fashioned idea that for two things to be comparable in the mind, they must somehow be superimposed on the same temporal instant. For all his talk of the stream and the fringe, James finally has no real account of how one temporal experience might imply or refer to another, and so he is stuck in the end with the crude demand that the instant of awareness must somehow *contain* those other moments of which it is aware. But this is to impale the instant on its own most obvious contradiction, since a dimensionless "spot of time" can't actually contain anything. Furthermore, such instantaneous superimposition could occur only in an immaterial mind, quite divorced from its brain.

Since its publication in 1890, James's account of the specious present in *The Principles of Psychology* has come to be seen as one of the most serious attempts to disentangle the problem of temporal consciousness from the larger and more forbidding problem of time itself. Despite its rather disparaging name, the specious present was taken up fairly quickly by other philosophers, including Bertrand Russell, C. D. Broad, and Edmund Husserl. Nowadays, it can seem as though James's account survives precisely because it is so woolly, since most discussions of it focus relentlessly on its weaknesses and inconsistencies. As early as 1908, J. E. McTaggart found it impossible to accept the idea of a present that is variable in length.[88] As long ago as 1954, C.W.K. Mundle presented his reconsideration as a final attempt "to get the last nails in the coffin of a suspicious character."[89] And yet the corpse continues to walk, so that it can be slain again by recent authorities like Barry Dainton and Robin Le Poidevin. It has been temptingly easy to drive stakes, if not into the heart, at least into some of the vital organs of James's argument, particularly his account of the experience of succession.[90] Though it may seem easy to see where James is inconsistent or even wrong, it is not so easy to improve on his version of things, and most of the problems that trouble him recur in the philosophy that follows.

IV

It could be argued that the problem of the present is the defining problem of phenomenology and thus of the continental philosophy that is generally held to have started with it. Having split itself off from the physiological psychology of the 19th century, phenomenology aimed to investigate the structure of experience itself and not its psychological or biological causes. Methodologically, then, phenomenology looked at the mind from a first-person perspective, and from that perspective time appears to be much more than a feature of consciousness: it is the medium in which consciousness exists. But not necessarily the whole of time, whatever that may be, since experience must by definition be concentrated on, if not limited to, the present. Therefore, a definition of the present would also seem to entail a definition of consciousness itself. As Derrida put it, in his highly critical account, the "living-present . . . is therefore the founding concept of phenomenology as metaphysics."[91]

In this respect, the foundation of phenomenology would be located in the experiential present as defined by Edmund Husserl, who passed on to his successors a set of ideas influenced directly by James and the empirical tradition behind him, as well as the psychophysiology of the 19th century.[92] Husserl objects most basically to a restriction of perception to the dimensionless boundary of the present, which may offer references to, or associations with, or even images of past and future, but not perceptions of them. For Husserl, then, imagining the past and future as constantly modifying the present is not enough as long as that present is still defined as having no duration of its own. For a present without duration, in Husserl's view, makes the experience of time impossible.[93] As he sees it, then, the "pure now" is only an "ideal limit" and is surrounded by a "'rough' now" that is actually experienced in an extended state.[94]

Filling in this "'rough' now" with something sensible turned out to be a lifelong task for Husserl. His simplest version is a metaphor: there is "a comet's tail that attaches itself to the perception of the moment."[95] This is a powerfully subtle metaphor, insofar as the comet's literal tail seems to resemble the visual afterimage of a moving light source. The metaphor thus uses the common experience that phenomena can last some time in physical form to substantiate the idea that they must also do so in the mind. But it is difficult for Husserl to describe the nature of this mental comet in literal terms. The comet's head, as he puts it, is the "'source-point'" of perception, and though he tries to sequester this concept inside scare quotes, it still nonetheless suggests that, in its primary form, experience at least begins at a point.[96] But this jumping-off point is always trailed by a "running-off," a gradual fading like the fringe that James imagines in a similar situation.[97] What this "running-off" consists of and how it relates to its origin are the great questions left by Husserl's account.

It does not help that the published version of *On the Phenomenology of the Consciousness of Internal Time* is a literal grab bag of selections from various points in Husserl's career, one that muddles distinctions that Husserl worked hard all his life to refine. Earlier in his work on the subject, Husserl used the term "primary memory" for the "running-off" that trails the first moment of perception. But there were significant problems with this term, since it invited confusion with the everyday concept of memory, which Husserl demoted to "secondary memory." Later, he used the term "retention," which helped to avoid the implication that the contents of the "running-off" period have to be recalled, as if they were ordinary memories.[98]

For it is the essence of Husserl's argument that the comet's tail is apprehended directly, if perhaps more faintly than the head. What this means, though, as Husserl puts it, is that "we have, then, characterized the *past* itself as *perceived*."[99] We may perceive it *as* past, and this is why the experience of time is not a single mush of perception, but we do perceive it. The idea of perceiving that which is not actually present, however, is so counterintuitive that even Husserl commented: "But 'perceived past,' doesn't that sound like wooden iron?"[100] Even re-named as retention, the concept of primary memory never loses that sense of paradox, since Husserl is concerned not just to distinguish primary memory from what is ordinarily considered to be memory but actually to oppose them. Between perception and memory, then, there is a temporal faculty that has the immediacy of the first and the retentive power of the second. For his successors in the phenomenological tradition, this is the solution that finally explains how the experience of time is possible. For his critics, among them Derrida, this amalgam of perception and memory involves a contradiction that collapses the entire system.[101]

One common practical objection to Husserl's account of retention is that, having connected the immediate past so securely to the present, it then needs some way to re-distinguish them so that the "running-off" can be apprehended *as* running-off. How, that is to say, does "the past come to be represented as past by an impression that is completely present?"[102] Is there a temporal mark or sign of some kind that the retention can wear as an ID badge so it will not be confused with the present itself? Or is it enough to suppose that the retention is weaker, fainter in its running-off so that it can be properly situated in the sequence? But here there is another problem, for it is not enough to describe a single passage of one comet's tail, as if experience were a series of neatly discrete events. Clearly, the comets keep on coming, and the tail of one must necessarily intersect in some way with the head of the next, and so on. How to prevent a train wreck of retentions as they pile up, one on top of another?[103]

It is hard not to feel that a great deal of trouble has been caused by Husserl's revulsion at the idea that the extension of perception in time might be accomplished by some sort of reference or re-presentation. There is a very basic opposition in Husserl's work between presentation and re-presentation that seems to make it hard for him to allow re-presentations into the present. For a re-presentation seems to involve conscious recall and thus to divide the unitary moment of immediate experience.[104] But this insistence on immediacy seems to mean that in order to be extended, the present moment must be expanded, to become a thickened or "big" now. It is hard to manage this if the now is also to remain immediate, all parts of it equally present to consciousness. Despite their necessary relation, the comet and its tail actually seem to be stuck in a paradox: if they are different, then they cannot occupy the same moment, and if they are the same, then they seem to deny the passage of time.[105]

Perhaps this paradox arises from a more basic inconsistency. On one hand, Husserl insists that the present is extended, with a duration of its own. On the other hand, however, he also insists that the original sensory impression and its retention must be experienced together, superimposed, in some way, on top of one another. This seems to mean, as Jean-Paul Sartre was to charge in *Being and Nothingness*, that consciousness is still restricted to the instant, so that the retentions and anticipations that should extend it are stuck "like flies bumping their noses on the window without being able to clear the glass."[106] For all the effort expended to pry open the present, for all the thought given to how and why it must be extended, it actually remains just as small a pinpoint as it was for Descartes. The requirement that the original impression and its extensions be perceived immediately was criticized almost from the beginning, on the grounds that it counterintuitively packs the experience of change into an instant of time.[107] Critical awareness of the same issue by Husserl himself is probably one of the reasons his struggle with the present was so protracted, and he came in the end to a highly complicated solution in which the stream of daily experiences floats on top of another, deeper stream formed of the pure consciousness of time.[108] But it is fair to say that he was never really satisfied with any solution, which is one reason why the Husserlian corpus on this subject is such a dither of documents.

In a way, Husserl was free of some of the conflicts that bedeviled James and the psychophysical research before him because he had bracketed off from consideration any purely physiological considerations. By the same token, though, this may have made it that much easier for him to preserve from Descartes the essentially immaterial mind centered on its single time-point. Though everything in Husserl's phenomenology is meant to question that concept, it still seems too fundamental for him to dispense with. At the same time, bracketing the physiological also left Husserl open to objections about the physical plausibility of his model of experiential time. Is it at all plausible to imagine the dense network of anticipations and retentions demanded by Husserl's model, produced, as it must be, many, many times a second, given the fairly limited speed and firing power of the human neural network?[109] This, at any rate, is the sort of question that has continued to interest the investigators of the experiential present in the 20th and 21st centuries.

V

To a significant extent, contemporary psychological and neurological research into experiential time is conducted within a context determined by James, Husserl, and the psychophysiologists of the 19th century. As Eric Kandel puts it in *Principles of Neural Science*, "the aim of cognitive neural science is to examine classical philosophical and psychological questions about mental function in the light of cell and molecular biology."[110] A number of psychological studies have been mounted to test specific parts of the models of James or Husserl.[111] Even when these authorities are not cited directly, the laboratory practices in use often replicate the 19th-century conditions and practices that conditioned their work. Optical illusions remain a major focus of interest, as they were for James, who was apparently one of the first to report on the "falling-water" illusion. Reaction time experiments are as much a stock-in-trade of the modern psychology laboratory as they were for Helmholtz and Wundt. And yet the general effect of contemporary neurological and psychological science has been to cast a harsh light on most of the assumptions supporting the models of the 19th century, even perhaps on the notion of the experiential present itself.

One of the most basic assumptions of past notions about the experience of time, one that goes all the way back to Locke's magic lantern and Stewart's time microscope, is that the human sensorium has a kind of sampling algorithm, sipping at regular intervals from a stream of time that, if not strictly continuous, is at least much more finely divided than human experience. Though the metaphors have been updated from the magic lantern to the video camera, it is still sometimes asserted that the human visual system is governed by some such sampling system, turning time into discrete bits such that some resolution must inevitably be lost.[112] Discrete time units of some kind, on the model of the specious present, are also a feature of some current explanations of the experiential present.[113] And yet there is also a growing body of suspicion about these time quanta, even beyond the quibbling about how long they might turn out to be. Despite a great deal of work, centered on a range of optical illusions, there does not seem to be any particular interval that consistently explains them all. In other words, no one sampling rate has been found that might explain how experience is packaged into extended present moments.[114]

One basic question that is raised by optical illusions in general is whether it can be assumed that physiological processes and sensory experience will necessarily correspond to one another in temporal order, duration, or pace. As Bruno Mölder puts it, there are actually three temporal sequences to consider: the objective sequence of "environmental events"; the sequence of "brain events"; and "the temporal properties of events as experienced."[115] If these are not necessarily isomorphic, then the psychophysiological project of deriving information about "brain events" from "events as experienced" must fail. And yet, as Konstantin Moutoussis asserts, "we are still far from knowing where, when, and how perceptual experiences arise from neuronal events, and it would thus be inappropriate to translate any neuronal time delays to perceptual time delays."[116] Certain optical illusions seem to show, in fact, that what Mölder calls "brain events" do not even occur in the same order as "events as experienced." Thus Mölder concludes that "consciously represented temporal properties need not match with the temporal properties of the neural processes that underpin these representations."[117]

This actually makes sense once it is realized that various different types of temporal evidence are processed at different rates by different parts of the brain. This is true not just of the different senses but of, say, different aspects of the visual field, such as color and motion. In fact, information from the other senses seems capable of influencing the processing of visual information.[118] If, as Dean V. Buonomano insists, "the detection of the temporal features, order, interval, and duration of both simple and complex stimuli can occur in different parts of the brain on an as needed basis," then it stands to reason that the experiential timing of very similar "environmental events" might differ from instance to instance.[119] This would shed a harsh light back on the hopes of the 19th century. As Buonomano puts it, "historically, the understanding of the neural mechanisms of how the brain tells time has been complicated by the fact that we have at times failed to take into account that distinct mechanisms are likely used to tell time on different scales."[120]

Increasingly, then, it is common to think of the human perceptual system as a distributed "neurocracy" rather than a single, hierarchical unit. In the "neurocracy," as Valtteri Arstila and Dan Lloyd put it, "nothing exactly corresponds to 'seeing a coffee cup.'"[121] In other words, the classic binding problem, the old Aristotelian question of how the milk comes to be perceived as both sweet and white, is not solved but dismissed. According to Moutoussis, "an alternative, although somewhat extreme, solution to the binding problem is to adopt the position that what we refer to as binding does not really exist, and thus there is no problem to begin with: if each visual attribute is perceived independently and at its own time, perception is indeed characterized by segregation, not integration."[122] This, of course, would solve, more or less by dissolving it, the problem that haunted both James and Husserl, which was how to put the parts of the specious present together again after having spread them out over time. The integration of past, present, and future into single instants turns out to be not just conceptually difficult but physically improbable.

Though this may seem a reductive, even a destructive, conclusion, it does serve to remove the most abiding contradiction that haunted the temporal models of James and Husserl. For the most serious issues arose in those cases when the extended experiential present had somehow to be shoehorned back into the tiny space of the abstract instant. Many contemporary researchers no longer feel the need to do this in part because they are working with models that are much more thoroughly physiological than those of their 19th-century predecessors. It is much harder to imagine how to focus a series of temporal events on a single infinitesimal instant without an immaterial mind to do the work. But the other feature that has lost its hold is the Aristotelian common sense, preserved by Descartes and Reid and thus passed on in a diminished and partially occult form to James and Husserl. The common sense had been so thoroughly identified with the experiential present that it came to be an inevitable part of temporal models that otherwise had little to do with Aristotle. Unfortunately, the common sense also brought with it a basic contradiction, since it was supposed to be an experiential feature that occupied no actual time. This was a contradiction even for Aristotle, and this contradiction was imported into every model that followed Aristotle's example in focusing the broad empirical present onto a single temporal point. Indeed, the power of the Aristotelian model may have inhered in this very contradiction, which it seemed to resolve, for it combined the prestige of the instant, which had always seemed the most logical abstract version of the present, with the appeal of the empirical present, which had the support of experience. However, any model that wanted to have both inevitably ran into the basic problem that one could not take up any time, while the other had to.

What does this mean for the experiential present? According to at least a few contemporary researchers, the experiential present itself has become an untenable concept. As Marc Wittmann puts it, "events are perceived at present, experiences are confined to the present, but the present is not experienced— *being present* is not a phenomenal property of experience."[123] In other words, we may perceive things, and even perceive them together in time, without necessarily having any separate awareness of their temporal commonality. If contemporary research is correct, then this sort of awareness is not necessary for us to function effectively as sentient creatures. Though this might seem a drastic and even an impoverishingly reductive view of human experience, it might also shed some light on one very prominent part of the history of the experiential present: the consistent reliance of temporal investigators on metaphors of a particular kind.

Locke leads the way in this practice by likening the human sensorium to the camera obscura.[124] Because the camera obscura fixes its user at a single point in space, one that doesn't seem to take up any space itself, the mind by analogy comes to seem disembodied and immaterial. From the Renaissance, the eye had been diagrammed as the apex of a cone of collected light; the Enlightenment imagined the entire sensorium as the apex of a similar cone, dimensionless and without extension.[125] The camera obscura is also focused on a single point in space, unlike the eye itself, which is constantly roving.[126] Therefore it seemed to make sense that observations made by means of such a device would also be limited in time, though images seen through an actual camera obscura are not fixed but fluid. The metaphorical camera obscura thus helped to substantiate the notion of a unitary present, focused on a single point. When it came to representing a longer stretch of time, Locke had natural recourse to the magic lantern, which reconstructs temporal experience as a series of still images strung along a line.

It is part of a longer tradition, then, when James sums up his discussion of the experience of succession by calling it "a sort of *perspective projection* of past objects upon present consciousness, similar to that of wide landscapes upon a camera-screen."[127] What he seems to mean is that the mind brings successive temporal experiences to bear on a single point, as a camera lens focuses a considerable extent of space through its lens. In this case, the metaphor takes for granted the temporal status of the photograph itself, assuming an instantaneity for it so as to illustrate the way the mind fuses successive impressions together. Here the example of the camera helps James to think about the specious present, as the example of the camera obscura and the magic lantern had helped

Locke. Later, James would use the same metaphor in a much more critical sense, decrying the tendency of other philosophers to abstract moments from "the stream of time, snap-shots taken, as by a kinetoscopic camera."[128] Even in critique, though, James shows how deeply the camera had come to be implicated in the human experience of time.

Perhaps James had been influenced in this respect by the original discussion of the specious present, in the course of which "Clay" wonders, "How is it possible for us to have experiences as of continuous, dynamic, temporally structured, unified events given that we start with (what at least seems to be) a sequence of independent and static snapshots of the world at a time?"[129] Here it seems that it is actually "Clay" who "starts with" static snapshots, since the metaphor seems to precede and inflect his empirical understanding of the processing of time. Later, the snapshot metaphor would fall out of favor, to be replaced by the video camera or the computer.[130] Such devices are metaphorical equivalents of the psychophysiological instruments of the 19th century, and both actual and metaphorical instances seem to perform the same function, which is to give embodiment to a category of experience that otherwise threatens to disappear.

At this stage, though, it is worth remembering that, at least in some cases, the measuring devices of the 19th century did not just reveal certain stages in the experience of time but actually vouched for their very existence. Perhaps this is true as well of the long tradition by which visual devices are brought in as ostensible illustrations of the experiential present. Despite itself, this tradition may confess that the experiential present has always been a metaphor. If contemporary science is to be believed, the disorganized and temporally disparate stuff of the senses is not focused on a single point of any dimension but rather is swept together in untidy piles. Though there may be various kinds of periodicity in the nervous system, though there may even be sensory quanta of some more or less regular kind, there is no reason to believe that these would necessarily stack up and arrive at fixed intervals. Perhaps the present is not a datum of experience to be investigated but rather an abstract concept that has made investigation of experience more difficult.

One problem with such a drastic conclusion is that, as the history of the kairotic moment has shown, the present is not just a scientific issue but also a moral and ethical one. What happens to the prestige of the present if it is dissolved into a cloud of dust motes? Formulas like Augustine's threefold present and James's specious present have mattered not necessarily because they adequately accounted for the way time is experienced but at least in part because they appealed as patterns of living. These models of the present functioned as metaphors in a much larger sense to figure the temporal life of an individual or a culture. Definitions of the present at the largest scale, as in the present time or the present age, are built on the example of these smaller, briefer presents. Part of the reason we care about the nature of the private, small-scale present, then, is because it helps us substantiate the larger common present, which is even harder to grasp.

3

The Longest Now:
A History of the Historical Present

I

When Anthony Trollope published *The Way We Live Now* (1875), he meant his adverb to cover a period much longer than an instant, much longer even than the extended present imagined about this time by William James. In fact, it is hard to say just how much time the *now* in Trollope's title is supposed to comprehend. He uses the word to designate an indeterminate temporal extent surrounding the date of publication, stretching at the very least some months into the past and, he must have hoped, some months into the future. This is not the present of philosophy or psychology but that of common parlance, closely akin to the vulgar present recognized since Aristotle. But it also has some characteristics that are not included in most descriptions of the vulgar present from Aristotle's to Reid's.

Though Trollope's *now* is vague and indeterminate, it must also be bounded. The implication of his title is that the present differs in some important respect from the past, and perhaps from the future. *Now* is commonly used in this vaguely antithetical sense to mean something like *nowadays*, with the implication that other days were otherwise. Though this version of the present might be quite long, perhaps even covering a period of some years, it is also unified, at least in some important respect, and identifiable as a period. As a period, this version of the present poses in an especially difficult way the basic challenge of the present in general, which is, as Norbert Elias puts it, to experience "at the same time what has not happened at the same time."[1] The longer the time span, the harder it is to accomplish this trick, which is already pretty daunting, at least to explain, at the much simpler level of the moment.

Trollope's *now* also has one characteristic that fundamentally differentiates it from the other versions that exist at shorter timescales. As the title implies, it is collective in nature. This indeed seems to be a necessary characteristic of the kind of present that takes up some extended period of time, that it should also comprehend some significant extent of human space. No one has this kind of present alone. Investigations and explanations of the other, shorter presents have taken place in an artificial environment inhabited by at most one person, but any understanding of a time period covering some months must face the reality of the social. The very notion of *nowadays*, of the contemporary, implies a society in which conditions change in a general way. Thus it is often suggested that the literal meaning of *contemporary*, times together, pertains to the times of various different people, brought together in one general sense of the present as an identifiable period.[2] Thus a present that means something like "the contemporary period" poses the problem of coordination in a different and even more difficult way than the one Elias identifies. It adds to the basic problem of temporal unity another, the problem of aligning the disparate temporal experiences of different people.

Given these challenges of coordination, and remembering that even the very limited unity of the private, experiential present has been quite hard to establish, it would seem that, where a now like Trollope's is concerned, the shorter the better. But this is not the case right now, when it is common to complain that the present is not nearly long enough. A whole foundation, Stewart Brand's The Long Now, has been set up to extend the attention span of the present into the farthest reaches of the future. Brand's project is based on the prevalent notion that the contemporary present has withered to a mere shadow of itself, mainly because of the sort of digital devices that Brand was among the first to celebrate. Though digital devices are a popular target and this shrinkage of the present a common complaint, it is also often said that the present has come unglued from the past, and this separation is dated as far back as the French Revolution and sometimes farther.[3] If this condition really has persisted since the 1780s, it would make for a very long now indeed. Sometimes, though, it is charged that the present is simultaneously too long *and* too short. "Such are the major traits of this manifold and multivalent present, a monstrous time," as François Hartog puts it. "It is at once everything (there is nothing but the present) and almost nothing (reduced to the tyranny of the instant.)"[4]

Though it seems clear that the now we live in now is not the one they lived in then, whenever that was, it is not so clear exactly how our now has gone wrong. At the most general level, what these complaints have in common is the idea that the contemporary present is simply too much itself, that it has come loose from past and future and/or that it has come to dominate or even eliminate them. Whether the time period at issue is called now, the contemporary, or even the postmodern, the argument is really about modernity, for this is the basic model of the break with the past in favor of the present, the original sin with which sin itself begins. As Reinhart Koselleck puts it, in what is currently the most influential analysis of these issues, modern experience corresponds "to a state of reality which increasingly allowed the dimensions of past, present, and future to break away from one another in the progress of time."[5] Despite the metaphor of breakage, modernity for Koselleck is really a long, drawn-out process of separation that is finally stretched to the breaking point only at the French Revolution, a world-shaking event whose unpredictable course convinced everyone that the past could not be relied on nor the future predicted. The present, in a sense, is all that is left.

Concentrated as he is on this historical break, Koselleck does not actually say a lot about what preceded it, but the very notion of a break implies a past in which things were quite different. Generally, he refers to this preceding state as "the traditional experiential space, which had previously appeared to be determined by the past, but which would now break apart."[6] Traditionally, then, the past informs the present, and because it does so, the present can in turn form useful expectations about the future. "Experience," Koselleck says, "is present past, whose events have been incorporated and can be remembered." And "expectation also takes place in the today; it is the future made present."[7] The traditional present, then, is threefold, constantly incorporating into itself bits of the past and projecting these forward into the future. If this model seems familiar, it is because it is explicitly based on two sources: Saint Augustine and Martin Heidegger.[8] There is no other evidence on which to establish the necessary baseline from which modern experience is supposed to have deviated.

There are two significant problems with this reliance on authority rather than demonstration or example. First of all, the models of the present offered by Koselleck's authorities are normative rather than descriptive. Heidegger does not believe that most people experience the present as a three-part compact. He views the present in its already broken state, at a time when most people live in a degraded version of time without proper reference to past or future. Thus he argues from the absence of such a concord that it should exist. In fact, it seems safe to say that the very notion of the threefold present, in this case at least, is a back formation, constructed as the opposite of the unhappy state that actually exists and projected back into the past as an ideal. Augustine's testimony might be taken as evidence for the actual existence of that ideal, except that his account is, in its own way, as haunted by distention as Heidegger's. The role of attention is to overcome the ordinary distention of time and thus bring a human consciousness somewhat closer to the eternity of God. Secondly, it is not at all clear how either of these accounts of individual experience might be expanded to cover the situation of experience in general. As Koselleck concedes, "it remains an open question whether the intersubjective temporal structures of history can be adequately adduced from existential analysis."[9] But this is, in fact, exactly what he does.

Despite its argumentative thinness, Koselleck's example has been influential in discussions of what is sometimes called the "historical present."[10] Basically, the term *historical present* is an awkward synonym for what Trollope simply calls *now*: the collective sense of a longish contemporary period as distinct in some way. But the term also includes a three-part argument. It implies that a particular understanding of this longer present has prevailed generally in history. In this sense, a better synonym might be *traditional present*. It also implies that this traditional present is historical in a second sense, in that it has ceased to prevail and has now passed into history. The title of Harry Harootunian's essay on this subject is, therefore, "Remembering the Historical Present." Finally, this traditional present is historical in that it always includes history. In other words, the traditional present was not cut off from the past but incorporated it, so that the present was a fluid part of the transmission of the past into the future.

This understanding of the historical present as a traditionally normative form seamlessly incorporating past and future into itself is now quite widespread. For example, Peter Osborne identifies the "phenomenological present" as a basic structure that the "historical present generalizes and complicates."[11] For Osborne, this phenomenological present is "always threefold."[12] Here he relies on Augustine and Husserl for support, as Koselleck had relied on Augustine and Heidegger. In a slightly more normative tone, Helga Nowotny calls on the example of James to argue that "the 'specious present' is not just interpreted as a phenomenon of individual psychology, but becomes socially and politically interpretable."[13] Here Nowotny ignores the doubts that James had built into his own term for the extended experiential present, as Osborne takes for granted the tortured speculations of Husserl as if they were matters of settled fact. As Paul Ricoeur points out, though, the difficulties that Husserl had in explaining how the three parts of time could converge on a single point are only amplified if his model is expanded to the more general level of intersubjective time.[14] Thus the historical present turns out to depend on a prototype, the experiential present, that is itself in need of much better explanation and support.

It seems odd, in any case, to rely primarily on modern authorities like James, Husserl, and Heidegger for models of what the present used to look like. On one hand, this would seem to involve reading back into history observations made about the present in modern times. On the other hand, the detectable existence of the threefold experience of the present in the researches of James and the investigations of Husserl would seem to contradict the idea that the present had freed itself of past and future as far back as the French Revolution. If the present had already dwindled to a pinprick, then why were these authorities so convinced that it must take up some measurable time? In fact, what James hesitantly called the "specious present" is itself a modern idea, developed slowly in the course of the 19th century against the traditional notion, passed on from Aristotle, that the true present is but a single point. The real problem for James and Husserl is that they cannot quite free themselves of the traditional authority of the strict present, the infinitesimal point, so that they can formulate a more modern notion of the present as a differentiated space.

In the absence of any real support for the authority of the historical present in these arguments, the basic question still remains: what was the present? Is it really the case that for much of history, human temporal experience was a successful amalgamation of the three parts of time that James and Husserl struggled so mightily to compose? Of course, it is easy to see why this question is not usually asked, much less answered, since it is hard to imagine what kind of evidence would settle the issue. We cannot exactly poll the dead about a present that is long past. However, even some speculative evidence might tell in an argument that has heretofore relied mostly on authority and a priori reasoning.

II

What, then, was the present? Hartog, like Koselleck before him, takes Augustine as a norm of measurement, if not exactly a constant in human history. As he puts it, "Augustine's phenomenological description of the three times still remains essential for apprehending and expressing these experiences."[15] But Hartog is also aware that the anthropological evidence does not always support the notion that Augustine's threefold structure is the essential substrate of temporal experience before the modern break. His example is the Maori of contact times, for whom the future was behind and not in front.[16] What actually lies behind in this case is a vast fund of possible actions, all of which exist more or less out of time and from which actions in the present are chosen. Time thus runs from potentiality to actuality, toward what European tradition calls the future, and not from that future through the present into a settled and no longer existent past. Thus it seems, from this one example at least, that the most fundamental aspect of the "historical present," the order within it of past, present, and future, is not an experiential given.

Presumably, such examples could be multiplied, since it stands to reason that the wide variety of human societies would have had a similarly wide variety of time schemes and timescales. But, according to some sociologists, it is not necessarily given that human beings need a time scheme at all. According to Elias, experiential time in the absence of clocks and calendars is discontinuous and episodic.[17] Time is told in terms of significant events, which succeed one another without establishing any particular relations of succession or priority. Early timing, as Elias puts it, is "point-like and discontinuous."[18] Where there are external time schemes, these are not meant to distinguish and order particular times but simply to establish the "right time," as in the right time to plant or worship. Thus the important distinction is not between past, present, and future, but between right and wrong, as in the ancient Greek distinction between *kairos*, the appropriate, and *akairos*, the ill-timed.[19]

Something similar is suggested by Georges Gurvitch, who has established an especially complex typology of social times. In his schema, archaic societies superimpose a cyclical mythological time onto the more or less steady state of nature, which is itself inflected by the unpredictable tempi of rudimentary social organizations. Since even ecological time is full of its own surprises, as in the case of storms and droughts, and since mythological time has a tendency to leap forward from cycle to cycle, the result is an especially complex mixture of stasis and uncertainty. As Gurvitch puts it, "this is a deceptive time, where time leaping forward and sudden crises are hidden behind delay and where erratic time seems to play a more influential role than would be expected."[20] In other words, time in such a situation is an unpredictable mixture of stasis and crisis, with purely episodic transitions from event to event, even as most things seem to exist in a steady state.

Gurvitch's model is so complex that it is a little hard to imagine what it would have been like to live in such a society on a daily basis. But the basic point he makes is the one also made by Elias, that societies without clocks or calendars need not necessarily have a single time scheme at all. Without this prior establishment of a single time-line, the distinctive ordering of past, present, and future makes little sense. Perhaps this is why Jack Goody claims to have found so little narrative in the oral societies he has studied, why he believes that the "intercalation of the past and the present" is raised as a problem in an acute form only with the advent of writing.[21] At the very least, then, there is some reason to believe that the ordered trinity of past, present, and future is not a primordial aspect of human experience.

The evidence of recorded history suggests that locating the present in any very precise way would have been very difficult for most early societies. Ancient Greek timekeeping, for example, was variable and inexact, as the day was broken up into unequal periods and the nighttime was not divided at all. Until about 159 BCE, daytime hour divisions were not observed in Rome.[22] The very concept of abstract punctuality was difficult to enforce when the shortest measurable unit of time, the *punctum*, was twelve to fifteen minutes long.[23] The minute, as the sixtieth part of an hour, was not generally recognized as necessary or useful until the end of the 16th century.[24] But, in fact, precise time-reckoning was not generally recognized as necessary or useful until quite late in recorded history. On the very threshold of the 20th century, Field General von Moltke observed complacently to the Reichstag that "practical life rarely demands a punctuality reckoned in minutes."[25] What *was* recognized, especially in highly organized units like monastic communities, was the rule of sequence and order. Where timing methods were developed and applied in such communities, it was not to tie observances to particular times but to make sure that they did not run too long or too short and thus interfere with one another.[26] As David Landes points out in his history of timekeeping, human beings got along for many centuries without having to know the time, which is to say, without having to locate the present moment in a larger or wider context.[27]

In fact, it makes more sense to think of the present as the imposition of a particular kind of society, as a forcible simplification of the almost chaotic time scheme outlined by Gurvitch. Having to do so is the effect of a larger, more organized society. Thus Elias maintains that the present is not a natural aspect of human consciousness in the raw but rather the result of a certain kind of social conditioning: "The concept of the present . . . represents the timing of a living human group sufficiently developed to relate a continuous series of events, whether natural, social or personal, to the change to which it is itself subjected."[28] Only in this social sense are individuals able to "distinguish as the present what they are doing here and now . . . both from what is over and subsists only in memory, and from what they may possibly once do, experience or suffer, that is, from the past and future."[29] The present, by this account, is not given but developed, and its first effect is to interpose itself and thus divide time into three parts.

The present may very well be a latecomer to a temporal system founded on the more basic distinction between earlier and later, before and after. These work quite well, in theory and in practice, without an absolute division between them. They provide all that is needed for a reliable sense of consequence. In fact, as McTaggart pointed out, before and after are much more reliable than their threefold counterpart, since the relations of before and after do not change, while the same event can be and is future, present, and past in turn. That which is before some later X is always before that X, but that which is before now will sooner or later be behind it.[30] The present is therefore a relatively specialized time tool, added as a division between before and after. Since its purpose is to transform these by division into past and future, it makes little sense to complain that the present has come to divorce us from the past. The present *is* a division. Logic dictates that it can only reintegrate past and future into itself if it has already divided them, so it makes little sense to think of the integrated, threefold present as primordial and the merely divisive one as a later degeneration.

There is at least some evidence to suggest, then, that anthropology and sociology may reinforce the findings of contemporary neurobiology, which have tended to undermine the notion that the present is an experiential given. At the very least, it seems safe to say that it is not necessary to organize human temporality on the trinitarian model of the present, or perhaps on any model of the present at all. Reconsidering the present in this way, making it optional, as it were, would at least have the salutary effect of explaining why it has always been so hard to understand. But this would, in its turn, raise another set of questions. If the present is not an eternal fact of human consciousness, if it is something more like a social category, then when, how, and why did it come about? Thus the question "What was the present?" might be rephrased as the even more puzzling "When was the present?"

III

Hartog is not the only one to note that some societies existing in historical time have not seemed to need a concept of the present much like the one taken for granted by European philosophy and science. He says that for the Maori "the divide between [past and future] which inaugurates modern Western history does not exist. It would be better to say that past and present coexist, and that the 'past' is 'reabsorbed' into the 'present.'"[31] The picture thus painted resembles quite closely that usually offered in accounts of the heroic age of the ancient Greeks. Hartog develops such an account at length, relying at points on the famous chapter in Erich Auerbach's *Mimesis*. For Auerbach, the *Iliad* takes place in "a pure present, without temporal perspective, in which there is 'no development.'"[32] Hartog insists that Achilles does act and in so doing creates effects not already comprehended by the past, but, he says, these effects are always folded back into the old present, which is so absorptive that it can include these without changing. The result of this circular process is "the perpetual present of epic time."[33]

This version of epic time is a kind of constant in European histories, so old as to seem almost perpetual itself, about which more will be said in a later chapter. But it is worth asking, despite the great authority of this account, whether the time scheme so described is all present or no present at all. Gurvitch maintains against the consensus that the epic tradition always projects "the present into the past."[34] In its attempt to ensure the stability of things, these heroic societies "make the past endure by dissolving the present and future in it."[35] In the end, though, it doesn't seem to matter much whether this singular time zone is called the past or the present, since any one of these terms in isolation is meaningless. The present, in particular, has its meaning and purpose only insofar as it keeps the past and the future apart. Without them—in isolation, as it were—it is not the present but just time, albeit time that does not pass. To see this static time as a perpetual present, as natural as it may be for a modern European, is, in fact, to read a past society by means of the very concept it is not supposed to have had. "Perpetual present," then, is not just a semantic contradiction in terms but also a historical one, in that it forces a modern name onto a past society that, by all accounts, had no use for it. It is a bit like taking an ancient celebration of the winter solstice and calling it Christmas.

If societies like that of the ancient Greeks of the heroic period, on the very edge of recorded history, did not observe the present as a social fact, then when did it develop? It might seem that any useful concept of the present must require a single, unified social subject, the *we* in *The Way We Live Now*. If this now is not shared, then it loses most of its usefulness and its significance. The construction of the present, though, cannot be the result of the self-consciousness of a unified social subject but must rather be an essential part of the creation of that consciousness. The present, in this respect, would not be a part of time or a kind of time but an approach to time, what Gurvitch calls mastery, an approach that involves representing, symbolizing, measuring, and quantifying time. As Gurvitch says, "mastery means *to unify time* in a definite manner."[36] What Gurvitch generally means by this term is the mastery of time, the unification and regulation of an otherwise inchoate process. But it must also involve the mastery of *times*, that is to say the elimination of the sort of temporal multiplicity that, for Gurvitch at least, is the ordinary state of human experience. Thus it must also mean the mastery of individual subjects, the unification of their individual time zones into one. This unification is also necessarily a synchronization, one that is more or less synonymous with the present as a social fact.

It probably goes without saying that another indispensable feature of such an organized time scheme is some abstract accounting system, independent of events in the particular and external to all individuals. When Locke complained that it is not possible to compare two different times, he meant that it is not possible to compare them directly. He had probably not forgotten about clocks, which make it possible to compare the experiential times of different individuals by reference to a measurement independent of them. Without some such standard against which to compare, it is hard to see what meaning could attach to *the* present. Perhaps this is why Elias finds it hard to locate any sure sense of the present apart from clocks and calendars, and why Goody finds it absent apart from writing. Even with these devices in hand, though, at least according to Gurvitch, the unification and simplification of time is always relative and perhaps even intermittent.[37] The underlying multiplicity of times is not erased but merely dominated.

Even in historical times, the Greeks found this basic task of synchronization inordinately difficult to accomplish. In the ancient world, according to Denis Feeney, "each city had its own way of calibrating past time, usually through lists of local magistrates, just as they had their own currencies, their own weights and measures, and their own religions."[38] Basic communication thus required a certain amount of agile synchronization. But this did not involve translating between calendars, because the ancients did not, for the most part, use dates. What they used for correlation instead were events. Decisive battles or notable reigns were not located within some neutral grid of dates, because such a thing did not exist. Instead, battles and reigns were used as markers to build up a common sense of historical time.[39] A classical author as late as

Cornelius Nepos gauged historical time by counting back and forth between certain fixed points: the first Olympiad, the foundation of Rome, the birth of Alexander the Great.[40]

Building up a sense of historical synchronicity in this way was a very difficult matter, but it was also an important project, first in order to give the various Greek states some way of conceiving their common history and then of integrating Rome into that commonality. Ancient history is thus replete with synchromatic tables, parallel columns of important events, counted down according to the Greeks, the Romans, and sometimes the Asian or North African worlds beyond. In this context, according to Feeney, each synchronism is a simile, a comparison of apparently distant things.[41] Like a simile, though, a synchronism inevitably raises a question about the basis of the comparison. Aristotle was probably the first to object that mere coincidence in time does not imply any causal connection or common purpose.[42] But the whole point of these synchronisms in the first place was to envelop the various Greek states and the republic of Rome in a common history with a common meaning. The fact that two distant battles seemed to happen at more or less the same time implied that the armies involved were part of a single struggle.

As this account already implies, the unification under Roman rule of the world it knew made a large-scale synchronization at least theoretically possible. The historian who most grandly proclaims this possibility is Polybius: "How, when and why all the known parts of the world were brought under the domination of Rome is to be seen as a single action and a single spectacle, which has an identifiable beginning, a fixed duration and an acknowledged end."[43] Polybius makes it clear how a single subject makes possible the narration of a single action, which can then be divided into the Aristotelian categories of beginning, middle, and end. These do not, of course, correspond in any exact way to past, present, and future. An Aristotelian action has a rather large middle, while the threefold time scheme has a very narrow one. For Aristotle himself, as Paul Ricoeur has argued at length, the three parts of the tragic plot are logical and not temporal categories.[44] Still, it is possible to see in Polybius the beginning of the adaptation of the tragic plot so that it can serve in temporal and even historical situations. To live in Rome between its beginning and its coming end was to live in a social present, albeit a vague and distended one, quite different from anything available before.

Polybius also attempted to convert the old synchromatic tables into a dated calendar.[45] Marking time in this way was especially important to Rome, which tended to identify itself with recorded history and measurable time. Still, the

Republican calendar was a hash of asymmetric months in which dates were not counted forward from one, but backward and forward from the three ceremonial markers: kalends, nones, and ides. For a number of reasons, one of them that the calendrical year did not correspond very closely to the solar year, it was essentially impossible to use numerical dates to mark particular events in time. Thus these still tended to be associated with festival days.[46] Because they were not anchored to particular dates or days of the week, these festival days could seem to exist outside of time, setting up a different system of accounting that could run in circles as the rest of the calendar marched forward from the founding of Rome. In fact, the pre-Julian calendar was so far out of sync with the solar year that seasonal festivals did not coincide with the parts of the year they were supposed to celebrate.[47] In other words, the establishment of Rome as a dominating world subject did not necessarily lead to a uniform mastery of time. In addition to the presence within Rome of various different time-lines along which counting might proceed, there was the consciousness, even for Polybius, that the sway of Rome was not, in fact, universal, that there were empires beyond it, perhaps with histories of their own.

The Julian calendar, of course, was supposed to change all this, and it did certainly establish a consistent accounting of time that corresponded more exactly than any system before to the patterns of the sun and moon. This is perhaps the most obvious example in European history of the mastery of time as the mastery of a people, and vice versa.[48] But there were other, ancillary calendars in use even after the Julian reform, so that it was still possible to live in several todays at once. The advent of the Julian calendar coincides, more or less, with the Advent itself, and this pivotal event became the center from which past and future are now calculated. This, in itself, would seem to give time a meaningful synchronization it had not had before. It is also sometimes asserted that monastic discipline, with its rigorous observation of regular times for prayers and other observations synchronized daily time in a similarly meaningful way.[49] Gerhard Dohrn-van Rossum shows in great detail, though, that monastic time organization was not meant to respect either time or punctuality in the abstract, but rather to make it possible to handle all the religious duties of the day without scanting any.[50] As to time itself, according to Thomas Aquinas, "the Church does not strive for restriction through the clever study of time. One does not need to use an astrolabe to know when it is time to eat."[51]

As for the calendar, the BC/AD system was not proposed as a universal system until 1627, and the century did not become a common means of reckoning until about a century after that.[52] The general sense of Christ's birth as the comprehensive midpoint in time, in other words, did not very immediately translate into a necessary system of organizing dates. Hannah Arendt maintains, in fact, that early Christianity was indifferent to these in general.[53] She points to Augustine's *Civitas Dei*, with its principled disinterest in secular history. For Augustine, the uniqueness of the Incarnation was absolute, and thus it made all other dates more or less identical in their insignificance. Since earthly events matter only against the background of eternity, they need not be organized or understood backward and forward in relation to other earthly events but only in relation to the constancy of God's plan. It makes little sense, in other words, to look to Christianity for a general observation of the social present. The messianic now, as Giorgio Agamben defines it, is neither in nor out of chronological time but is the time that time takes to conclude, like the time it takes us to realize what has just happened, only raised to a higher power.[54] This is not a present marked in time but one lifted out of it. As Paul puts it, the Christian lives "forgetting what lies behind, but straining forward to what lies ahead."[55] The present, according to this diagram, is not a point or a dividing line but a vector leading always in one direction. In any case, the time of the Church was not the only time, even in the Middle Ages, when the Church itself recognized the claims of ordinary chronological time alongside Paul's time of constant expectation.[56]

When it came to accounting for historical time, the early Christians used the same sort of synchromatic tables that had served the ancient Greeks. The most influential of these was the *Chronicle* of Eusebius, who set out in the 3rd century CE to coordinate the Jewish and Christian scriptures with the histories of the secular nations. Eusebius arranged his historical matrix in nineteen parallel columns, one for each tradition, a system that narrowed as early empires passed into dust and the Romans came to dominate the world.[57] The result was so influential it established a tradition of tabular parallel histories in which the Roman Empire gradually came to be the dominant column.[58] Unfortunately, this tradition lasted longer than the Roman Empire itself, so that the tables gradually acquired more columns again, and the problem of coordinating different world histories emerged in the very attempts to graphically solve it. One problem that became more stringent over time was that of reconciling the apparent history given in the Bible with that provided by other sources. Even the Hebrew and Greek versions of the Bible itself gave different accounts of the amount of time between the Creation and the Flood. Then, when Europe acquired more complete knowledge of the past histories of civilizations like the Egyptian and the Chinese, the account of past time became even more complicated.[59]

Daniel Rosenberg and Anthony Grafton have shown that such tabular, parallel histories were by far the dominant graphical form in which history was visualized well into the modern period. Though the ostensible purpose of such tables was to provide a sort of Rosetta stone for the translation of one time-line into another, what they tended to expose was the incoherence of the time-line as a metaphor. Even the apparent mastery of Rome over other chronologies was temporary and to a large extent illusory. What the tables showed, then, was that for the greater part of human history, there were multiple times running simultaneously and thus multiple historical presents. Or, to put it more accurately, the very notion of a historical present as a single synchronizing point to which all could refer made no sense.

In fact, it seems quite possible that a universal synchronization in terms of a single present was not really available until Newton offered it to the world in a purely abstract form. As Locke formulated it at the end of the 17th century, "this present moment is common to all things that are now in being, and equally comprehends that part of their Existence, as much as if they were all but one single Being; and we may truly say, they all exist in the same moment of Time."[60] This particular definition of the common present is not just different from but actually diametrically opposed to all previous versions of that category. From the time of the Greeks, at least, events had conferred dignity on dates, such as they were. The subjects of history—Greeks, Romans, or Christians—had given history its meaning. In fact, without such significance, dated time had no particular purpose, and there was no reason to observe it. In Locke's formula, though, time itself precedes those who might observe it, and dates exist whether anything happens on them or not. Time itself is the universal subject, and it enlists "all things," conscious or not, and makes of them "one single Being" in a way that no actual civilization could even imagine.

Something like this must have been a prerequisite before Kant could even propose his project for a universal history: "A philosophical attempt to work out a universal history of the world in accordance with a plan of nature aimed at a perfect civil union of mankind."[61] This history would transform "an otherwise planless *aggregate* of human actions" into a system, recognized as a whole.[62] Locke's abstract sense of all beings as one in the light of time makes it possible for Kant to propose a universal human subject, which is itself quite abstract since it exists only as a promise, as the end of the historical system of accounting. Redeemed from its past state as a planless and episodic aggregate, the human story ceases to be episodic and assumes the shape of a plot. This plot is then called history, in that purely modern sense of the term that uses it to designate not the story of events alone but rather the invisible course of time that subtends it. This is what Koselleck refers to as "history as a collective singular without reference to any associated subject," and which he dates as a general project to about 1780.[63]

Without some such conception of history, the very notion of the present as a point of universal synchronization makes no sense. But it is also worth noting the priority that Locke gives to the present itself. For Locke, it is not the common past that makes all existence into one being, or the expectation of a common future, but rather the reality of the common present. That all things share the same now is our best evidence for their commonality and thus for our belief that they share a common past and future, neither of which we can actually witness. In much the same way that the coordination of the different senses just *is* the present for Aristotle, the unity of all beings just *is* the present for Locke. It seems possible to say, therefore, that the present as a social fact, apart from its scientific or experiential versions, did not emerge until sometime in the early modern period, somewhere between Locke and Kant, and that it did not arrive by separating itself from the past and the future. Rather, it seems safer to say that locating the present is the primary step in the coordination of social time and that the establishing of the past and future as linear history, in Kant's terms, follows from that.

Still, it is hard to say with any certainty that Locke's version of the universal present has ever been much more than a convention. For one thing, history continued to be represented primarily in tabular form well into the modern period. Joseph Priestley, for example, produced a widely influential *New Chart of History* in the late 18th century that was supposed to allow viewers to locate historical events in "universal time."[64] But he did not himself believe that this concept was anything more than a useful convenience.[65] For him, "universal time" was really nothing more than the empty space containing the various histories. It did not itself have any substance, any power, or even any meaning. In fact, as Priestley's example inspired more and more such tables in the following centuries, the space of universal time became more and more crowded and thus more and more chaotic. Bringing the histories of different cultures, religions, and places together did not, in other words, have the effect of unifying them but rather of dramatizing their differences. The great project of "synchronology," to adapt the title of Stephen Hawes's 1869 chart, ultimately showed how asynchronous historical times had always been.[66]

IV

Perhaps this brief history of the present as a social fact can help clarify the terms and stakes of contemporary complaints about our present. First of all, charges that the present has changed in some way presume that it is a given, a constant and primordial fact of human sociality. But this does not seem to be the case. Negotiating the world in terms of before and after does not necessarily require a fine line between them, and organizing a social polity on a local basis does not necessarily require calendrical time with a moving present at the center of it. Philosophical concerns about the now are, of course, very old, but these tend to concentrate on it as a logical or experiential puzzle and not as a feature of social organization. People with any historical sense at all will have some notion of the difference of their time from other times, but this does not imply the existence of a unified social present. In this form, it seems that the present is fairly young, as human institutions go, and that it did not change in modern times but arrived with them. The imposition of the present, in and as modernity, might seem to divide a previously unified temporal continuum. But it seems that such a continuum had not been part of the human understanding of historical time, at least not until Kant proposed it as a project. Perhaps this project makes no sense without the present to anchor it, as the past and the future, unlike before and after, really make no sense unless the present intervenes between them.

Perhaps, then, the problem is with the present *as such*. General unhappiness with it may not have to do with its being too long or too short, too disconnected from past or future, or with any other quality, but precisely with its lack of qualities. Locke's sense of all being as one being unified in the moment was not just abstract but also ideal, in the sense that it did not actually exist in reality. Nowadays, at least if philosophers like Peter Sloterdijk are to be believed, that unity exists inescapably. As Sloterdijk puts it, "the globalized world is the synchronized world; its form is produced simultaneity, and it finds convergence in things that are current."[67] One of the reasons this is a deleterious situation for so many is the source of the synchronization. As Walter Benjamin says in *The Arcades Project*, expanding on Marx, "simultaneity, the basis of the new style of living, likewise comes from mechanical production."[68] Kant's grand project of universal human history is realized by industrial capitalism, by and for its technologies, and thus its character is purely mechanical.

If the old synchromatic tables used by the Greeks produced a global simultaneity that was essentially metaphorical, contemporary technologies produce one that is definitely metonymic. Where the Greeks did not actually need a date unless some significant event sanctioned it, dates and times now come constantly and unbidden, prior to their significance.[69] Simultaneity seems to require explanation, to demand meaning, and so people get restive if the year or the decade does not readily offer its own interpretation. Constant attempts to define the spirit of our age simply expose the fact that the age precedes its spirit, as the calendar precedes events. The present, above all, precedes any explanation of itself. We have been given this sort of social present without having any particular need or use for it, and now we labor under the necessity of finding a place for it. This may be why the present is now such a topic of anxious discussion.

One thing these discussions tend to ignore, however, is their own constant presence in the modern period. Romantic opposition to the abstraction of time coincides with Kant's plan to achieve it, and the tradition of critique that Berlin calls the opposition of quality to quantity is a steady component of modern philosophy from the early German Romantics through Kierke-gaard and beyond. In other words, there have been many time-lines and other versions of the present within and against the apparent global synchronic-ity. Koselleck himself was fond of the notion of "the contemporaneity of the noncontemporaneous, or perhaps, rather, of the nonsimultaneous occur-ring simultaneously."[70] For Koselleck, this is a fact of history, each portion of which will contain different, noncurrent time-lines. It seems, however, that the advent of modernity, with its single time-line of progress, tends to exacerbate the traditional tendency to arrange these different time-line hierarchically, as the Greeks did when they banished the barbarians to a time behind.[71] The unsynchronized still exists, somehow, within the synchronous and beneath its domination.

For Gurvitch, on the other hand, the mastery of any one time frame over the others is always illusory. He quotes from Maurice Halbwachs the prin-ciple that "there are as many origins of different times as there are different groups. No one time is imposed on all groups."[72] What passes in the modern period for the universal time of technology and science is the attempt of the bourgeois class to impose "its own scale of time as universal."[73] But its preten-sions are only partly successful, and modern time has more parts to it, more layers, more tension and competition than that of any earlier period.[74] Gur-vitch might warn us, then, that what is sometimes advertised as "a world-wide condition of simultaneity" is not by any means what it is cracked up to be.[75] For anyone who has to make a phone call from Sydney to Los Angeles, the abstract ideal of a universal synchronization is not of much relevance. Surely one of the effects of standardized world time zones is to dramatize how far apart Sydney and Los Angeles actually are.

From this point of view, the apparent simultaneity of all contemporary time-lines may look like the empty abstraction it was for Priestley, not a fact of experience at all but a convention. One reason we tend to feel otherwise may be the continuing influence of the concept of modernism, which has always served to convert modernity's empty simultaneity into a meaningful synchronism. In the beginning, of course, *modern* was a deictic, a synonym for *now*, designating the present.[76] Even in its celebrated quarrel with the ancient, the modern was still a relative term, and thus it was capable of moving in time to keep up with the present. Sometime around 1927, though, with the publication of *A Survey of Modernist Poetry* by Robert Graves and Laura Riding, the term *modern* lost its deictic quality, its relativity, and its freedom and became attached to a particular stretch of years. Once it was provided with a beginning, whether it was identified with Baudelaire, Wilde, or Eliot, the modern also necessarily needed an end, and once it was defined by these it could no longer function as a synonym for the contemporary. Thus the rather odd situation in which the modern is no longer present and the present is apparently no longer modern.

In its young and innocent days as a simple deictic, the modern did not have any particular character. Arbitrary and relative, it simply designated whatever was happening right now, a random and therefore meaningless collection of events. Losing its connection to the present and becoming fixed in historical time, losing its essentially arbitrary quality and acquiring a particular significance, the "spirit" that is usually associated with an "age," all happen as functions of one another. However, these changes do not just happen to the modern, now converted to a period concept, but to the more general concept of the present, with which it had been synonymous. Though the modern has been severed from the present, ideas about the present are still strongly conditioned by the modern. All the terms for *now*, including *contemporary*, seem to have lost their deictic function, their purely relative significance, and are expected to have a particular quality, on the model of the modern. The technological synchronicity that allowed the modern to think of itself as a distinct period of time was purely metonymic in nature, and thus it lacked almost by definition any particular significance. In a sense, it was no more meaningful than the deictic it had replaced. Modernism is the concept that converts this empty set of relations into a significant simultaneity.

One impediment to this effect is the empty circularity of the term itself. Since modern*ism* intrinsically means nothing more than commitment to the modern, it can hardly lend to modernity the significance it lacks. Another problem is modernism's own lack of meaningful simultaneity. It is worth noting at this point that Rosenberg and Grafton end their history of the historical time chart with an extensive examination of some exemplary graphs of modernism, including the famous flowchart of modern movements that Alfred Barr printed as the cover of the catalog for the MOMA exhibition *Cubism and Abstract Art* in 1936.[77] Though Barr's chart is often denounced as an attempt to impose a single interpretation of the modern movement, it actually shows how disparate the modern movements were, at least in time. In any one year, say 1910, cubism, futurism, expressionism, orphism, and suprematism all jostle for the same space in the historical continuum. The historical present thus pictured is just as various and asynchronous as the world histories of Eusebius or Priestley. And Barr's is only one of several rival charts, all attempting to coordinate the histories of various tendencies and movements into a single entity that might be called modernism.

This attempt has never been successful. In fact, it is now quite common to insist that there are different national and regional versions of modernism across the globe. For example, Fredric Jameson notes the presence within modernism of "various national traditions" with "a certain order and logic specific to each one."[78] Modernism does not arrive at the same time or move with the same tempo in Latin America as it does in France. In fact, the wider the geographical net is cast the more various are the time schemes, so that modernism in Japan may coincide only very briefly with what passes by the same name in much of Europe. Of course, the natural end of this exercise is to decide that the very concept of modernism, as the work of a particular time, is faulty, and that its uniform imposition on the globe is a historical injustice. Pluralizing modernism is one way of saving appearances, but this also pulls it away from the temporal simultaneity that was the basis of modernity in the first place. There is hardly any need for a concept like modernism if the historical singularity of the modern has disappeared.

It might be said, then, that modernism has left us the expectation of a meaningfully synchronized present without providing a very good example of how to realize it.[79] If nothing else, though, the common assumption that modernism should be followed by a successor movement, like it in form but different in content, shows how the notion of a common, social present persists in the absence of any particular evidence for it. Presumably, if the contemporary were such a present, then there wouldn't be so much anxiety about how to characterize it, what to call it. Current debates about this issue assume that one of the more important offices of art and literature is to declare the meaning of the present. A closer look, taken in the next three chapters, at painting, narrative fiction, and film, will show instead how these arts have tended to question the assumptions on which the traditional notion of the present has been based.

Part Two

4

The Present in Pictures

I

What does the present look like? At first, this may seem a rather daft question. After all, what else do we see *but* the present, staring us in the face every day? We can't see the past or the future, so what we see, by process of elimination, must be the present. Or perhaps it would be more accurate to say that what we see must be *in* the present. But if so, what visual quality marks it as such? Apparently, there are disorders in which the ability to discern the present is lost. In his essay on déjà vu, Henri Bergson recounts the case of a patient who "has not completely succeeded in apprehending the actual; he cannot say with certainty whether now is present, past or even future; he will decide for the past if that idea be suggested in the questions put to him."[1] The way Bergson phrases this is rather curious, since it implies that the patient is still seeing now but cannot recognize now as the present. What sort of sensory evidence is required to recognize the present? The easy impressionability of the patient in this case seems to suggest that the present is an idea added on to the sheer immediacy of the now. But, if so, how does the additional notion of the present change what he experiences already?

Generally speaking, philosophy and common sense tend to agree with Kant that time itself cannot be apprehended directly. As Kant puts it, time "cannot be a determination of outer appearances; it has to do neither with shape nor position, but with the relation of representations in our inner state."[2] Time, in other words, is a condition of experience, a necessary context for it and, as such, is no more apprehensible than air. But does this necessarily mean that the present cannot be apprehended directly? One of the basic requirements for any kind of experience, as Kant sees it, is that the manifold presented by the outer world to the senses be unified in time and space. He calls this "the synthesis of apprehension," and its chief duty in the whole process of experience is to weld impressions into the "absolute unity" of a "single moment."[3] Being organized into successive presents, then, is a necessary attribute of experience, but this organization, according to Kant, is not really a process but rather an a priori condition, without which there could not be representations of time or space at all.[4]

Temporal experience is more specifically organized by what Kant calls a schema, a kind of template laying down the conditions under which intuitions can be matched to concepts.[5] A schema is something like the requirement that a triangle have three sides, a sort of experiential funnel by which the moiling stuff of intuitions is sifted into categories like *triangle* or *square*. The most basic schemata are temporal in nature, and they match concepts like substance and causality. What Kant calls the schema of actuality "is existence at some determinate time."[6] In other words, if something exists, it must exist at some time. In contrast, if it is possible, it exists at some time or other, and if it is necessary, it exists at all times. The schema of actuality, then, seems to govern our apprehension of the present, of things that exist now. But the schemata in general are not to be confused with images, and, in fact, Kant goes to some lengths to oppose them. Images, he says, are never adequate to concepts and must always be connected to them via the schemata. In other words, "existence at some determinate time" is not something we can see but rather is part of the format in which we see. There is no image of the present as such.

For Kant, of course, these are a priori conditions of experience and not empirical facts. But other, more recent philosophers have considered in a more immediate and practical context the question of whether or not we can see the present. Craig Callender, for one, wonders if there is some phenomenal property that corresponds to the concept *being present*. For a number of reasons, he decides this issue in the negative. He points out, for example, that the night sky includes light many eons old that does not look any different from that reflected off the planets, which is itself from a much more recent past. He also notes that most useful phenomenal properties allow us to make distinctions such as that between loud and not so loud or between red and blue. But if every perception is in the present, then it cannot be used in this way.[7] The situation in this case is a little like that in the Land of Oz, where everyone wears green spectacles. But if everything is a just a shade of green, then green is the one color that cannot be distinguished, and so the Emerald City would only seem emerald to outsiders.

Callender does not consider other basic facts of human vision. The eye is not fixed but constantly moving and blinking, so that the field of vision is not received all at once but built up out of a number of brief, partial glimpses. Though it is sometimes said that the constant sight of things together in space is our visual warrant for their common temporality, the fact is that we actually assemble this spatial simultaneity from a collection of shorter, more restricted visual reports. The essentially discontinuous nature of saccadic vision means that what passes for the present is actually punctured throughout by infinitesimal fits of inattention and shifts in focus. The fact that we do not see these must cast a certain shadow over what we do see, which can hardly be the unitary, immediate entity we call the present if it is neither unitary nor immediate. Callender does end his argument by citing other evidence from cognitive neuroscience and physics to the effect that phenomenal properties come into the nervous system from a number of different directions and at different rates.[8] The effect of this sort of evidence is to suggest that the present is not a raw aspect of perception but more a belief about it.

If we cannot actually see the present, then what is it that we do see? Kant's argument, which has been definitive in this respect, is that we must represent time by means of spatial analogies. The problem with space as such, though, is that it is temporally invariant. Kant suggests that we tend to represent the passage of time as "a line progressing to infinity," but lines don't actually progress anywhere. They just sit there. Kant says so himself, insisting that a line is just like time "with this one exception, that while the parts of the line are simultaneous the parts of time are always successive," as if that one exception didn't make all the difference.[9] In order to effectively represent time, then, we have to add to space the factor of movement. This is why so many ancient definitions of time were based on celestial motions and why opponents of these were able to argue that they were circular since the concept of motion already includes time within it.[10] Be that as it may, in ordinary experience, we certainly do tend to represent time by means of spatial movement. Clocks are simplified, abstract versions of the ordinary movement that supports our sense of time. This basic fact has serious implications for our sensory experience of the present, though, since it would seem to mean that there is no readily available sensory version of it. Though we cannot see time itself, we do at least have a constant image of its existence, but even this cannot be said of the present.

Perhaps this is one reason why the present has always been so hard to grasp for definition. In phenomenal terms, the present can only be intuited by reference to the continuum from which it has been abstracted. Deriving the still from the moving, the discontinuous from the continuous, the unitary from the dispersed, has always been difficult. It has been so hard, in fact, that it makes sense to wonder if the whole project hasn't started from the wrong end. The hardest part, even for those like James and Husserl, who have given the problem its most substantial solutions, is, having started from the standpoint of the present, how to explain the experience of motion. The answers to this question have been so tenuous they have made the fact that we do sense motion seem almost miraculous. Perhaps it would make more sense to start with the evident fact of the experience of motion and then wonder how the experience of the present might be derived from that. Looking at the world as it happens doesn't seem to yield much obvious evidence for a concept that has been so easily taken as the fixed point from which all analysis of temporal experience must proceed.[11]

Given these evident facts of ordinary sensory experience, the best chance we have to see the present might lie in pictures. To say so, however, would seem to contradict the commonsensical idea that every picture is a picture of the past. Though this is true in relation to the viewer, in itself every picture is a picture of some present. Surely this is one source of the uncanny power of photographs, that they hold time still, as it never is otherwise, so that a present can be kept to be viewed again later. In a photograph, some part of the past is *still* present, though its subjects may be many years in the grave. Jacques Aumont, like many commentators, maintains that in a photograph "*I see time*,"[12] but this can hardly be true, since time, by definition, is not static. Rather, what is seen is a part of time that doesn't change, which is what we tend to think of as the characteristic feature of the present.

At certain points in human history, holding the present in this way has been the purpose of pictures. In 1833, John Constable advertised his aims as a painter in this way: "To give 'to one brief moment caught from fleeting time' a lasting and sober existence, and to render permanent many of those splendid but evanescent Exhibitions, which are ever occurring in the changes of external Nature."[13] Here Constable quotes from Wordsworth, who praised a painting by George Beaumont for giving "To one brief moment caught from fleeting time / The appropriate calm of blest eternity." In this familiar formula, time is always "fleeting," which is to say in constant, incessant motion, and the job of painting is to snatch some portion of it as it passes. The implication of the formula is that the portion of time rendered in the picture is captured from a prior existence in the wild, as it were. Moments, in other words, exist as units of time. But this is at least paradoxical, since it implies that ever-flowing time is fundamentally made up of static parts. How much more sensible it would be to assume that the painter gives the moment its stillness, as he gives it the quality of perdurability. In fact, this is not so inconsistent with Constable's claims or with the reality of painting, which makes time still so that it can endure. This would mean, though, that the painter does not capture the moment but makes it, by abstracting the still from the constantly moving. In other words, the painter produces the present, and the painting is not a retrospective record but a temporally creative act.

If we want to know what the present looks like, then, we should look at pictures, not because they are so many records of a present already in existence but because they are the means by which the look of the present is established in the first place. Where else is there any phenomenal evidence of that strange aspect of time that is moving and still at once? This might seem a fantastic notion if the present is considered to be a primordial fact of human existence. But the evidence of the preceding chapters has suggested that the present is not a given, that it is, in most of its versions, a metaphor covering a relatively formless temporal situation. There is certainly no need to believe that the present is older than the habit of making pictures, since this may be almost as old as speech. In any case, the known history of pictures is also a history of attempts to conceptualize the present, to find an image for something whose very nature makes it not just hard to see but also difficult to imagine.

II

The classic account of the nature of pictures also necessarily involves a theory of the present, if for no other reason than that the effect of pictures is supposed to be confined to the present. As E. H. Gombrich puts it, perspective painting abides by the negative rule that "the artist must not include in his image anything the eye-witness could not have seen from a particular point at a particular moment."[14] In his well-known essay, "Moment and Movement in Art," Gombrich quotes Lord Shaftesbury to the effect that the artist, having chosen his moment, is "afterward debar'd the taking advantage from any other Action than what is immediately present."[15] A proper painting is, therefore, as James Harris puts it, "of necessity a *punctum temporis* or instant."[16] As Harris noted, though, this restriction makes any very complicated subject matter difficult to represent without the application of information about preceding and succeeding moments. Painters had solved this problem for centuries in various ways, mostly by suspending their figures at what seemed to be crucial moments in a legible arc of action. Such moments are, in the canonical words of G. E. Lessing, "fruitful" enough to give the imagination free reign.[17]

Lessing's *Laocoön* is usually cited as distinguishing painting from poetry on the grounds that the former cannot convincingly depict time, as the latter cannot logically encompass any space. Lessing does, in fact, lay down a law that sounds a good deal like Shaftesbury's, to the effect that the single moment depicted in a painting "must express nothing transitory."[18] But even these momentary images can convincingly imitate an action, he argues, if the painter chooses an instant "which is most suggestive and from which the preceding and succeeding actions are most easily comprehensible."[19] A painting of a properly poised runner, for example, will exploit the viewers' experience of running in order to suggest parts of the action that aren't actually there. Elsewhere, Lessing cautions his reader that such techniques do not allow the painter to combine two different points separated in time, as the poet can routinely do, but he almost immediately begins to waffle and qualify this statement, until he finally decides that a very great painter, such as Raphael, may occasionally combine "two different moments into one."[20] What he seems to mean by this is, as Robin Le Poidevin puts it, that paintings "can represent aspects of time that they are unable to depict."[21] Though a painting may only show a runner in midstep, it can also use the general fund of human knowledge about running to make that image into a sign for a full gallop.

Because Lessing was writing about paintings and not about human sensory physiology, he did not move on to the next logical question, whether paintings work the way they do because human perception always superimposes bits of the past and future on what counts for the immediately present. But this is certainly the assumption that took hold in the decades after *Laocoön* was published in 1766. The "specious present" that James developed toward the end of the 19th century has an obvious ancestor in the "fruitful" moment that Lessing describes in the 18th century and in the whole tradition of perspectival painting that had preceded him. This, then, is the canonical version of the present in pictures and sensory psychology, the threefold structure centered on a dimensionless instant. This model of the present governs ideas about visual experience well into the 20th century, as evidenced by Sartre's version of it in *The Imaginary*: "Retention and protention constitute, in every way, the sense of the present visual impression—without these synthetic acts, one could hardly speak of an impression at all."[22] But the extension of this version of the present from aesthetic standards to phenomenology does raise at least one question. Why is the task of the painter so tricky if ordinary experience always superimposes past and future onto every present impression? If *every* moment is a fruitful moment, then doesn't that more or less define Lessing's category out of existence? This is a question that could only be answered once photography established the principle that any moment at all could be the source of a picture.

The whole project of photography might be described as an investigation of the moment. The desire to capture the moment as it passes is one that preceded photography and that must, in some sense, have brought it into being. Even before Wordsworth, William Cowper expresses it in *The Task*: "To arrest the fleeting images that fill / The mirror of the mind, and hold them fast, / And force them sit, till he has pencilled off / A faithful likeness of the forms he views."[23] Thus Cowper seems to describe, sixty years before the fact, the ambition that drove the British originator of photography, William Henry Fox Talbot, who was frustrated by his inability to transcribe the images cast by the camera lucida, a portable version of the camera obscura that was usable outside. Looking back on his first ambitions, Fox Talbot remembers thinking "how charming it would be if it were possible to cause these natural images to imprint themselves durably, and remain fixed upon the paper!"[24] A similar expression turns up in a story passed down from his French counterpart Joseph Niépce, who almost came to despair from his inability "to fix the images of the camera."[25] When Daguerre announced his invention to the world public, Samuel Morse thought back to experiments of his own "to ascertain if it were possible to fix the image of the *camera obscura*."[26] To be sure, other expressions are used, and it is not uncommon for early experimenters to confess a desire to capture or store the images made by the camera obscura.[27] But the idea of fixation is so pervasive in these early accounts of the drive to develop photography that it hardly seems a pun when a report to the French Academy describes Niépce as having an "idée fixe."[28]

As Lady Elizabeth Eastlake informed her readers in 1857, the expression *fixing the image* is "photographic language" for making it permanent, and the pervasiveness of the expression arises from the essential difficulty faced by would-be photographers, since it was easier to cause an image to appear than it was to make it stay.[29] But "fixing" must have *become* photographic language, with this specialized meaning gradually narrowed from the one Fox Talbot originally had in mind. For the first and most basic problem he faced was that of stilling the image cast by his camera lucida. Even set up before a distant and mostly static landscape, the camera lucida would convey a good deal of movement, including the gradual progress of the shadows as the day advanced.

Thus his lament over the "fairy pictures, creations of a moment, and destined as rapidly to fade away" that the camera cast before his hapless pencil.[30] To fix is, first of all, to arrest the moving image and then to fasten it durably to a medium. As the London *Literary Gazette* put it in reporting on Daguerre's announcement: a method "has been discovered to fix these wonderful images, which have hitherto passed away volatile—evanescent as a dream—to stop them at our will and . . . render them permanent before our eyes."[31]

To capture the moment means, on one hand, to stop the seen before it disappears. Gombrich quotes Ruskin's regret that he cannot catch a wave so as to give an exact description of it as the daguerreotype can.[32] On the other hand, capturing the moment as the early photographs did also revealed something that had never been seen and which therefore could not have been regretted as it passed. When Eastlake marvels at the hypernormal detail of Fox Talbot's photographs, she means to include the temporal as well as the spatial, "the fall, not of the avalanche, but of the apple, the most fleeting smile of the babe."[33] A year after Eastlake's article was published, Thomas J. Kaife presented a rapid-fire camera that, he claimed, could make visible "epochs of time inappreciable to our natural unaided organ of vision."[34] Photography, in other words, does not merely record vision but also improves on it, and the speed with which claims like Kaife's surfaced suggests that exploring unseen increments of time was one of the earliest ambitions attached to photography. In this sense, the camera is a popular version of the time microscopes that were filling the psychology laboratories at just this time.

The camera, in other words, does not just stop and record time but also investigates it. Geoffrey Batchen maintains that, for Talbot, "the primary subject of every photograph was . . . time itself."[35] In a fairly basic way, this is seriously counterintuitive, though, because the photograph improves on the camera obscura precisely by subtracting time. Looking at a photograph may help us sense within ourselves the passage of time, but this is surely not inherent in the image itself, which is unnaturally still. In temporal terms, then, the real subject of every photograph is the present, isolated for examination from the tracts of time around it. The present is not directly available for examination because it doesn't last but also because we cannot register the present and be in it at the same time.[36] To recognize the present is to make it into something else, something no longer present to us in the same way. In other words, photographs captured what had not been seen before, what could not have been seen, and the picture of the present they produced turned out to differ in important ways from the one they had been invented to record.

This new version of the present turned out to violate preconceived notions to such an extent that it demanded a specialized name: the instant. To some extent, the notion of the instant seems intrinsic to photography, appearing in Fox Talbot's first description of it: "The most transitory of things, a shadow, the proverbial emblem of all that is fleeting and momentary, may be fettered by the spells of our 'natural magic,' and may be fixed for ever in the position which it seemed only destined for a single instant to occupy."[37] Fox Talbot also attempted to make good on this boast, which was hardly realizable with the technology of 1839, by experimenting with flash exposures, produced by electric discharge.[38] Ordinary photographs of moving subjects were commonly described as "instantaneous" by the 1850s, even though the exposure times were still fairly lengthy and great cleverness had to be employed to get everything in focus.[39] When roll film was finally introduced, toward the end of the century, "the golden age of the ordinary instant" could commence, though, as Tom Gunning points out, this "age" was hardly more than an instant itself.[40] Thus the research-oriented projects of Etienne-Jules Marey and Eadweard Muybridge were not in advance of the popular market but actually arrived as it reached its height. When Muybridge was hired by Leland Stanford in 1872 to take his celebrated pictures of a horse in motion, he was expected to produce an instantaneous photograph, an already well-known species, though one with which Muybridge himself had no experience.[41]

For most of the 19th century, definitions of the instantaneous were remarkably elastic. Even Albert Londe, who was a professional and might have been expected to try harder, provisionally defined the instant as "a very brief period of time."[42] Elsewhere, bound to put a number on it, Londe chose a quarter of a second.[43] But the term implied, for many, a truly impossible standard, an exposure of infinite quickness capturing a single point in time. Thus an 1895 manual called *Instantaneous Photography* tried to restrict the art to exposures "beyond the limits of measurement."[44] The manual did not specify how this was to be verified, but it is clear from this demand that popular photographers were conducting their own series of experiments, parallel to those in the psychology labs, on the human experience of time. For the instantaneous photograph to realize its potential, it had to be made entirely by mechanical means, without the intervention of the clumsy hands or the blurry eye of the photographer. This was necessary if the instantaneous photograph was to record sights that human beings cannot ordinarily see, to meet Londe's most persuasive definition: "We propose to call *instantaneous* every photograph taken in a fraction of a second that our senses do not allow us to perceive."[45] By this definition, then, the instantaneous photograph had to reveal the invisible, and thus it tested, by implication, the temporal acuity of human eyesight.

Using the camera to find an exposure time shorter than the instant of time discernible by eye turned out to be technically easy but conceptually paradoxical. The experiments proved to be rather difficult to validate for the rather ironic reason that the instantaneous photograph had to be *seen* to exceed the limits of sight. There was no such thing as an instantaneous still life, for reasons that must be fairly obvious, though they seem, on examination, to be a little odd.[46] For an instantaneous photograph to achieve its purpose, it had, in a sense, to fail a little, to show some awkwardness of pose, some apparent violation of the laws of physics, some motion blur, that would prove that it had delved within the ordinary moment of vision. The results of the camera's perfection as a surrogate, in other words, would show to the eye itself as imperfections in the photograph.

The fad for instantaneous photography turned on this paradox. There was a powerful novelty value in these pictures, which seemed to realize for the first time the truly revolutionary powers of the camera.[47] The off-balance, oddly suspended scenes they showed were taken as visible evidence of rapid temporal change, all the more persuasive for the violent distortion it took to make them still. The snapshot, in particular, seemed to make the present visible and thus to vouch for its existence and dramatize its brevity at the same time.[48] Thus it seems inevitable, in retrospect, that the snapshot fad and the first real discussions of the present should have coincided in the 1890s. These were not coincidental beginnings, though, but rather culminations, since the present had been under concerted study throughout the century and even the term "snapshot" dates to 1860 and Sir John Herschel.[49]

The full complexity of these snapshots was probably revealed most effectively by the opposition they excited. From the beginning, rapid-fire photography was criticized as unrealistic, non-mimetic, since it represented sights that the unaided eye could not see. Even the painter Jean-Louis-Ernest Meissonier, who had been inspired by Muybridge's horse pictures, considered them little more than raw material, since a true artist "no more has the right to put on canvas what is visible with the aid of a sole lens than to paint what a microscope would show him."[50] The rift created within the ancient partnership of vision and art was felt with almost visceral pain, and many artists and even some photographers reacted as if betrayed. Marey, for one, mounted a defense of his methods that relied on the example of Lessing, as if these new pictures were simply validations of classical standards of picture making. The most legible phase of any human movement, he instructed the painters, was to be found where the body has just changed its direction. These segments could be lifted from chronophotographs and used with full confidence.[51] But he did not make it clear how the viewer is to deduce from a single frame, without the surrounding evidence, that the body in question is at any particular moment in its progress, that it might be turning left rather than right, rising rather than falling.

In fact, the craze for instantaneous photography had systematically refuted the assumptions on which the notion of the fruitful moment had been based. As Marta Braun shows, there is a necessary trade-off in these photographs between analysis and synthesis, between the clarity of the first and the smooth integration of the second. The more finely time is sliced into instants, the more difficult it is to see how these might be reintegrated into a legible arc of action.[52] Gombrich points out that the production stills used to advertise commercial films are not usually actual frames but rather posed shots taken after the fact. Frame grabs are not always legible enough to portray the important action at a moment.[53] In short, the evidence of photography suggests that the fruitful moment is not a judicious selection from nature but an aesthetic convention.[54] The picture of the present that had been accepted as an aesthetic standard since at least the 18th century was not relevant outside painting because it could not be generalized: every moment is not a fruitful moment. Is it any wonder that this period of European aesthetic history coincided with the psychological investigations of the present that culminated in the work of James and Husserl?

The passage from painting to photography had exposed the fact that the present, at least as Lessing had defined it, is not something to be captured by a clever and judicious eye but is only to be found in pictures themselves. It turns out that painting had been compensating for its essential stillness by all sorts of stratagems that simply aren't necessary in ordinary sensory experience, which does not need reintegration because it does not come piecemeal in the first place. Photography exposed the artificiality of the present stripped of the adjustments and justifications with which painting had surrounded it. Thus it tended to call into question not just the fruitful moment but also the moment itself. But the passage from painting to photography, from Lessing's formulation of the fruitful moment to the rage for instantaneous photography, is a relatively brief episode in the history of the visual arts. And the relationship that Lessing assumes must obtain between a picture and the present, the representational relationship, though it is the one most usually associated with art as such, is not the only one available. In the long run of the history of pictures, the present has often meant something quite different.

III

Lessing's assumption that art necessarily occurs in the present may have been conditioned by much older ideas about the nature of art. According to the ancients, it is not just works of art that exist in the present but aesthetic experience itself. According to Plato, in the *Philebus*, any kind of pleasure is "unlimited, and belongs to the kind that does not and never will contain within itself and derive from itself either beginning, middle, or end."[55] For Aristotle as well, pleasure, like sensation in general, is "at any moment complete, for it does not lack anything which coming into being later will complete its form."[56] What is true of pleasure in general is certainly true of aesthetic experience, which is commonly constituted by the co-presence of different perceptions—color and shape, for example—in a single sensation.[57] Such sensations are not just limited to the present, but their singularity is one of the defining features of the present as such.

It is not too far from this descriptive account to a normative ideal in which the perfect convergence of perceptions in the present is the feature that makes aesthetic experience the finest kind of experience in general. The Peripatetic, the Epicurean, and the Neo-Platonic schools, despite their various differences, all agreed that aesthetic pleasure was the highest kind, "corresponding to the richest possible grasp of a moment."[58] The intrinsic identity of pleasure with that "grasp of the moment" then became a conscious ideal, as though it were not an inevitable fact of experience. Beauty was to be apprehended all at once, not just in a moment but even in an instant, and the brevity of the present ceased to be a problem as it became an index of a very particular kind of pleasurable certainty. The obvious fact that we must encounter any work of art, novel as much as photograph, in the present, thus becomes a measure of art's particular excellence as experience.

This did mean, though, that the "binding problem," that nagging question as to how the different sensations are to be combined, reappeared as a threat within aesthetic theory. Aristotle worried about this early on, and in worrying about it, he produced yet another set of ideas about the extent of the present. Very small things, he said, cannot be beautiful because our apprehension of them approaches zero in terms of time, while very large ones cannot be beautiful because we cannot see them in their entirety all at once.[59] Aristotle arrived at the same solution to this problem as Goldilocks, with the successful work of art installed firmly in the happy middle. The beautiful takes up just as much time as an ordinary person can apprehend at once, which is to say that it is coterminous with the present, as measured by some implicit norm. But this model of aesthetic experience, and the version of the present that corresponds to it, were always to be haunted by the extremes on either side. The instantaneous photograph is one example of an aesthetic object that seems to reduce our apprehension to the vanishing point. On the other side, where the time required for apprehension exceeds the beautiful mean, lies the sublime.

Burke, for example, produces a physiological explanation for the fact that "visual objects of great dimensions are Sublime."[60] If all the rays of light reflected by some huge object strike the eye at once, it must necessarily be overwhelmed by the effect. If, on the other hand, the eye processes rays of light one by one, then it is clear that it must soon be exhausted by the labor of composing all the rays reflected by some huge object. In either case, the eye's inability to receive all the rays at once causes it pain and pushes the experience into the realm of the sublime. Though the evidence and reasoning differ considerably from that of Aristotle, the identification of the beautiful with the experience of a unitary present is the same. Kant's explanation is similar to Burke's, though less physiological. For him, "the effort to take up into a single intuition a measure for magnitude requiring a significant time for apprehension" results in a kind of violence insofar as it impresses us with the limits of our comprehension. Feeling this limit, painful though it might be, is also the condition for realizing that we can actually extend our comprehension beyond the limit, which is the source of the curious "pleasure that is possible only by means of displeasure" that Kant calls the sublime.[61]

The definition of the beautiful, then, depends on a certain version of the present, one in which experience is perfectly centered on a moment of just the right size. Louis Marin cites a certain landscape by Poussin, in which a "single time, that of simultaneous presence, governs the contemplation of the things that are co-present in the space."[62] There is a kind of blissful, utopian enjoyment inherent in such scenes, what Marin calls "the sovereign delight of the present," that comes from feeling as if all the past and all the future were concentrated somehow in a moment so that they could be taken in all at once. Paintings like this are visualizations of the classical repose and calm that Goethe called "that splendid feeling of the present."[63] A very different kind of present appears, however, in another painting by Poussin, in which a storm crackles in the background. This irruption of the sudden into the static calm of a classic landscape exemplifies what Marin calls "the meteoric instant of sublimity."[64] The flash of lightning is a perfect representation of the paradox of the pictorial sublime in that it is huge and scary but also infinitesimal in its temporal extent. In fact, Marin implies that the lightning flash becomes huge and scary by first being too quick for the eye to catch. The time it takes to happen is so much shorter than the time that is necessary to see anything, much less paint anything, that the calm symmetry of the beautiful is torn apart from within. Thus the phenomenological evidence that was to become notorious in the instantaneous photograph is visible within painting itself in a natural effect that is "*incommensurable* with the present of the gaze that contemplates it where it has been deposited on the canvas."[65]

When such effects had been formulated by Burke and Kant, the sublime could become a catchword for experiences that exceed the bounds that classical aesthetics had placed around the present. One of the most prominent examples in this respect is Barnett Newman's mini-manifesto "The Sublime Is Now." Newman's dictum is based on an experience that seems designed to illustrate Kant's theory of the sublime. Visiting some ancient Native American mounds in Ohio, Newman feels simultaneously his own small presence, "here I am, *here*," and the immensity of the cosmos beyond, "chaos, rivers, landscapes."[66] Being able to intuit that chaos, though, redounds upon the tiny individual, whose presence suddenly seems immense: "Man is present."[67] This present is one transformed by its passage through the immensity of the cosmos. It is not, Jean-François Lyotard insists, the conscious now of Augustine and Husserl, but one that defies the ordinary limits of consciousness.[68] It contains, in other words, the vast space of time intuited before the ancient mounds.

Newman's sublime now is meant to be exceptional and even subversive, though it relies on a set of ideas that had seemed second nature since the time of Aristotle. And it is also possible that the sublime now, the present that comprehends an experience of vast times, is more common in the history of art than fruitful moments. Aristotle worries about experiences that take too little or too much time, but he does not consider the very similar problem of experiences that touch on too many times. The canonical sublime experience, standing before the ancient Egyptian pyramids or Newman's Ohio mounds, is an experience of temporal vastness but also of temporal difference. It must certainly be a feature of seeing the pyramids to be impressed with their elemental presence right now, the inaccessible present of their origins, and the many, many times through which they have persisted. It must make the present seem both large and small at the same time, which is more or less what Newman

means by the sublime now. Despite the tradition that locates art in the mid-
dling temporal zones, this sublime present is the one more commonly found
in pictures, even perhaps those that restrict themselves to a single moment.

IV

In most traditional accounts, the presence of a picture is inversely related to
the absence of its subject. The canonical example in this respect is the story
of the Corinthian maid who traces her lover's shadow on the wall as a way
of keeping him in mind even when he is gone.[69] But a tracing of this kind
is a fairly minimal representation whose extreme schematism seems almost
designed to emphasize the absence of the subject. Would a photograph of
the lover have the same effect of absence, as most commentators on the art
of photography insist, or would it rather suggest two presences, two presents,
one being contemplated now and another, also visible and identical to the first,
located at the time of exposure? If one current definition is to be accepted, and
a picture is an *"image with a medium,"*[70] then wouldn't there always be these
two presents to contend with, one relevant to the physical substrate and one
implied by the image itself? Reducing this situation to a single moment is
one of the simplifications that Lessing's theory accomplished in concentrating
attention solely on the represented subject of the picture.

Even as a purely material artifact, though, a work of art intersects with time
in a number of different ways. Art exists most simply in immediate terms, as
what Jacques Rancière calls the "senseless naked presence" of the material substrate.[71] The stone, the paint, the print are there, first of all, in a pure present,
static marks on a page, paint left splashed on a wall. For all but the very newest
artworks, though, that presence has a curious quality, so solid in the now and
yet redolent of some stretch of the past. George Kubler claims this is true of all
artifacts, which have a specific kind of duration, "so durable that they antedate
every living creature on earth, so indestructible that their survival may, for all
we know, ultimately approach infinity."[72] Exaggerated though it may be, this
idea does suggest the way in which artworks may occupy a kind of extended
present tense, even as mere objects, quite regardless of any content. What else
is Benjamin's theory of the aura about but this awe that attaches to pictures
from the past, whose physical presence now seems a kind of mystery?

Originally, the image was inseparable from its medium, and the whole purpose of picture making was to attach the two to one another so that the image
might enjoy some of the durability of the medium. *Imago* referred at first to the

wax death masks that were carried in Roman funeral processions and that were sometimes worn by actors hired to imitate the illustrious dead.[73] For Hans Belting, the negative, empty space of the mask indicates the absence of its subject, but it must also be significant that the impression records the actual touch of the one who passed away.[74] Even when it is removed and carried aloft, the mask retains a connection with the body of the deceased. The cavity inside the mask, therefore, is the original impression, and this antecedent shows why impressions have always been understood with some literalness, as if they always resulted from the impress of a touch. The medium, then, retains the original present of the image, which is one reason why such masks remain powerful in later generations. In a larger sense, the continuing connection between image and medium allows for a temporal cooperation between them, a kind of relay between the immediacy of the medium and the timelessness of the image, and between the pathos of the image and the durability of the medium.

This sort of temporal exchange is most apparent in the pictures that were produced as ritual objects before art became art. Artifacts and architectural monuments, according to Alexander Nagel and Christopher Wood, were understood "as belonging to more than one historical moment simultaneously. . . . They stitched through time, pulling two points on the chronological timeline together until they met."[75] This was possible because the time in which the artifact had been created, the time in which it was appreciated, and the time it depicted were put in touch with one another, so that they could indicate one another without becoming the same. This is especially true of the icons produced for the Byzantine church. The icon, as a physical object, was thought to be identical to the sacred personage it represented, which is why it was able to perform the same kind of miracles. Thus, according to Georges Didi-Huberman, it would be wrong to say that the icon represents: its purpose is to make present.[76] It exists in order to create a connection between two different modes of the present, the eternal present of God and the immediate present of the mortal observer.

In his work on Fra Angelico, Didi-Huberman argues that this complex temporality is characteristic of at least some Renaissance art as well. In his long analysis of the theme of Annunciation in the Renaissance, Didi-Huberman maintains that "all times and all tenses are thus at work in the moment of the Annunciation."[77] The event itself is virtually instantaneous, as Mary comes to realize the truth almost before it is announced, but it also embodies a present as old as Creation itself, in a garden that is often evoked in paintings on this theme, and also another present that will finally bring an end to time. Such paintings tell a very brief story, with the gesture of the angel toward the virgin, but superimpose on that moment others that are connected to it by leaps through time. Jean-Luc Nancy says something similar about a painting of the Visitation by Pontormo. Here there is also an instantaneous revelation, as the unborn John the Baptist leaps in the womb of his mother, Elizabeth, when she greets Mary. As a revelation, this moment reaches forward to the life that John can herald even before he is born and beyond that to the celebrations of this moment repeated in Christian ritual. The painting thus establishes what Nancy calls a "double presence . . . a present that comes from nowhere and from no time." As the two women gaze at one another, two times also exchange gazes, the time of the observer and the time of the painting, "the view across which the immemorial considers us and, so to speak, sees us coming and even offers us its own visitation."[78]

As these discussions imply, the model for the relation of the image to the medium, of the presence of the image to the present of the medium, is the Incarnation itself. Didi-Huberman quotes the dictum of Giovanni di Genova, whose definition of *imago* ends with the notion that every image allows the viewer to participate in the mystery of the Incarnation.[79] Along with all its other mysteries, the Incarnation binds the eternal to time, so that every moment of Christ's life on Earth resonates with a past that goes back to Creation and a future that extends to Apocalypse. All of this is contained within what Didi-Huberman calls a "virtual present," an instant that is produced "outside any historical law," one that shows "how a 'linear' notion of the present moment is radically overturned and superseded."[80] Though it incorporates past and future, then, this version of the present is almost the opposite of the one institutionalized later as the fruitful moment. In literal terms, the picture still occupies but a moment, the instant of recognition in Annunciation or Visitation, and it also contains a past and a future. But these are not the moments lying immediately before and after, not perhaps moments at all, but vast stretches of time that come to be superimposed on the unchanging plane of the painted surface.

The close association of this virtual present with the sacred might suggest that the situation changes when, as Hans Belting puts it, art ceases to serve a religious function and becomes art. Certainly, the separation of the picture from any ritualistic context, and, in the form of easel painting, from any context at all, must mean that it comes to be located more simply in a particular version of the present. But this is not necessarily the case. According to Rancière, at any rate, "the present of art is always in the past and in the future. Its presence is always in two places at once."[81] The picture plane, then, is inherently a kind of interface between two times equally present that confront one another in the moment. Surely this duality becomes even more apparent as the image comes to be more temporally representational. The location of the image in a distinct moment always makes it an instantaneous anachronism. The very details that once made a painting by Caillebotte so topical now make it seem all the more remote. Thus Didi-Huberman maintains that the attempt to contain a historical moment within a painting always fails: "We could say that a historical painting never captured any 'real moment,' that the most beautiful *istorie* in painting represent time as an equivocation about succession, as an aporia of the instantaneous."[82]

Even classical history painting, though, according to Marin, contains strategic equivocations about the present. The fruitful moment itself might be understood as an "interval, not represented except by the cut that sharply punctures the unity of the present."[83] The instantaneous pause so central to such pictures might seem less like an intimation of the narrative moments around it and more like an "unrepresentable, invisible flash-instant, the *punctum temporis* of the mortal cut."[84] On the other hand, even conventional history paintings might include gestures toward the vast present indicated by sacred art. Didi-Huberman's contention that the purpose of sacred art is to *present* is matched by Marin's notion that representational art "*presents itself as representing something.*"[85] In other words, a painting does not necessarily dissolve itself in service of the image represented, to assume the classic role of the window giving on reality, but also always presents itself as an act of depiction. Whenever a painting emphasizes the presence of the picture plane or brings the background out of its appropriate position behind the figures, or even when it acquires a frame, then it identifies itself as a depiction. Whenever the image openly relies on its medium, then the picture turns on and brings out its own temporal identity. When description prevails over narration, detail over design, facture over mimesis, then the painting becomes an act of making present and not a representation.[86]

Even within the image, though, there are devices that Marin describes as presentational. Figures within the painting that gesture toward the focal point, sometimes by explicitly pointing, sometimes just by gazing intently, establish a deictic relationship within the image that reproduces the relationship established by the picture itself as it gestures toward its subject. This sort of pointing out, Marin says, establishes "an atemporal present," an "unassignable present," quite separate from the "categories of time and space."[87] Not the fruitful moment, or the blissful present of Poussin's calm landscape, this is the present in which the medium instantiates the image, lodging its time in another time that endures, though it does not last any longer than the instant of the image. If, on one hand, this atemporal present seems to harken back to the eternity of the icon, it also anticipates, in its self-reference and dependence on the medium, the development of modern art. Among Marin's examples are the geometric abstractions of Frank Stella, in which successive bands of color frame themselves, instead of framing a representational image. In so doing, he says, the painting "presents itself representing something."[88] It is a picture of a picture pointing at itself and thus staging the flat, atemporal present in which it will exist, hanging on the wall.

The farther away we get from the era in which easel painting was the norm and into a period dominated by installations, performance art, and new media, the more the classical form of the fruitful moment comes to seem an episode in art history, delimited, on one side, by the eternal present of sacred art and, on the other, by the atemporal present identified by Marin. Alexander Nagel makes this argument in a book that assembles a number of parallels between medieval and modern art. He sees installation art as itself a norm, as the ancient practice of fitting an image to a particular site is only briefly interrupted by the development of galleries.[89] Echoing an argument also made by Didi-Huberman, Nagel argues that the original type of the image, the index, in which there is a physical, causal link between referent and result, has once again become the norm, as artists after Duchamp lose interest in iconic resemblance.[90] In this analysis, conceptual art appears as a continuation of the long engagement of art with the mystery of the Incarnation, of the containment of ideas somehow in bodies and objects.[91] On all these counts, the present of the work of art assumes a much more complicated aspect than it has in its ostensibly canonical form as the fruitful moment.

This is the version of the present found in much contemporary art. The photography of Hiroshi Sugimoto, for example, involves a purposeful expansion of the time frame of the instantaneous snapshot. In one project, Sugimoto records the full duration of a film, as shown in a classic 1970s theater, combining every frame in one still image, so that the screen becomes a soft, luminous rectangle floating in the dark. A whole narrative, in other words, comes to be present in one instant of time. As Lutz Koepnick puts it, "Sugimoto pictures the presence of a past as one extended now in whose space we can enjoy the pleasures of losing our normal temporal bearing."[92] Among Koepnick's other examples of this effect are the glacier photographs of Nina Subin and Olafur Eliasson. Since a glacier is, in a sense, flux frozen in time, photographs of these can be seen as affording "a timeless present existing in a state of suspension."[93] Of course, a great deal depends on whether we see such examples as representative or exceptional, and Koepnick tends to see them as part of a countercurrent to the otherwise dominant trend of the present. But it is also true, as he argues, that the most common forms of contemporary art, including installation and video art, tend by nature to probe "the temporality of producing and attending presentness," to explore the nature of the present rather than taking it for granted.[94]

From this point of view, even easel painting might be seen to occupy a more extensive present. According to the curator of one of the recent now-based exhibitions, MoMA's *The Forever Now*, this situation obtains not just in performance art, installations, or video, but even in the ostensibly more traditional practice of painting. For Laura Hoptman, the painters in this exhibition place their works in an "eternal present" that she explicitly links to that of Saint Augustine.[95] According to this argument, contemporary painters have available to them all the resources of the entire history of painting, arranged not in some narrative order but rather in a vast simultaneity, from which they are free to choose without reverence or irony. In a sense, this reference to a larger present frees these artists from the local present and from the demands of critics and scholars that their work help to define it. Thus Hoptman is quite upbeat about a present that otherwise causes such distress in the art world, but only because this present is coextensive with another, much larger one.

The situation of art in general, then, might be said to resemble the one laid out in George Kubler's *The Shape of Time*. Kubler defines the time of art by reference to a more general theory in which the present is informed by signals relayed from the past. "The nature of a signal," he says, "is that its message is neither here nor now, but there and then. If it is a signal it is a past action, no longer embraced by the 'now' of present being. The perception of a signal happens 'now,' but its impulse and its transmission happened 'then.' In any event, the present instant is the plane upon which the signals of all being are projected."[96] The present, in other words, is a one-dimensional medium on whose infinite thinness the whole of time depends for its existence. Since the past is flattened out against the membrane of the present, there is no question of narrative or even of sequence. All "thens" are potentially equidistant to one another in the context of the single "now." This strikingly modern metaphor also applies quite well to the situation of medieval and Renaissance art as described by scholars such as Nagel and Didi-Huberman. Perhaps, then, it is the most satisfactory account we have right now of the present to be found in pictures.

5

Narrative and the "Unexplained Instant"

I

Toward the beginning of Elizabeth Bowen's wartime novel *The Heat of the Day*, the unreflective nature of the rather strangely named character Louie Lewis is described in this way: "Her object was to feel that she, Louie, *was*, and in the main she did not look back too willingly at what might have been said or done by her in pursuit of that."[1] Louie, in other words, lives in the present, but the simplicity of her devotion to the here and now is qualified considerably by the complexity of Bowen's account of it. Some of this convolution is due to Bowen's insistence on a prose style as twisted and indirect as the motives of her characters, but some of it is endemic to narrative fiction. For the most striking oddity of the passage is certainly the way it calls upon the past tense in order to assert Louie's existence in the present. According to settled stylistic convention, narration of a character's thoughts shifts the verb tense into the past, so that Louie's simple and immediate desire to affirm that "I am" appears in a very different form as the statement that "she, Louie, *was*." Anyone reading this novel will accept the conversion without even needing to understand it, and yet the italics applied to the second *was* in the sentence trip the eye and awake a skeptical attention. A clash between the existential and the narrative present appears, and what is meant to affirm Louie's life in the present sounds as though it were consigning her to the literal past.

The peculiarly convoluted present that appears in this instance is not just endemic to narrative but definitive of it. The speaker in a lyric poem or a character in a play is free to announce her existence in the present tense, and if Louie had been allowed by her creator to speak at this point, she too would have said, "I am." Because her thoughts are narrated and not transcribed, however, she must, by convention, slip into the past tense. Traditionally, the present tense itself appears in narration only in relatively specialized cases, almost all of them involving first-person narrators. Even there, its use is complicated by the practical fact that it is difficult "to record instant happenings at the instant they happen."[2] Even in such cases as Samuel Richardson's "writing to the minute," the gap between experience and record cannot literally disappear, a fact that parodies such as Fielding's *Shamela* made much of. In this case, convention seems to respect a basic fact of human life, that having an experience and recording it must be temporally distinct. Even those, like Louie, who live in the present, must narrate that fact in the past tense.

A similar example from Willa Cather's *The Professor's House* illustrates another aspect of this traditional practice. When Cather's protagonist, elderly professor Godfrey St. Peter, willingly faces the prospect of death late in the novel, he decides, "It was the truth."[3] Here, the underlying statement, what St. Peter must be understood to have thought to himself, employs what is sometimes called the gnomic present. Pronouncements like "it is the truth" are meant to be atemporal. In this case in particular, the existence of the abstraction in question is meant to be absolute. Shifting the gnomic present into the narrative past, as Cather does, has the weird effect of making the statement seem to contradict itself. It is hard to imagine a situation in which something was atemporal and absolute at some point in the past and then stopped being so. What kind of sense would it make to say "God was good"? If Nietzsche is right and God has died, then this can only mean that he was never himself in the first place.

In this case, though, more is involved than simple conventions about the narrative use of tense. The ghostly presence of the present tense beneath the past-tense verb sets up an ironic tension between the character's thoughts as they must have occurred and as they are transcribed by the narrator. The reader senses the narrator in the transposition from present to past and in so doing senses a difference in point of view, which in this case is almost an opposition. What is involved here, then, is the kind of free indirect discourse often applied in modern novels to a character's thoughts, with the implication that these are to be approached with some critical wariness. This technique often sets up a kind of temperamental distance between narrator and character, but it also dramatizes the necessary fact that these two inhabit different time zones. Even in the case of eternal and timeless truth, it seems, the narrator is behind the fact itself and must deliver it to the reader in the past tense.

Extreme cases like these, in which characters trying to think in the present about the present are formally prevented from doing so, show that managing the present is a challenge for any traditional narrative organization. Storytelling sounds like a simple, even childlike, practice, but the very concept of *telling* adds to *story* a complication in time. There are always at least two nows in any narrative, one for the events and one for their enunciation. If that enunciation is written and not oral, then there is another now, that of the reader. Though common sense might seem to dictate that these are arranged in sequential order, with the events before the narration and it before the reading, this is not necessarily the case.[4] Even in a traditional novel like *Jane Eyre*, the older Jane, the narrator, must have a certain priority in order to introduce her younger self, and this older Jane exists in a kind of hovering present over all the events of the novel, so that she can interpose her famous comments to the reader, a few of which are given in the present tense. It is clear to us, then, that *as a story* the events of *Jane Eyre* come at the end of the narrator's journey through adolescence, only when Jane has acquired the perspective and experience to transcribe them. According to Käte Hamburger, the events of a story, considered in relation to the time in which they are narrated, lose their temporal quality altogether and merge into an undifferentiated present.[5] Of course, for the reader, the entire novel exists in a kind of present, since every bit of it is equally available at any moment in readerly time.[6] On the surface, though, this complicated situation in which three nows are superimposed on one another reads as if there were no present at all, since everything is traditionally expressed in the past tense.

It is no wonder, then, that the role of the present in narrative time and the relation of that present to the present as such are controversial issues in critical theory. On one side is the notion, chiefly advanced by Paul Ricoeur, that the purpose of narrative is to rescue experience from the grip of the present, to help us rise above the sort of life that Louie seems to revel in. On the other side, emphasizing the inevitable difference between presence and the present, is a body of work that starts with Derrida's critique of Husserl. Beginning from fundamentally different suppositions about the present, the two sides then arrive at diametrically opposed conceptions of narrative time. For one side, Louie's *was* can easily be read as designating the temporal present particular to her, and the convention we follow in doing so can be interpreted as the mind's triumph over the distention of time. For the other, the italicized past-tense verb betrays the inevitably belated nature of all temporal experience, a displacement that happens even when the speaker says, "I am."

This disagreement has implications beyond the theory and criticism of literature, for narrative is widely held, in a number of disciplines, to be pervasive
in human experience. History, psychology, law, political science, sociology—
most human disciplines in fact—have decided that people are inevitably
storytelling creatures.[7] In philosophy, this effort was pioneered by Arthur
Danto, who emphasizes the pervasiveness in human thought and action of
"interreferential connections of the sort we find in *stories*."[8] Evidence of these
is embedded in language, in the web of "beginning and endings, of turning
points and crises and climaxes" that we throw over the world of phenomena.[9]
These referential implications, holding together the disparate parts of a temporal existence, are both evidence of and reinforcement for a connected and
continuous sense of time that is apparently necessary to effective human life.

However, Danto does not think that these connections are apprehensible in
action. Stories, by nature, are told later, after the fact, and narrative consciousness for Danto is one that consciously perceives the present as "part of a story
later to be told."[10] Even the present, in other words, is experienced through a
kind of proleptic retrospective, as it may appear from the standpoint of some
possible future. This, for Danto, is the advantage of a narrative consciousness,
that it enriches and expands the present by superimposing on it perspectives
derived from past and future. But his theory also includes within it the other
possibility, that every moment is instantly evacuated of meaning and significance by reference to another, later moment, on which it is dependent, so
that the full meaning of any moment can never be determined until time itself
comes to a halt. What Peter Brooks calls "anticipation of retrospection" may
be "our chief tool in making sense of narrative," but it is also a practice that
threatens to drop us into a state Brooks calls "narrative interminable."[11]

The stakes in this engagement between narrative and the present are not just
literary or even philosophical, for the notion that the present is constantly processed into some sort of narrative form in many cases is not just a descriptive
claim but also an ethical imperative, a demand inherent in ethical standards
that the present always be referred to causes and consequences beyond it. The
common complaint among cultural critics that contemporary consumers have
come to live in an idiotic here and now, that everyone is like Louie Lewis, rests
on the assumption that a responsible, fully conscious human existence must
transcend the present in which it seems to live. In these accounts, at least, the
question of the present is relevant not just to written narrative but also to that
larger experiential narrative that is supposed to give meaning and significance
to everything we do.

II

Though storytelling is commonly thought to be both pervasive and ancient, the classical tradition has very little to say about its temporal complexities. Plato sees all verbal art as narration of "past, present, or future events," but he has nothing else to say about the ways in which narrative handles time.[12] For him, the main feature distinguishing one kind of narrative from another is the identity of the speaker, which is openly that of the poet in epic but that of an imitated character in tragedy. The temporal implications of the first situation, the fact that the narrator must inhabit a different present from that of the story itself, do not seem to concern him. When Aristotle comes to consider epic poetry, he applies the dramatic standard of unity in action, which is superior in his mind to mere temporal unity. When he explains the famous and influential trio of beginning, middle, and end, his analogies are curiously static. The order constituted by a satisfactory plot, he says, is like that of a painting or the body of a living creature.[13] In fact, the dramatic unity of the single action constituted by beginning, middle, and end is fundamentally different from the merely temporal unity of a string of events. Thus Ricoeur's complaint that Aristotle does not simply ignore time but explicitly excludes it from his consideration of the tragic mythos.[14]

The influence of Aristotle was such that unity of action continued to seem the goal of all narrative art, even in periods that were more self-consciously concerned with time. When Goethe and Schiller developed their account of epic and dramatic poetry, both forms were subjected to the rule of unity, with this basic difference, that epic was restricted completely to the past and drama completely to the present.[15] Thus the epic poet surveys from a distance, with "calm self-possession," all that has already happened, while the dramatic "mimic" immerses us in the moment.[16] In developing what he calls "the idea of narration," Schiller emphasizes the freedom of the reader, who can start or stop at will, unlike the audience imprisoned within the time of a play, and the similar freedom of the narrator, who, because he comes after the events, has the calm equanimity of one for whom every moment is the same.[17] Schiller is therefore aware of what Aristotle ignores, the temporal difference between the present of the story and that of the storytelling, but for him this difference has a simplifying effect. For the past of the story is defined as *completely* past, every part of it equally far from the present, and the present time of the narrator is not imagined as progressive but rather as punctual, as the point made timeless by its equal relation to all other parts of time. Thus the calm freedom of the epic poet arises from the epic's exclusion of passing time.

Schiller adds, however, that the forms of epic and tragedy, past and present, must necessarily complicate one another. Since all poetry, even that of the epic, needs a certain concrete sensuousness that can only exist in the present, and since tragedy, in order to be noble, must acquire some of the ideal timelessness of epic, the two forms constantly strain toward their opposites.[18] Tragedy struggles upward to a freedom out of time, while epic aspires downward, as Schiller rather oddly puts it, to a timeliness at odds with its usual home in the past. All of this happens, in the best and most successful instances, without stress or strain, and the mixture ends up almost magically achieving the unity it might have seemed to violate. But Schiller's account also suggests another possibility, that the present occurs as a crisis in the timelessness of epic narration, that the calm freedom of the narrator cannot survive an exposure to the harsh brevity of the actual present.

This possibility, refigured in historical terms, forms the basis of Georg Lukács's theory of the novel. Lukács explicitly adopts from Goethe and Schiller the idea that drama exists in a "normative present tense," while the epic exists "completely in the past."[19] But the mixing that Schiller thought was necessary for both epic and tragedy now occurs in the novel, and not as a routine fact of composition but rather as the result of a historic trauma. "Time can become constitutive," he explains, "only when the bond with the transcendental home has been severed."[20] At some indeterminate point between the present and the high point of Greek civilization, the wholeness of life became partial, and meaning was no longer given but problematic. The calm freedom from time characteristic of the epic became anxious and self-conscious, and narrative began a long struggle with the incursion of time. What Lukács poignantly calls "the present, the unexplained instant" lodged itself in the midst of narrative and refused to capitulate to the demands of meaning.[21] In relation to the epic past, the present is no longer a necessary tincture of dramatic sensuousness but a break, an interruption that marks a fundamental crisis.

The difference that Lukács sees between his world and that of the Greeks may be entirely imaginary, but the difference between his account of narrative and that of Aristotle is not. Somewhere between Goethe and Lukács, the distance between the narrator's present and the story's past started to matter in a newly negative way, and the conflict between the two introduced temporal difference into narrative as a problem for it to solve. Lukács's account is both romantic and tendentious, but it is not particularly idiosyncratic. For Mikhail

Bakhtin as well, the epic takes place in an "absolute past" that is not so much a time as "a temporally valorized hierarchical category"[22] Even the Hellenistic romance, the source of so much of what we now think of as story, does not really take place in time, according to Bakhtin, because events in the romance change nothing but simply reveal what was always true, though obscure.[23] Only with the novel does narrative come into conflict with "the inconclusive present," and when it does, the open-endedness and sheer contingency of that present, "taken as a starting point and center for artistic and ideological orientation, [mark] an enormous revolution in the creative consciousness of man."[24] The novel, in other words, is a different kind of story, one in which that slight admixture of the immediate, that reference to the present, which for Schiller was a benign necessity, has become a subversive feature that tips it over into time.

Bakhtin, like Goethe and Schiller, imagines a total temporal separation between the epic story and the telling of it, a separation that ensures the uniformity of the epic past and the relative timelessness of the epic narrator's position. There is no question here of interference between story and teller or of self-consciousness on the part of the teller. With the novel, on the other hand, the time inhabited by the teller and the timeless past of the epic story come into direct contact. Where the epic had no now at all, the novel suddenly has at least two, as the self-conscious separation of story into story and teller divides the time of narration into two, as if each side had given temporality to the other by offering itself in comparison. For Lukács, this seems a single traumatic episode, but for Bakhtin it is simply a moment in a process that has happened several times, between classical antiquity and late Hellenism, between the Middle Ages and the Renaissance, and late in the 19th century. Surely the important point, though, is that this is a historical process, that the relative timelessness of stories in antiquity had to be qualified by some exposure to the contingency of an "inconclusive present." Thus the present becomes the mark of a certain kind of modernity, as the feature that turns ancient storytelling into narrative as we know it.

According to these experts, then, the present is a kind of necessary threat to narrative, inimical to it and constitutive of it all at once. The puzzle that the present imports into epic calm is a problem, the solution of which is narrative itself. The present thus comes to have a privileged, though controversial, place in contemporary disputes about the nature and necessity of narrative. For Ricoeur, the most influential proponent of the idea that narrative is fundamental to human self-understanding, the basic purpose of narration is to solve the problem of the present. Philosophy, Ricoeur maintains, is incapable of resolving the basic conflict between the cosmological instant and the extended present, both of which seem to have a claim on our understanding. Augustine's notion of a threefold present, "a present of future things, a present of past things, and a present of present things," is a start, and it is, according to Ricoeur, the "most elementary inductor of narrative," but it remains to novelists to flesh out this bare diagram with real experience.[25] The novel as a genre, then, is a vast encyclopedia "of the infinitely varied way[s] of combining the perspectives of time that speculation by itself fails to mediate."[26]

Novelists can work as they do, though, only because human experience is already structured into something like a series of rudimentary plots. Relying on Husserl and Heidegger, Ricoeur argues that human experience is structured by "an explicit or implicit phenomenology of 'doing something.'"[27] Any action, that is to say, necessarily depends on implicit assumptions about what is prior and subsequent to it. This is one reason why the present can never make sense to us as a dimensionless, isolated instant. From this implicit sense of an extended present, the novelist makes a more elaborate structure, which is then fed back into the general fund of human understanding, to form our future expectations of both life and literature. Ricoeur's three-volume exposition of this process is extensive and elaborate, but it is not particularly idiosyncratic. Frank Kermode, for one, also appeals to Augustine's threefold present and uses it as a model for "our way of bundling together perception of the present, memory of the past, and expectation of the future, in a common organization."[28] This constant bundling is, according to Kermode, the source of narrative plot and the explanation for its pervasiveness in human culture.

Ricoeur and Kermode, then, advance the common notion that narrative is more or less synonymous with temporality, the human experience of time as opposed to the mechanical measurement of it. In a way, though, their explanations make too much sense, for it is difficult to see why there should have been such a contradiction—between temporality and cosmological time—for the novel to resolve if, in fact, human experience is always so deeply structured into narratives. How did the notion of a dimensionless instant, the foundation of what Ricoeur calls cosmological time, come to impose itself on a consciousness so constantly entwined with past and future? If, in this sense, the novel offers a solution that seems too strong, in other respects it may seem too weak, since novels so often harbor temporal discontinuities that tear the present apart. Louie Lewis's past-tense pronouncement of her existence in the present is just one example of a split caused by the narrator's constitutional separation from all the time in the narrative. In such cases, as Ricoeur says himself, there is a "split between the discourse of the speaker (narrator, fictive author) and the discourse of the character."[29] By giving us more than one present to contend with, the novel may seem to take apart what Ricoeur says it is supposed to compose.

In any case, Ricoeur himself has substantial doubts, which help to make the third volume of his study seem both retrospective and a little regretful. He notes the fact that Husserl himself was never satisfied with his own phenomenology of time, particularly as he tried to extend it beyond single episodes to the whole of duration itself. How, he asks, is it possible "to draw, from a phenomenology applied in the first place to the continuous expansion of a point source, a phenomenology of the whole of time?"[30] How do the individual moments, fringed as they are with retentions and protentions, add up, sequence themselves, overlap, or otherwise combine without at some point becoming a train wreck of temporal accumulations? Like Husserl as well, Ricoeur runs up against what he calls "the ultimate unrepresentability of time, which makes even phenomenology turn to metaphors and to the language of myth."[31] What had at one point in the analysis seemed an advantage, that human beings can create figures for time, now seems a very basic disadvantage, that we cannot approach time except by way of figures. This shift then leads Ricoeur into a very chastened reconsideration of narrative, which cannot, he finally decides, usher us into the very heart of time, where it no longer passes at all but simply persists, beyond all the lives that have ever tried to contend with it.

For all Ricoeur's self-aware skepticism, there is one problem not discussed in his retrospective reconsideration: the historical status of his own account. As a phenomenologist, Ricoeur is not making limited, empirical claims about particular individuals at a particular time, which is why his own story, linking Augustine and Aristotle together so as to make way for narrative, is not a developmental sequence but a formal schema. And yet, all of his privileged examples are novels, and modern European novels at that. Of course, Ricoeur constantly notices historical differences between his examples, and he monitors a great many short-term historical shifts, including the quarrel within historiography that takes up half of his first volume. But he does not seem to say that the problem/solution structure, by which narrative resolves the temporal contradictions left by philosophy, occurs within time itself. In this, in fact, he is typical of narrative theorists in general, who undermine their own position insofar as they insist that narrative is always and everywhere the human way of processing time.

One of the most recent attempts to work out these conflicts in the narrative role of the present is that of Fredric Jameson. In *The Antinomies of Realism*, Jameson argues that narrative and the present are not just related but are actually necessary to one another. He starts by identifying a "narrative impulse" in all sorts of written and spoken products, and though he does not construct a phenomenological or sociological substrate for this "impulse," the very term implies a general human tendency. Checking the force of this tendency is what he first calls "a painterly moment," a scenic or descriptive imposition that stops the narrative in its tracks.[32] Apparent from the first in episodes like the description of Achilles's shield in the *Iliad*, this moment gains in prestige and influence until it comes to dominate literary modernism. Between these historical extremes, literary realism establishes a tense standoff between narrative and this "painterly moment." It is, in fact, this "compact between chronology and the present that makes realism possible in the first place."[33]

A long line of literary philosophy from Goethe and Schiller to Lukács remains implicit in the background of Jameson's argument, as is a shorter history of practical critique that positions novelistic realism as a compromise between plot and scene, narrative and episode, or diachrony and synchrony. But Jameson's account departs from these traditions by identifying the second term in all these oppositions with something he calls the "existential present."[34] What he apparently has in mind is the instant as defined by Sartre in *Being and Nothingness*, a kind of present that is not connected to past and future but rather defined by its symmetrical difference from them, from the past insofar as it is a new beginning, from the future insofar as it has to be determined by a past. This present is "an ambiguous, temporal reality . . . limited by a double nothingness," as if it were an exact inversion of the present installed within a narrative, always connected as it is to both past and future.[35]

The present that Jameson finds embedded within narrative is therefore something other than scenic description, metaphoric elaboration, or episodic dallying. In fact, the problem with Jameson's account of this present is that it is so much more than these merely practical effects that it seems indescribable. At two points he calls it an "eternal present," as though Sartre's existential instant had become an atemporal category and not a concrete moment of choice.[36] What Jameson is trying to describe, in terms he confesses are awkward, is some description of consciousness devoid of temporality, of the pure present in which there are no moments, just consistent, extended wakefulness. Throughout the argument, he identifies this state with "affect," which he defines as a basic ground tone of bodily awareness, situated beneath the named emotions and their psychic counterparts.[37] Prior to any specification, this raw sense of being a body is not just resistant to narrative but even to description. Thus, although Jameson is able to find it in many realist narratives, particularly in Zola, it is a feeling for which there is no name.[38]

It is quite possible, therefore, to come away from Jameson's account with the sense of having been shown the answer, but only in a flash and from a great distance. To further define the present, he has recourse to "what Alexander Kluge calls 'the insurrection of the present against the other temporalities.'"[39] But this does not seem a particularly apposite reference, since Kluge does not associate the present with affect, and because he has a solidly conventional disapproval of anything that looks like living in the present. In the essay published in *New German Critique* as "The Assault of the Present on the Rest of Time," Kluge cites Piaget to the effect that a healthy human consciousness forms connections between past, present, and future, while only a sick modern consciousness fastens on the present.[40] It is hard to see in this prejudice any place for the vast, indescribable bodily present that Jameson finds so powerfully at work in realist fiction.

It is also hard to accept Jameson's association of the body with an atemporal present. Sartre identifies the body with the past, "*the passed-beyond*," and not the present, existential or otherwise.[41] Literary theorists, especially Peter Brooks, have tended to associate the body with narrative, with the drives and desires that make us tell and attend to stories.[42] And this seems to make sense, if only because bodily reactions necessarily take time. A purely ideal state might be imagined as timeless, or instantaneous, but a physical one must be located in some kind of time. Affect, as Jameson imagines it, is a great molten magma of bodily sense, barely stirring below the level of namable emotions, and thus devoid, somehow, of change. No doubt the difficulty he has in describing this kind of affect comes from its lack of change, for an affective state without any change in it is a deeply counterintuitive notion.[43]

Balancing the present against narrative as he does, Jameson actually gives us a taxonomy and not an explanation. It is never clear in *The Antinomies of Realism* why the present exists as a constant tug against the progress of any story. Finding it as early as he does, in the oldest narrative we know, has the effect of installing it as a constant, born with stories themselves and just as little in need of explanation. This also means, though, that there is no explanation for the increasing power of the present over the history of narrative. How and why do narrative and the present strike their truce, for the brief moment of the realist novel, and why does this balance of forces slide into the imbalance visible in literary modernism? Does it make sense to think of the "painterly moment" first installed within the *Iliad* as more or less identical to the effects achieved by Zola in a time dominated by the invention of photography?

Jameson's account may be hampered in this respect by its reliance on Lukács at his most reactionary. What Jameson calls the "painterly moment" appears under some different names in Lukács's "Crisis of Bourgeois Realism." In that essay, Lukács describes with high dudgeon the influx into narrative of "pictorial effect" and "photographic authenticity."[44] This sudden emphasis on scene and description has a number of lamentable effects: the separation of detail from design; the separation of the individual moment from the developmental flow of narrative; the estrangement of the individual from the mass of humankind. All of this is more or less synonymous with "the severance of the present from history," the result of which is to make it an incomprehensible puzzle.[45] In short, the picturesque or the photographic functions for Lukács as the "painterly" does for Jameson, as an index of the indescribable present that invades narrative and tears it apart.

In this way, perhaps, Jameson's analysis comes to be haunted by a traditional aversion to the present, despite his sense of the insurrectionary powers of it in the form of affect. According to this long-standing literary critical tradition, the present is the necessary irritant that causes the epic to form a narrative, but it is also the constitutional enemy of that narrative. Belief in this last is the literary critical version of the philosophical prejudice against the punctual present that many theorists share with Heidegger. Literary narratives, then, are the artistic ancestors of the psalm analyzed by Augustine, the temporal object that externalizes and thus corroborates the very existence of the threefold present as an experiential fact. Literary and historical narratives exist, Ricoeur maintains, because human beings are basically narrative creatures, so that art forms a virtuous circle with life that constantly refreshes the essentially threefold nature of human experience. But if this is so, if narrative is so primordial, so basic to our way of thinking, then why does the "unexplained instant" remain such a threat? What might the persistence of this present tell us about the notion that human beings are essentially narrative creatures?

III

The idea that human beings are essentially storytelling creatures is so ubiquitous right now that even James Phelan, the editor of a journal devoted to the subject, has warned of "narrative imperialism."[46] Much of the current prestige of this idea can be traced to Ricoeur, who is frequently cited and referred to. In fact, there is a relative dearth of authoritative citations to works prior to Ricoeur's, which might raise a bit of doubt about what might otherwise seem the most obvious common sense. If narrative is so intrinsic to the human condition, then why wasn't this fact widely observed before, say, the mid-1980s? Recall that Ricoeur finds Aristotle distinctly lacking in real attention to narrative time, which was not an issue elsewhere in classical antiquity. Bakhtin notes that, even when the novel began to attract informed critical attention at the end of the 18th century, little of this had to do with stylistic or technical matters such as the manipulation of tense, sequence, or duration.[47]

If narrative has always been essential to human experience, this fact also escaped many of the great general anthropologists of the past. Vico, for example, thought that early human beings were distinctly nonnarrative creatures: "Now, since the minds of the first men of the gentile world took things one at a time, being in this respect little better than the minds of beasts, each new sensation cancels the last one (which is the cause of their being unable to compare and reason discursively), therefore their sentences must all have been formed in the singular by those who felt them."[48] Civilization arises as human beings learn to collate and compare particulars, but this long and difficult process is, for Vico, a logical one that issues in law and philosophy, not stories. Hegel, too, felt that the development of a historical consciousness was an achievement with a history of its own, a development that occurs in some places and times and not in others, and which is to be thought of as an accomplishment and not a mere condition.[49] These are only two examples, but they are influential panoptic accounts of humankind, and they do not seem to conclude that storytelling is an intrinsic human activity. At least some contemporary anthropologists agree. In fact, what must be the very largest collection of essays ever assembled on the topic of the novel begins with an essay by Jack Goody that maintains that "narrative is not so much a universal feature of the human situation as one that is promoted by literacy and subsequently by printing."[50] Goody usefully distinguishes between storytelling, which is episodic and improvisational, and narrative as such. The latter, distinguished by extended sequences, especially fictional ones, is just "not a predominant characteristic of adult intercourse in purely oral (nonliterate) cultures."[51]

Perhaps it is foolish to look this far back in history, before the great upsurge of historical thinking that is commonly supposed to accompany the Romantic Age. Peter Brooks argues that narrative "as a dominant mode of representation and explanation comes to the fore—speaking in large generalization—with the advent of Romanticism and its predominantly historical imagination."[52] If so, it is a development that has only been noticed in retrospect, for very little of the early commentary on the novel put much emphasis on narrative issues. Since the novel commonly had to defend itself against standards derived from tragedy, it often made common cause with baggy classical epics like the *Odyssey*, which seemed to justify a loose and episodic treatment.[53] In other words, novelists like Fielding appealed to the authority of a long nonnarrative tradition to defend what seemed to some critics of their time a form in which the parts were not sufficiently related to one another. When the novel was preferred to the romance, it was generally on the grounds of verisimilitude or logic and not because it had a tighter plot. Even when Thomas Holcroft complains of the old romances, "plot they had none," he is judging in terms of logic and not in terms of temporal organization.[54]

A look at the philosophers most commonly cited as authorities on the prevalence of narrative also reveals an equivocal history.[55] The most ubiquitous such reference is to Alasdair MacIntyre's *After Virtue*, which has gone through three editions since its original publication in 1981. As it turns out, though, narrative actually plays a secondary role in MacIntyre's analysis, and it is not until quite late in the book that he states in forthright terms a "concept of selfhood, a concept of self whose unity resides in the unity of a narrative which links birth to life to death as narrative beginning to middle to end."[56] MacIntyre is so certain of the prevalence and necessity of this kind of selfhood that he cites few sources beyond Barbara Hardy, whose claims in this respect, he admits, have been contested.[57] But the argument doesn't matter much, because, in fact, MacIntyre's own analysis shows that human beings have rarely been narrative creatures. Though he claims in his account of ancient Greece that "the narrative form of epic or saga" is fundamental to life in those times, what he means by this is that epic provides a structure in which everything finds its place: "Heroic social structure *is* enacted epic narrative."[58] As structure, epic form is necessarily static, governed by rules, MacIntyre says, that are like the rules of chess, so that lives do not develop so much as gradually reveal the necessary conditions of their being. The heroic age, in other words, takes place in a kind of eternal present, in which nothing changes, and this, it must be said, provides much of its glamor for MacIntyre, as it apparently did in very different circumstances for Lukács.

The definition of virtue that *After Virtue* is meant to promote is derived from Aristotle, but Aristotle himself was not, MacIntyre admits, much interested in narrative. Taking the standards of his own time for granted as he did, thinking so deeply within his tradition as not to sense it *as* tradition, Aristotle did not think in historical terms, and this "severely limits what he can say about narrative."[59] Only when Aristotle himself became a historical figure, in the Christian Middle Ages, did his work emerge as the basis of a system that connected "the distinctly narrative element in human life" and the vices and virtues that define morality.[60] But this turns out to have been a tragically brief episode in the overall human story, for ever since the Middle Ages, according to MacIntyre, the narrative impulse has been lost. The separation of narrative from life, the segregation of it into the specialized realm of aesthetics, which MacIntyre finds such a distressing fact of contemporary philosophy and literature, is the "outcome of a long history from the later middle ages until the present."[61]

If, then, narrative is fundamental to human life, it must be that human beings have rarely been human, since, by MacIntyre's reckoning, they have mostly failed to achieve narrative. Before the Middle Ages, people were too good for narrative, their system of virtues so solid that nothing was needed except a constant measuring of individuals against a static yardstick, and then after the Middle Ages, people were too weak for narrative, and lived purely episodic lives, without beginning, middle, or end. Even within the Middle Ages, though, what MacIntyre considers narrative is not very much like the form studied by experts like Ricoeur, Chatman, and Genette. For MacIntyre, narrative means "quest," and quest means the gradual realization of purpose, of a goal postulated teleologically at and as the beginning of life. Lack of virtue impedes one's progress toward the given end; virtue smooths the way. The twists and turns that generally constitute a story, therefore, are defined as errors, and the separation of beginning and end is a defect to be overcome. Stories themselves are mistakes, intervening between the pure identity of purpose and fulfillment. The emphasis that MacIntyre always puts on the "unity of the epic quest" is appropriate, for it is not change or development that makes narrative for him but rather the static revelation of the given.

Taking MacIntyre seriously, then, would lead to the conclusion that human beings have never actually been narrative creatures. And this, in fact, is what some of his most notable followers have said. Chief among these is probably Charles Taylor, who cites Ricoeur and MacIntyre to the effect that it is "a basic condition of making sense of ourselves, that we grasp our lives in a *narrative*."[62] This basic condition then makes for a very small part of the massive argument to follow, for one reason at least, which is that it has very rarely been fulfilled. Ever since Locke, it turns out, people have suffered from "an erroneous understanding of the self," an understanding that makes the

self "punctual" and not narrative at all.[63] When each present moment is conceived in isolation, without its traditional ties to past and future, then stories
have to be made, as they are no longer given. But this sort of "self-making"[64] is
not what Taylor thinks of as narrative, though he is aware that it is characteristic of the novel as a literary form. For him, as for MacIntyre, a true narrative
is a quest, and a quest is the gradual realization of a goal given at the outset,
a search in which the time passed does not produce the outcome but stands
in the way of its realization.[65]

One way of summing this up would be to say that the argument for narrative has generally been normative and not descriptive. Narrative, according
to MacIntyre and Taylor, should organize human life, but, sadly, it does not.
One thing to observe about the argument, then, is that it is not organized nar-
ratively itself, except perhaps as a narrative of decline. But even this is not quite
right, since MacIntyre and Taylor tend to see departures from virtue in terms
that are just as atemporal as those they use to define virtue in the first place.
Since the standards they admire are never produced but always exist as given,
human history simply pivots around a single pole. At the center is a point
of perfect stillness, an eternal present, and around the periphery are all the
individual, isolated presents that deviate from it. In this sense, MacIntyre and
Taylor agree with a large body of contemporary critics, some with quite different political allegiances, such as Paul Virilio, who charge that people nowadays
are trapped in a temporal prison of their own devising. Narrative has such a
powerful claim in such arguments precisely because it does not characterize
contemporary life.

What supports the narrativity thesis in the absence of historical evidence
for it is the ubiquitous assumption that the phenomenological present is
essentially narrative in character. For Louis Mink, as for most everyone else
who writes on the subject, narrative is ubiquitous because it corresponds to "a
contingent fact of empirical psychology," that we live in a specious present lasting about a second, and to a necessary phenomenological fact, "that we could
not even form the concept of the specious present were we not able to hold
in mind, through *this* sequence of presents, right *now*, the thought of past and
future, of past futures and futures past."[66] Narrative consciousness, in other
words, is the specious present raised to the next temporal level, as though the
experience of a lifetime were the experience of a second at a higher magnification. There are, to be sure, arguments in favor of narrative that are essentially
logical and not psychological or phenomenological. But the most common
assumption by far is that traced out explicitly by David Carr, whereby the

experience of the specious present is a scale model for a concept of human action, a definition of the self, and a graph of human history.[67] Given this genealogy, it is no wonder that the self turns out to be a normative ideal and the history is universal.

A great deal has been built, then, on what is, after all, the shakiest part of the arguments of both James and Husserl, the capacity of this present, however extended, to combine with the others around it and yet still retain its own character as a discrete experience. Even the most determined contemporary opponent of the narrativity thesis, Galen Strawson, accepts this general notion of the nature of the experiential present.[68] What he objects to is the magnification of that present to encompass a human lifetime.[69] A more fundamental objection has been raised by Owen Flanagan, who points out how conveniently the demand for narrative matches "moral and legal practices in the post-Enlightenment North Atlantic."[70] The whole point of the requirement of narrative, according to Flanagan, is to produce accountable human beings, selves that Flanagan calls "forensic" after Locke.[71] And it does seem as though the suspicion that attaches to the present among thinkers such as MacIntyre and Virilio comes from its unaccountability, its tendency to escape, as if to allow those in the present to escape the rightful judgment of some end. Thus Flanagan concludes unsurprisingly that the narrative self has been "normalized by cultural forces, not by human nature as such."[72]

In other words, the narrativity theorists, like the narrative theorists before them, have tended to assume the three-part division of experience as a given, so that any other kind of present appears as a departure from the norms of humanity itself. The problem that the present poses to this model of experience is fairly easy to delineate. The present is necessary if the atemporal past of epic is to be turned into narrative at all, as it is necessary if past and future are to be distinguished from one another. Thus it is essential to the trinitarian models of experience and of narrative alike. But its purpose in these models is an oddly contradictory one, since it is supposed to exist only in the passage from past to future, so that it must interpose itself and cease to exist more or less at once. Unfortunately for narrative, the present is so effective at keeping past and future apart that it easily comes to seem the only actual aspect of time. The present is experientially so strong, so *present*, that it has a tendency to persist and thus to block the narrative development that was ostensibly its purpose in the first place. Lukács calls this the "unexplained instant" because it undermines the logic of narrative and turns experience into a puzzle. But his phrase also confesses the fact that an inability to explain the present haunts and hampers his theory of the novel. Narrative theory assumes that the present has been explained, but its inexplicable qualities remain as inconsistencies in that theory.

IV

If the very existence of the present instigates a kind of crisis in storytelling, then that crisis has persisted for a very long time. Its effects are all the more apparent right now, if for no other reason than that present-tense narration in the third person has become rather common, in violation of all previous standards of literary decorum. Contemporary authors like David Mitchell, who write primarily in the first person, have found it so natural to write also in the present tense that they carry this practice over even into third-person narratives. Thus a historical novel like Mitchell's *The Thousand Autumns of Jacob de Zoet*, though it is set in the late 18th century, is narrated in a kind of cinematic present tense. Though the chapters are dated and in some cases timed, the action always happens now, the same now for every date and apparently the same now for the very distant narrator and the characters. To a well-disposed reader, the effect is to resolve the tension that exists in instances like those quoted from Bowen and Cather, who felt some sort of responsibility to speak of immediacy itself in terms of the past. The present *tense* at least, doesn't seem like much of an imposition, and it is easy to read for quite some time without even noticing it.

It is to explain this situation that Armen Avanessian and Anke Hennig have offered their recent study *Present Tense: A Poetics*, which overturns all the assumptions that have traditionally governed discussions of the narrative present. For them, novels like Mitchell's are not exceptions to an ancient rule but rather investigations of the conditions of time in narrative form. Thus they challenge the assumption that the past tense is the privileged form in which narration should take place and with it the idea that the present is some sort of foreign imposition.[73] One of the main reasons that present-tense narration in general has been deprecated is because it ostensibly sets up a problematic synchronization between narrator and character. In other words, Bowen keeps her distance from Louie by pressing her words back into the past, even when they pertain to the present as such. Without this distance, all sorts of uncomfortable questions would arise about the status of the narrator and the relation of the narrator to the character. The whole structure of fictional temporality, in which Jane Eyre as narrator is kept carefully separate from Jane as a character, would collapse, and with it perhaps the orderly succession of time itself.

Avanessian and Hennig begin to dismantle this traditional argument by calling into question the apparently commonsensical assumption that no one can experience and relate that experience at the same time.[74] Or, rather, they question the relevance of this apparent fact to literary narrative, which is not, of course, the reflection of some prior reality but rather the creation of that reality. In other words, Avanessian and Hennig simply remind us of a blindingly obvious fact that is often left out of discussions of the present and literary narrative, that the narratives in question are also fictions. As they put it, "what does not exist, and in that sense is fictive, cannot be past."[75] Against the common notion that telling is something that happens after the events are over, that discourse necessarily follows story, they advance the post-structuralist alternative that since discourse actually produces the events of the story, the story does not exist without the discourse and cannot therefore precede it.[76] It might be best to say, then, that telling and the story exist in the same moment, in the present together, since the story events only exist just as they are told. This understanding of the story-discourse relation would, in fact, give us a better understanding of the odd way in which Jane Eyre the narrator permeates her own account and often seems to speak in a kind of undertone through herself as a character.

In fictional narrative, then, tenses in general do not refer to positions in some preexisting temporal continuum, but instead serve to constitute that continuum. Actually, Avanessian and Hennig state this categorically and in general: "The tenses of language do not depict the future, the present, or the past. Nor do they refer to time. Tenses create an understanding of time in the first place."[77] In support of this notion, they cite a number of philosophical linguists, including Harald Weinrich and Gilbert Guillaume.[78] If this is so, then it is not enough to say that tenses create time within literary fictions. It would be more accurate to say that tenses are fictive in their own right. This would be particularly true of the present, a tense that has been hard for every authority to explain and account for. Thus Avanessian and Hennig speak of the "present's lack of unity, uniformity, and synchronicity," terms that might be applied to any tense but which are particularly telling in respect to the present, which has always tended to ground the unity, uniformity, and synchronicity of time in general.[79]

The traditional notion that the present is an existential threat to narrative is founded on the idea that tenses are fundamental to experience. To speak of past events in the present tense is therefore to violate the order of time and the necessary shape it gives to experience. For Ricoeur, the role of narrative is to arrange this order around the present such that its necessary three-part structure is unified and made sensible. According to Avanessian and Hennig, the effect of present-tense narration in contemporary fiction is to desynchronize the parts of time. Instead of bringing some part of the past into the present by narrating it, the present tense narrator actually makes something present into the past.[80] Until the story is told, in other words, there *is* no past. The present tense used in contemporary fiction thus contains within itself a basic asynchronicity. This "non-contemporaneous present tense,"[81] this positing of *is* and *was* together, is for Avanessian and Hennig the elementary inductor of narrative, which is not founded on a three-part sense of time arranged in successive and yet exclusive compartments but rather on the basic contradiction in the idea of the present itself, on the disunity that always persists despite all efforts to establish its unity. It is thus the off-beat nature of the present that makes narrative both possible and necessary.

When Bowen displaces Louie Lewis's ruminations about the present into the past, she simplifies a very complex temporal situation. The narrator's present, Louie's present, and the present that Louie thinks about are different and yet happen at the same time. One of the purposes of the traditional manipulation of tenses in narrative is to straighten out this situation by placing Louie and her thoughts in the past. This is in line with the general assumption about fictional narrative that the story events are to be treated as if actual, with the inflections of fiction coming only at the level of discourse, which is conventionally treated as an interpretation. To keep the story events in the present is to expose their fictionality, their logical contemporaneity with the discourse that has created them. Of course, the story events are still different from the event of narration, but this difference is not accounted for by the linear temporality of past, present, and future. It is accounted for by their fictionality, by their purely conjectural existence in the present. It might also be said that this is true outside of fiction, since the past is always conjectural, even when it has not been created by a novelist. Seriously considering such possibilities expands the debate about narrative and the present beyond the literary into a wider context, where many of the same assumptions have long applied.

To support their notion that the tense structure of language is itself a work of fiction, Avanessian and Hennig draw on a large body of testimony from linguists and philosophers. Their chief example of the former is Guillaume, whose position they summarize in this way: "Our chronological understanding of time does not originate in everyday life. It is acquired through language and reactualized in every usage of tense. Our poetics of narrated fiction refers to this grammatical event."[82] In other words, language is not a mimetic replica of a preexisting temporal situation but rather a process by which temporality is constructed. The practical fact that tenses in many languages, certainly in English, can be used in almost any way of any aspect of time would tend to reinforce this abstract maxim. As Mark Currie points out, our ability to use and understand such odd locutions as "I am leaving for France tomorrow" is evidence of the very loose relationship between verb tenses and the times to which they seem to refer.[83]

Perhaps this is not so far from what Ricoeur and other narrative theorists are saying, that experience comes to us already constructed by language in a particular temporal formation. According to at least some analytic philosophers, though, experience does not come constructed in that way. As Craig Callender puts it, "once the distracting features of temporal indexicals are cleared away, there is very little in experience suggestive of a tensed present."[84] By this reasoning, there is nothing internal to events that places them in any temporal relation to other events. This relation must be constructed by reference to yet other events, and so on. Thus, according to Bas Van Fraassen, the facts always "*underdetermine* the time order, unless we include purported *modal* facts about what might, would, or could have happened."[85] This is one reason why many philosophers besides Strawson have resisted the idea that narrative continuity is essential to the existence of the self, because such continuity has been under suspicion at least since Hume.[86]

The relationship that obtains in fiction between story and discourse, therefore, is not so different from the one constructed by language for experience in general. In both cases, the story does not come before the discourse but afterward, as an effect of it. Or, as Avanessian and Hennig put it, "it is the simple *usage* of language that accomplishes the transformation of an amorphous perception of time into a chronological image of time."[87] The disruptive version of the present that Lukács calls the "unexplained instant" seems like such a threat because it exposes the basic fictionality of this chronological structure. When the narrator and the events are put into the same tense, the separation between story and discourse, reality and mimesis, collapses, and both seem to exist on the same level. If this is a slightly queasy situation in relation to the novel, it is far more upsetting in relation to the apparent chronology of actual time. For it seems that artistic institutions like the novel exist in part to help support conventional assumptions about chronology. When the present persists, instead of yielding up the past and the future as it is supposed to, the status of that chronology seems shaken. The "unexplained instant," in other words, unexplains time itself.

V

Until recently, resistance to the present in fiction was largely theoretical, since the present was more of a tendency or a principle than an actual presence, and the present tense was at most an intermittent, local effect, used for emphasis. As Avanessian and Hennig have noted, though, the present tense became much more prevalent as the 20th century turned into the 21st, to such an extent that it has become the subject of a minor controversy. Philip Pullman began the fuss with a complaint that was published in the *Daily Telegraph* in connection with the Man Booker shortlist of 2010. As Pullman later clarified, he was not opposed to the traditional use of the present in past-tense novels, where it achieves a particular effect by way of contrast. What he did want to proscribe, though, was the wholesale abandonment of the common literary past tense in favor of the present, which he said made him feel "claustrophobic, always pressed up against the immediate."[88] Writers who do not use "the full range of English tenses," according to Pullman, forfeit a valuable resource and lose a powerful method for adding contrast and interest to their writing.[89]

Though Pullman's complaint is largely phrased in practical terms, it depends on a number of implicit assumptions and value judgments. Since he assumes that the present tense has traditionally been used for emphasis, as provided by an increased immediacy, he believes that contemporary writers who rely on the present are overusing it in an attempt to achieve a more heightened realism. In fact, though, the 19th-century writers he cites often used the present tense to break the reality effect, since an interruption in the present almost always exposes the presence of the author. When Brontë breaks into the present tense in *Jane Eyre*, it is usually to address the reader directly, and thus to advertise the fact that there is another Jane, the narrator, for whom this particular moment of tension is actually part of the settled past. And this Jane is, of course, a very thin stand-in for the author herself, which is why these intrusions were reprehended by later critics, who wanted the surface of the fiction to remain untroubled by any traces of its actual production. Dickens goes even further when he interrupts *A Christmas Carol* to say that the Spirit of Christmas Past appearing at Scrooge's bedside is "as close to it as I am now to you, and I am standing in the spirit at your elbow."[90] Here Dickens turns himself as author into a weird version of the Spirits, suggesting that like them he inhabits a present entirely out of time. And this, of course, turns out to be true as later generations of readers hear his ghostly voice and feel his ghostly hand.

Since it is not true that the present tense has always been used in the past to achieve a heightened realism, Pullman's charge against contemporary use of the present may thus seem rather weak. In fact, though, there is a deeper and less explicitly stated motive behind this criticism. Use of the present tense, Pullman says, is "an abdication of narrative responsibility." In his opinion, storytellers must "say what happened, and let the reader know when it happened and what caused it and what the consequences were."[91] Stories, in other words, are causal structures. To restrict them to the present is to eliminate the elemental before and after that reflects the necessarily causal nature of human action in general. Writing in the present, like living in the present, is an evasion of responsibility because it severs cause from effect and postpones the consequences of our actions. It is refusing to pay the bill.

Criticism of the present tense in fiction thus forms up ranks with criticism of the present in general, as both tend to generalize a very specific kind of accounting as if it were a universal human imperative. Asked to respond to Pullman's criticism, one of the writers he may have had in mind did seem to reinforce a certain stereotype. David Mitchell says of his novel *The Bone Clocks* that "I liked the idea of a narrative that surfed the crest of the present moment for six decades."[92] Figured as *surfing*, writing in the present sounds a lot like the sort of irresponsible flitting that critics of the present associate with social media and the Internet. But Mitchell, who is particularly known for writing in the present, is also known for an almost painful earnestness, an anti-postmodern lack of irony. Thus it may be that, instead of fatally severing time and ethics, as Pullman seems to think, his work with the present may simply offer a different version of their relationship.

Mitchell has written a number of novels entirely in the present, including *Number9Dream*, which he says was originally drafted in the past and then translated, verb by verb, into the present.[93] The change seems appropriate in this case since the present has the effect of protecting the naïveté of the narrator from any interference by a more experienced narrative consciousness. *The Thousand Autumns of Jacob de Zoet*, also written in the present, features a similar character, but in this case that character is not the narrator, and so the novel presents the more complicated situation of third-person narration in the present. Like Hilary Mantel's *Wolf Hall*, published to great acclaim at about the same time, it is also a historical novel, at least in the sense that it is set in the distant past. The present tense in *Wolf Hall* can actually have an oddly distancing effect, since we know what the characters don't: what will happen to them. *Jacob de Zoet* does not concern real historical figures, but the general historical situation is real enough, and so the present still has the odd effect of marooning the characters on a floating island of temporal ignorance.

Mitchell's most complex approach to the present, however, comes in a novel that is only intermittently written in the present tense. Still his most highly acclaimed novel, *Cloud Atlas* is presented in eleven sections, six moving forward in time from the middle 19th century to the distant future and then five more retracing the same steps in reverse order. Each of the six narratives is a pastiche of a particular literary form, and several of these forms are generically retrospective: a diary; letters; an interrogation; an oral storytelling session. These are thus necessarily written in the past tense with occasional interpolations in the present, especially in the diary. One narrative, a pastiche of a James Ellroy novel set in the mid-1970s, is written in the present. But the gist of Mitchell's novel, and of its approach to the present, is to be found in the links between the narratives, which are effected by reading. Each narrative contributes a story in some form to be read in the next narrative in the historical line, so that the 19th-century diary of Adam Ewing is read by Robert Frobisher in Belgium in the 1930s, and Frobisher's letters to Rufus Sixsmith turn up in the Ellroy-style thriller in the 1970s, and so on. In other words, each narrative turns out to contain the one before, so that the whole structure resembles a set of matryoshka dolls, a metaphor that the novel is perhaps a little too eager to offer for itself.

When it does so, though, *Cloud Atlas* also offers itself as a model of the present. Thus Isaac Sachs, the rather hapless scientist in the 1970s thriller, theorizes: "One model of time: an infinite matryoshka doll of painted moments, each 'shell' (the present) encased inside a nest of 'shells' (previous presents) I call the actual past but which we perceive as the virtual past. The doll of 'now' likewise encases a nest of presents yet to be, which I call the actual future but which we perceive as the virtual future."[94] The way the novel actually works is a little different, since each narrative includes within its present the previous narratives, in written form, so that time is a steadily fattening matryoshka doll, always looking the same but always containing more versions of itself. The present is the doll we can see and hold in our hands, but it includes within it all the other seemingly identical dolls, back and back until time disappears. The past, in other words, does not come before the present as its cause but exists within it as one of its components.

Still, there is a great deal of causal impetus in *Cloud Atlas*, most especially the narrative curiosity that drives the characters to find the rest of the interrupted story that precedes theirs. Mitchell constructs his novel so that the reader's experience of it mimics that of the characters: each narrative is interrupted by the next at a crucial point and is not resumed until the structure swings back around to that narrative, at which point the lost portions are restored. Frobisher finds the rest of Ewing's journal, Frobisher's final letters are mailed to Luisa Rey, and so on. The reader then is made to experience the almost visceral frustration that afflicts Frobisher when he realizes his copy of Ewing's journal stops mid-sentence, because the reader had faced that same gulf of white space just a few pages earlier. As Jameson puts it in his analysis of the novel, "we do want to find out what can possibly come next, in this series of stories broken off as surely as Sheherazade's."[95]

In this way, Mitchell seems to insist on the almost instinctive nature of narrative expectation. More importantly, he seems to give that narrative desire a socially redeeming ethical counterpart. For the string of readers (or viewers or listeners, since the media change from narrative to narrative) is quite purposely various in gender, sexual orientation, nationality, and class (and perhaps species, considering that the most important link in the chain is a futuristic clone). Why would Robert Frobisher, a decidedly louche homosexual composer, want to know anything about Adam Ewing, a repressed 19th-century clerk? Why would Sonmi-451, liberated from slavery as a service clone in the 21st century, want to waste her precious time watching a film based on the narrow-minded memoirs of Timothy Cavendish, failed publisher in present-day Britain? Mitchell apparently wants us to believe that the purely visceral desire to know what comes next overrides all differences and distances, that narrative curiosity corresponds in some way to a curiosity about those who are different from us, that it therefore transcends social divisions. Thus there is a rough parallel between the narrative desires of the characters and a string of selfless acts by which the characters reach out and help save someone with whom they have little natural sympathy. And this string of acts becomes a virtuous circle as Adam Ewing's kindness to the Moriori Autua works its way around the centuries and returns as Autua saves Ewing from a slow poisoning. The acts of selfless kindness that come in between have no real temporal relation to one another, but the way the novel is structured suggests that they lead to one another as surely as the first part of each narrative is completed by the second part.

This structure makes a strong plea for the ethical value of narrative curiosity and thus perhaps for narrative itself. But the novel also presents a very different judgment, contained within the metaphors by which narrative curiosity is lit-eralized as consumption. Thus Sonmi opines rather stuffily at one point that reading without experience is like "food without sustenance."[96] At her own first exposure to reading after a life as a mindless drone, Sonmi "devoured" the texts she was given.[97] These are commonplace metaphors, but they have a particu-lar resonance in this situation, since the clone system that originally produced Sonmi works by endlessly feeding the decommissioned clones to their succes-sors. And this vicious circle functions as an obvious figure for the economic system as a whole, the motto of which is "the weak are meat the strong do eat."[98]

The basic ideology of *Cloud Atlas* associates the curiosity that drives sci-entific investigation and invention with the baser demand for more food. All of these can be described as the simple "hunger for more," whether it is "more gear, more food, faster speeds, longer lives, easier lives, more power."[99] Narrative curiosity is therefore just one more of these demands for more, the accumulation of which drives society forward until it literally devours itself. The structure of the novel can thus be seen as a countervailing strategy with an oppositional ethical message. The interruptions in each story are, in this analysis, tests for the characters and the readers, who have to soldier forward without knowing what happens next. For the characters, action involves a leap in the dark, and their ethical interventions must all be carried forward in utter disregard of the consequences. Not knowing the end, not having an end in mind, acting without regard to the outcome, these are the hallmarks of the selflessness that the novel counterposes to the satisfaction of appetites that leads to apocalypse.

As a whole, *Cloud Atlas* makes its position on these issues fairly clear, since it puts the end of the story in the middle of the book and then requires its readers to work backward to the beginning. The simple desire to know what happens next is thus subjected to a considerable undertow, as the incomplete first part of each individual narrative is followed by the next incomplete narra-tive that contains it. This structure, and not the intermittent use of the present tense, is Mitchell's contribution to the contemporary debate about the role of the present in narrative fiction. For Mitchell, the present is not the infini-tesimal interval between past and present but the perspective from which we observe the whole of time. Each moment, this structure suggests, has all the others within it, as if time were a three-dimensional spatial structure, a sky-scape, a cloud atlas, and not a two-dimensional line. The novel is full of intima-tions of this, as bits and pieces of the narratives bleed into one another, as the schooner *Prophetess* that once carried Adam Ewing shows up as a museum piece in the 1970s narrative or the Swannekke power station of that narrative survives as a tribal name in the last, post-apocalyptic storyline. Responsibility, in this structure, is not just owed to local causes and effects but to the whole structure all at once. The reader's responsibility is not just to connect what happens now with what comes next but rather to notice these extratemporal links and thus to build up the present that contains them all.

The whole novel is offered to the reader in that impossible, atemporal present, at the chronological end of all the narratives, which comes in the middle of the book, when the final narrator says:

> Sit down a beat or two.
> Hold out your hands.
> Look.[100]

The book the reader is holding then becomes a futuristic holographic projection, viewed in an even more distant postapocalyptic future, with all the other narratives enclosed somehow within it. The most thoroughly neglected temporal aspect of narrative fiction, the time zone of the reader, for whom the whole of the novel really is available at any time at all, now becomes an analogy for a perspective beyond the end of history.

Calling attention to the book in the reader's hands also helps to identify the agency that makes such time-traveling possible. Mitchell rather casually presents one of the narratives in his chain as a novel and inserts it as such into the next narrative in the line. Luisa Rey is a fictional character, even in relation to the other characters in *Cloud Atlas*, including Timothy Cavendish, who reads about her in manuscript. In a way, this throws the entire structure off balance, since it is ontologically impossible for Frobisher's friend, Rufus Sixsmith, to appear as a character in *Half-Lives: The First Luisa Rey Mystery*, and it is equally impossible for Luisa to be biologically related to the other main characters, as it is frequently hinted she may be. In another way, though, this reworking of a hoary postmodern device makes the whole structure work. In fiction, all events are essentially coterminous. In *Cloud Atlas*, Mitchell extends this principle to historical time itself, so that the act of reading fiction operates as a model of temporal existence in general. Instructed to hold the book in our hands, we are introduced to a time zone in which all the narratives spread out from the center in both directions and exist simultaneously. For Mitchell, the present tense in which the reader reads, not necessarily the one in which the writer writes, is the appropriate basis on which to construct an understanding of time large enough to include even the end.

6

The Cinematic Present:
From *Intolerance* to *Interstellar*

I

In 1915, at the height of his fame, D. W. Griffith proclaimed the triumph of film over all other forms of art: "It is the ever-present, realistic, actual now that 'gets' the great American public, and nothing ever devised by the mind of man can show it like moving pictures."[1] Movies, he implies, have the advantage of immediacy. They show their subjects directly, without the intervention of signs or symbols, and without any lapse of time, unlike written narrative, which seems to admit its essential belatedness by conventionally telling stories in the past tense. Apart from its boosterish exaggeration, this may seem an unexceptional claim, especially in the context of 1915, when Griffith was trying to gain respect for a medium still disdained by many as a toy. But it may also sound a little strange now, when Griffith is considered the first director to have pulled together the basic elements necessary to film narrative. After Griffith did his work, according to the standard account, films no longer depended on a series of attractions, one pure present at a time, but coordinated their moments in a series, so that complicated stories could be told. The "actual now," in other words, was no longer "ever-present" in his work but was split up, delayed, displaced, and doubled or tripled in the service of suspense, pathos, social commentary, or other narrative demands.

A film as complex as *Intolerance* (1916) involves four different storylines, ranging over 2,500 years of history, with each storyline further divided in various ways, between characters and places, so that the conflict and suspense within each time period is counterpointed to that in two or three of the others. In what sort of "now" can all this be taking place? As the scenes shift from characters in modern dress to those in outlandish Babylonian costumes, how is the audience supposed to avoid the impression that the Babylonians are further away in time? And yet it was surely Griffith's notion that all of this, being present to the camera in the same way, was also equally present in time. The gap between the purity of his claim, that movies occupy a single, solitary now, and the formal and temporal ungainliness of his most ambitious movie raises a basic question about film itself. What kind of present does a film establish for its audience, and how does that present relate to the prevalent use of film to tell stories?

This turns out to be a controversial issue among film theorists, though it is not often raised as such. One thing that Griffith meant when he claimed that movie audiences can "see everything—positively everything" was that seeing everything has the effect of seeing everything *at once*.[2] This claim was frequently echoed by early commentators on film. Hugo Münsterberg, writing in 1916, describes the temporal effects of film as if shots were superimposed on one another and not arranged in sequence: "With the full freedom of our fancy, with the whole mobility of our association of ideas, pictures of the past flit through the scenes of the present. Time is left behind."[3] Ten years later, Terry Ramsaye said much the same thing: "The photoplay of today moves backward and forward through Time with facile miracle from the Present into the Past and Future by the cut-back, flashback and vision scenes." In this way, film satisfies "the human wish to live in the Past, Present and Future all at once."[4] Each film, then, is a modern *Christmas Carol*, turning the ordinary present into the eternal present, balancing all of time on the head of a pin.

Later theorists have offered a much more mundane version of this idea, based on the commonsensical notion that whatever a film shows at any moment must be shown as if it were happening in the present. So Seymour Chatman says: "It is commonplace to say that the cinema can only occur in the present time. Unlike the verbal medium, film in its pure, unedited state is absolutely tied to real time."[5] Stanley Cavell quotes Alain Robbe-Grillet to the same effect: "The cinema knows only one grammatical mode: the present tense of the indicative."[6] However obvious this may be, it has been disputed by many. For it is just as commonsensical, of course, to assert that, as a photographic medium, film only represents things that are no longer present. For this and many other reasons, Gilles Deleuze insists that "the postulate of 'the image in the present' is one of the most destructive for any understanding of cinema."[7]

Cavell and Deleuze are as influential as they are in part because of the complex negotiations they effect between these two commonplaces: that film transpires in real time and that it preserves what is now past. In *The World Viewed*, Cavell describes at length "that specific simultaneity of presence and absence which only the cinema will satisfy."[8] What he has in mind is something like this: the temporal and spatial absence of the filmed subject is overcome, turned into a conviction of its presence, by our confidence in the automatism of the camera, a confidence that depends, in its turn, on our absence from the negotiations between lens and subject. As he puts it, "photography maintains the presentness of the world by accepting our absence from it. The reality of a photograph is present to me while I am not present to it: and a world I know, and see, but to which I am nevertheless not present (through no fault of my subjectivity), is a world past."[9] So a film shows what is past but makes it present, not just because the film reels, the projector, and the screen are present with us, but also because the filmed subject itself exists in a present tense now coterminous with and indistinguishable from our own.

Deleuze objects to this very common and apparently sensible idea that film exists primarily in the present, but only because he also objects to common assumptions about the nature of the present itself. For Deleuze, following Bergson, the present must always be internally differentiated, since to be registered *as* a present it must also already be a past. In these two modes, the present is successive to itself, "still present and already past, at once and at the same time."[10] The image is that which allows us to see this internal successiveness in its full amplitude, extending out as it must to encompass all of time. As Andrey Tarkovsky says in his treatise *Sculpting in Time*: "The image becomes authentically cinematic when (amongst other things) not only does it live within time, but time also lives within it, even within each separate frame."[11] Even the smallest increment of film time, the single frame, thus contains some time within it, as does the smallest increment of actual time, the present.

This is not perhaps as radical as it sounds, nor is it necessarily very far from what Griffith had in mind. Münsterberg, at any rate, maintained that the separate scenes of a well-crafted narrative film seem to be "proceeding in the same instant." Three different times and places may be presented on-screen, but "it can hardly be said that we think of them as successive. It is as if we were really at all three places at once."[12] Münsterberg does not take this down to the level of the individual photogram, but Deleuze, following Tarkovsky, does: "What is specific to the image, as soon as it is creative, is to make perceptible, to make visible, relationships of time which cannot be seen in the represented object and do not allow themselves to be reduced to the present."[13] To see time transpire, even in the instant of a single image, is the apparently impossible feat accomplished by the great filmmakers that Deleuze lionizes in *The Time-Image*.

This inevitably means, though, that *all* the past and future are available in *one* present. Thus there is a tendency in some of the filmmakers that Deleuze prefers toward what he calls a "'perpetual present' cut off from its temporality."[14] Films that aspire to this temporal state do not necessarily need to have any of the internal organization usual in most films. As Tarkovsky admitted in relation to *Stalker*, "I wanted it to be as if the whole film had been made in a single shot."[15] The omnipresence of the "ever-present now" means that narrative devices are really unnecessary. Why should there be any elision, condensation, or rearrangement when the past and future are immediately available in the moment itself? Thus Deleuze has little interest, in *The Time-Image* at least, in narrative issues or methods, concentrating as he does on the description and analysis of moments in which the film has come to a virtual standstill. He warns that "the simultaneity of a present of past, a present of present and a present of future" does not mean the suppression of all narrative. But it does nonetheless abstract narrative "from all successive action," so that even narrative is rolled up inside the moment, along with the rest of time.[16]

In contrast to this kind of concentration, the splits, displacements, and rearrangements that characterize conventional film narrative must seem like diversions at best. Thus Raymond Bellour points out how little Deleuze has to say about "the interruption of movement. The often unique, fugitive, yet perhaps decisive instant when cinema seems to be fighting against its very principle."[17] For Bellour, the most basic fact about a film is that it is made up of still images and thus of interruptions. Though these interruptions disappear in the process of projection, they tend to reappear at successively higher levels of organization. It is even possible for some filmmakers to "pull or lure the film, cinema, toward the point they designate."[18] That point is the instant, a constitutive and yet alien stillness at the heart of film. In this analysis, then, film is essentially associated with the present, not because every filmed event takes place in the present, but rather because the present lurks as an inevitable presence within filmed movement. Where Deleuze sees the present as always immediately linked to past and future, Bellour understands it as a kind of invisible barrier between them, a stubborn independence in the instant that prevents it from being assimilated. If the basic cinematic tendency as Deleuze understands it is toward the film of a single shot, the films that Bellour favors are broken by interruptions. The question for Bellour, then, is "what kinds of instants does the interruption of movement imply?"[19]

II

Questions like this show how basic explanations of the structure of film inevitably involve assumptions about the nature of the present. Nothing demonstrates this more vividly than the stubborn persistence of belief in the persistence of vision. Though serious theorists from Erwin Panofsky on have started with motion in their attempts to define the specific powers of film, it is still not entirely clear how the illusion of motion is derived from a series of still images, and the explanation most commonly offered is quite wrong.

For serious investigators from Plateau to Marey, the answer to this mystery was fairly simple. The familiar presence of afterimages left on the retina by a particularly bright light or a vivid color suggested that *every* image left its impress on the eye. Thus a series of still images could fuse into the illusion of continuous motion because each frame left an afterimage on the retina to be fused somehow with the one following.[20] Marey successfully established this as the standard explanation of cinematic motion despite the fact that it violates common sense in several ways. There doesn't seem to be any way for an after-image, burned into the retina, to fuse with another, incoming image, so that an average of the two will be registered, a process that would seem to require the stimulation of parts of the retina by light that is not actually present. Nor does it seem logical that this process should continue for some steps, produc-ing clear motion instead of a blurry mess. Nonetheless, persistence of vision became the conventional explanation, trotted out in the opening paragraphs of film histories from Ramsaye to the present day.

Even as Marey was establishing retinal persistence in its position of author-ity, though, the optical and psychological science of the day had displaced it. Münsterberg, professionally aware of the latest research as of 1916, rehearses the familiar stories about stroboscopic discs and afterimages only to debunk them. He cites Sigmund Exner's experiments, which had also impressed Wil-liam James, to the effect that perception of motion is a specialized process, separate from perception of shape or color.[21] Exner's experiments with still and moving lights seemed to make motion perception an automatic process, even perhaps a physiological one, but Münsterberg also cites the later research of Max Wertheimer, which offered a cognitive explanation. As Münsterberg puts it, "the continuity of the motion results from a complex mental process by which the various pictures are held together in the unity of a higher act."[22] Wertheimer is still often cited in contemporary studies, though "complex men-tal process" has generally been replaced by complex neurological processes.[23]

But some basic conditions for understanding motion vision had been laid down by the time Münsterberg wrote: the perceptual process behind the movies is the same as that behind the perception of ordinary motion; both rely on sampling and summation that occur well after light hits the retina; motion is perceived in itself and not just as a feature of shape or color.[24]

These more complicated explanations have made little headway outside certain specialized sciences. Even Münsterberg, who went to great lengths in his book to give a scientifically respectable account, succumbed in the end to the theory he had debunked. When he comes to the "cutback," or what we would now call the flashback, he concludes: "The whole technique of the rapid changes of scenes, which we have recognized as so characteristic of photo-play, involves at every end point elements of suggestion which, to a certain degree, link the separate scenes as the afterimages link the separate pictures."[25] Afterimages persist in his account as they do in much film criticism of the pres-ent day, long after their very existence has been disproved. They retain their prestige, not just in undergraduate film surveys, but also in the most sophis-ticated studies of the visual arts. Rosalind Krauss, who has written a closely considered account of the optical unconscious, assured her readers in 2011 that "cinematic motion is based on the physiological fact of the 'persistence of vision' by means of which any visual stimulus induces a ghostly copy of itself (called afterimage) which remains on the retina, as though suspended before our eyes, masking the slippage from that stimulus to the next."[26] Münsterberg's slip suggests an explanation for such otherwise inexplicable ignorance: per-sistence of vision provides a vivid metaphor, visual itself, not just for the way in which film narrative links together its separate scenes, but also for the way in which ordinary temporal experience knits its moments into a continuity.[27]

The notion of afterimages must have appealed in the first place because it so strongly resembles one of the most ancient metaphors for memory: the imprint. Plato established a tradition by comparing memories to impressions on a wax tablet.[28] A popular medieval metaphor for memorial vestigia was the footprint.[29] This habit of imagining memory as an inscription in some medium was considerably reinforced by the advent of recording technologies, some of which, especially the phonograph, seemed to work just as Plato's wax tablet was supposed to work.[30] Thus it became increasingly easy to think of the appearance of successive recording media as a biological and psychologi-cal revelation, as the mind progressively externalized its methods of retention, revealing that it had been a sort of photographic plate or phonograph record all along.

If long-term memory worked in this way, by inscribing itself into some medium, it made sense to imagine that short-term memories would work in the same way, that everyday experience was given its continuity by the gradual and successive imposition of one sense impression on another. Thus the influence of Fechner's *Nachklange* on psychologists such as James. For Fechner, every sense impression was a mini-memory, with an echo trailing after that connected it to later impressions. The tendency of impressions to subsist for an instant thus made ordinary experience possible. This much longer and deeper tradition subtends and reinforces the purely optical theory of afterimages, supporting it even as science obliterates the basis for both. Thus Giorgio Agamben argues, in a masterful essay on Aby Warburg, that "alongside the physiological *Nachleben* (the persistence of retinal images), there also exists a historical *Nachleben* of images."[31] The purely optical afterimage would have been fairly easy to displace if it had not been an instance of a much more complex idea about temporal experience in general.

This is one of the things that film theorists from Münsterberg to the present mean when they say things like "the photoplay obeys the laws of the mind rather than those of the outer world."[32] Münsterberg, of course, would not have included in his equation of film and mind any of those ideas like condensation, representation, and displacement derived from Freud and used by later theorists, nor could he have included any of the Lacanian concepts that go into theories of the gaze. But, underneath these, there is fairly common agreement with a principle enunciated by Annette Michelson in 1971: "The illusionism of the new, temporal art reflects and occasions reflection upon, the conditions of knowledge; it facilitates a critical focus upon the immediacy of experience in the flow of time."[33] What this means is that the temporal relations that make up a film resemble those that make up ordinary experience to such an extent that they make that experience available in a way that is otherwise structurally impossible. At the heart of that experience is the relation between "immediacy," or the present, and "the flow of time," or the continuity of one present with the others around it.

Probably the most uncompromising version of this claim comes from Deleuze, who disdains the notion that film indirectly represents the flow of time. What he calls "direct cinema" achieves "a before and an after as they coexist with the image, as they are inseparable from the image. This is what direct cinema must mean, to the point where it is a component of all cinema: to achieve the direct presentation of time."[34] Though the philosophical background of this idea in Bergson is far from phenomenology, Deleuze is very nearly paraphrasing Husserl here, especially in his insistence that the flow of time is presented directly to us and not through representations. For Deleuze, film accomplishes something that Husserl felt was fundamental to ordinary temporal experience: it constructs a present in which the past and the future are immediate and immediately available. The now, in other words, is "ever-present," just as Griffith claimed. What happens, then, when Griffith's narrative methods divide and multiply the now, interrupting one now with another, stalling or speeding up the flow of the immediately present? Is narrative, in fact, a basic violation of the fundamental ontology of film? Or does it display for us a different present, one that does not flow but persists in its singularity?

III

For Münsterberg, the structure of the photoplay depends on a kind of persistence of vision, working at progressively higher levels of organization. Separate scenes, as he puts it, are linked together "as the afterimages link the separate pictures."[35] Two decades later, Rudolf Arnheim made the same point in reverse when he described film as "a montage of single frames." The famous montage effects associated with Eisenstein, he says, are achieved by carrying over the principle of persistence of vision to the "macroscopic" level.[36] In this analysis, the most fundamental unit of film criticism is the single frame, and the relationship of that frame to the frames around it is an analogy for all the other effects of film editing, not just montage as such. This apparently natural progression from frame to film motion to film continuity in general resembles the similar progression from present to temporal experience to history in general that is proposed by philosophers such as David Carr.[37] The similarity is probably not coincidental, given the general tendency to explain film on the analogy of human temporal experience. Barthes recognizes this when he describes the common belief that "the filmic world" and "the real world . . . continue to flow by in the same constitutive style."[38]

For Barthes himself, however, the photograph breaks this flow, since it is a present turned entirely to the past, without any visible relation to the future. The individual frame, then, remains stubbornly separate, and its stuttering relation to the frames around it might remind us of an essential discontinuity in ordinary temporal experience. Or, more famously, it might remind us of what Barthes calls "*flat Death*."[39] This apparently commonsensical idea, that the photograph, because it is still and distinct within the flow of time, inevitably represents death, is common to many distinguished theorists of film, including

André Bazin and Christian Metz.[40] The most vivid pieces of evidence for this view are portraits like the famous photo of Lewis Payne that Barthes includes in *Camera Lucida*, and the association of photography with death in general would seem to depend on a reduction of the full range of photographic representation to the particular case of the portrait. Metz, for one, admits that "there are other kinds of photographs: landscapes, artistic compositions, etc.," but this does not stop him from making the portrait exemplary.[41] Still, it is not entirely clear why a photograph of a landscape or an eggbeater should necessarily remind us of death, except perhaps in the way that everything can potentially remind us of it. Perhaps the stillness of the photograph, lurking within the flashing frames of a film, represents a different problem, present within a life and not just coming at the end of it.

From at least the time of Bazin's famous essay "The Ontology of the Photographic Image," film has been understood as repairing some essential damage done to human experience by the stillness imposed through photography. No longer is the object "enshrouded in an instant," as Bazin puts it, since film motion delivers it from its "convulsive catalepsy."[42] Behind this idea is a long history, especially prominent in France, hailing film as a transfiguration of the stillness of photography, a history that also extends forward to Metz, who considered film motion to be "a destruction of the photograph."[43] The most thorough critique of this tradition is to be found in the work of Garrett Stewart, who does not dispute the distribution of stillness and motion across the relationship of photography to film, just the idea that film can ever entirely subsume the still.[44]

Restoring motion to stillness as it does, film also rescues a real present from the past. Bazin offers a metaphor persuasive enough to have become quite popular: the photograph immures its subject "as the bodies of insects are preserved intact, out of the distant past, in amber."[45] To make these insects move is to animate them, once again, in the present, so that Metz, among many others, thinks of film as always happening in the present tense.[46] Some fairly large part of the general notion that films take place in the present must rest on this prior association of the still photo with the past. Popular anecdotes about the Lumière brothers astounding their first audiences by starting a film with a still image reinforce the idea that film kicks the photograph out of its immobile past and starts it living in a real present.

Lately, however, this canonical separation of photographic images into the still and the mobile, the past and the present, has been questioned. Under the influence of video and digital imagery, critics have rediscovered a whole range of forms that are intermediate in some way: printed sequences of photographs; film stills and other uses of the photogram; films published as illustrated books.[47] As Stewart and Bellour have shown how commonly the still photograph appears within films, partly as a reminder of the photogram that otherwise seems invisible, critics of photography have begun to insist that there can be a fair amount of movement in a "still" image. An early, influential essay in this respect is Peter Wollen's "Fire and Ice," which insists: "The fact that images may themselves appear as punctual, virtually without duration, does not mean that the situations that they represent lack any quality of duration or other qualities related to time."[48] A still image, in other words, can represent what it cannot depict, a more modest version of Deleuze's notion that still images within a film can directly depict times beyond their frame. In any case, it is much more common now to see photography and film as points along a continuum, rather than polar opposites, and to look, under the influence of Bellour, into the space between film and photogram, for degrees of motion or stillness.[49]

Taken far enough, this rethinking can result in a complete reversal of the hallowed association of the photograph with the past, film with the present. As Olivier Lugon points out, it was common in Germany between the wars to advertise photomontage as a film in stills, and to think therefore of the individual photo as the concentration of movement rather than its antithesis.[50] Reanimated in this way, the photograph could also be reinserted into a mobile present, pulled out of an immobile past. This is part, perhaps, of Barthes's idea, expressed in "The Third Meaning," that a film still "throws off the constraint of filmic time."[51] What Barthes means is that a projected film enforces a certain time scheme onto its viewers, while the still frees them into a present that, in a sense, is wider in scope than the time of the film. Meditating on the still, the viewer abides in the present, while the film piles up in the past. In "Observations on the Long Take," Pier Paolo Pasolini takes the same idea to the next higher level of film organization. According to Pasolini, film takes place in the present only insofar as it is limited to single takes: "The long take, the schematic and primordial element of cinema, is thus in the present tense." Once these are multiplied, subordinated to one another in an organizational scheme, "the present becomes past."[52] An immersion in time, of the sort also admired by Barthes, becomes a perspective on it, and the pure present of the single image is sacrificed to an organization that brings back the whole notion of before and after and thus plunges the film into the past.

On one hand, then, the individual photogram is an inescapable reminder of the past lurking within the flowing present of the film. On the other hand, though, the single frame, lifted out of context, has the full amplitude of an expansive mental present, while the film enforces a death march through time on a helpless consciousness. How far this conversation has come from Griffith's blithe assurance that film provides us with a limitless now. Perhaps the source of this disagreement and division is not to be found in the history of film criticism itself but rather in the terms it borrows from ordinary experience, as if we understood that. Appeals to the present or the past imply that these are known quantities, to which the structure of film can be matched and thus explained. Deleuze is one of the most powerful film theorists because his theory of the time image rests on a well-developed concept of the present and its relation to the time around it. But the Bergsonian account of time on which Deleuze depends is just one of several contending theories that have attempted to make sense of the present. Thus the contentious variety of ideas about the relation of still to film motion may derive from a more fundamental indecision about the experiential relation of one moment to the next.[53]

The present thus persists within film as a nagging problem, a constant reminder of our inability to understand what seems such a natural and fundamental aspect of experience, the progression from one instant to the next. In this sense, the individual film frame may represent death, as so many have insisted, but only insofar as the instant of death is a very drastic instance of a hiatus that is always possible within the apparent continuity of experience. With the invention of the photograph, Tom Gunning has argued, "the instant, previously only an abstract philosophical conception of an indivisible atom of time, now took on visible form."[54] The still photograph thus presented in a form that became ubiquitous and inescapable the problem of the present. Sergey Tretyakov once called the photograph "an infinitely fine scale that has been scratched from the surface of reality with the tip of the finger."[55] Bellour calls the photograph "a thin film of time in a pure state."[56] Both are groping toward a description of a magnitude just this side of zero, so close to it, in fact, as to be identical, while still somehow remaining a magnitude. This is a conundrum that is only exacerbated in the structure of a film, where the individual frame may very well seem to mark, not the instant, but the difference between instants, as if time itself were to be found between the frames.[57] But this then raises the other nagging issue, that of continuity between instants, since moments whose own duration vanishes toward zero can hardly establish an ideal basis for continuity. Inability to explain film movement is just an instance of a larger inability to explain the perception of movement in general, which itself rests on a profound lack of understanding of the continuity of time. The stillness found inside the moving image is, in this sense, a stubborn persistence in the present, a persistence of it as an unexplained fact at the heart of human temporality.

IV

Even as it organizes still frames into larger and more complicated units, film preserves all sorts of reminders of a recalcitrant present. In its earliest and most undeveloped form, according to the influential formulation of Tom Gunning, film is nothing more than a sequence of present-tense instants. The film of pure visual display, what Eisenstein called the attraction, is limited, in Gunning's words, "to the pure present tense of its appearance."[58] At this stage, a film is nothing more than a pile of instants, all at the same level of temporality. Anything like narrative development is discouraged in favor of a simple alternation: now you see it, now you don't. Such has been Gunning's influence that it is now a commonplace that the tension between attraction and narrative is fundamental to the history of film. Like most commonplaces, this has also attracted its share of critics, and even Gunning has not represented his dichotomy as an utterly exclusive situation.[59] So it is now generally agreed that the attraction represents one pole of a tension in all films between the present tense of pure display and the more complex temporality required by narrative.[60]

Contemporary narrative films therefore often contain residual instances of the pure present tense of the attraction. One of the more obvious of these is the freeze-frame, which Bellour and Stewart treat as a reminder of the photographic stillness at the heart of film motion. But the freeze-frame also demonstrates something uncanny in the photograph itself, the way it holds the present, allowing us to contemplate it in a way that is impossible for ordinary consciousness. Freeze-frames force the viewer to study the photograph for a fixed period of time, so that the instant comes to have an amplitude it never has as actual time passes. What is seen on-screen then is the paradox of an instant that takes some time, as if every freeze-frame were an essay on the perennial question, how long is the present?

There are many such moments even in the most conventional narrative film, in which the camera comes to dwell on something purely for its visual interest. Roberto Rossellini referred to the effect of such moments as "denarrativization," and he claimed that, for him, the narrative was just a means of getting from one moment of suspended contemplation to the next.[61] Probably the oldest and most common of such denarrativizing devices is the close-up.

In his famous essay on Griffith, Eisenstein focuses first on the close-up, and he marvels at its capacity to pack a whole set of ideas and reflections into a small space, to make the audience or reader see what otherwise would have to be explained. But this power of ocular concentration is precisely what makes the close-up a nonnarrative element, what made it such an unwelcome innovation, at least according to the creation myth as Griffith told it. He notes ironically that it was considered "anarchistic" because it broke up the obvious flow of action across a legible physical space.[62] Later, the close-up came to be celebrated, almost fetishized, for precisely this reason, because it broke up the integrity of the scene and cut into the flow of the narrative.[63]

This apparent opposition between the momentary stillness of the close-up and the flow of narrative rests on the assumption that the latter is achieved primarily by continuity. But it is one of the basic paradoxes of narrative organization that continuity is achieved by means of carefully modulated interruptions. In classic montage, the jump cut makes this interruption obvious. In doing so, it makes the viewer aware of an interval, a space between the images, which is technically atemporal and nonchronological.[64] In cases of maximum discontinuity, as in films like Dziga Vertov's *Man with a Movie Camera* (1929), the continuous time in which the film viewer is ostensibly situated is completely replaced by this blank non-time, which is the matrix within which the individual shots are situated. Instead of flowing, then, the film stands still within a static time frame constituted by the atemporal jumps from shot to shot.

The commonplace cuts in an ordinary narrative film apparently work in a very different way, constructing a coherent temporal space that supports the shots, floating them in a medium that flows onward even when the camera eye is closed. But this coherent space is not an automatic effect of a sequence of cuts. Cutting, as Kristin Thompson explains in the standard account of classic American cinema, was both an opportunity and a problem: "Unless the filmmaker finds cues for conveying the spatio-temporal relationship between shots, the effect of the cut is a perceptible break between bits of subject matter." Early filmmakers developed a set of rules and procedures the purpose of which was "taming and unifying" the otherwise anarchic effect of the cuts.[65]

Perhaps the most venerable of these rules is the one laid down very simply by Rudolf Arnheim: "If two sequences of the same action are to be understood as occurring at the same time they may simply be shown one after the other, in which case, however, it must be obvious from the content that simultaneity is intended."[66] Arnheim is careful to note that succession does not automatically imply simultaneity, but as the convention took hold, it became common enough that it came to seem automatic. Thus, according to a basic formula first proposed by Christian Metz, "alternating of images equals simultaneity of occurrences."[67] It is worth stopping for a moment, though, to note how odd this convention is, and what a kink it puts it the apparently automatic flow of film narration. To make the formula work, filmmakers must evoke in the minds of the viewers a discontinuous time zone, quite apart from the one visible on-screen, in which successive moments come to be simultaneous.

This odd, nearly atemporal present appears overtly in some of the earliest films in which Griffith established the norms of continuity editing. Griffith's first extended sequence of parallel editing, according to Gunning, comes in *The Fatal Hour* (1908), a film whose title announces its dependence on the clock. In it, a detective is captured by the criminals she has been pursuing, and she is tied up in front of a pistol, which is linked to a large clock and set to fire at 12:00. Apprehended at about 11:40, the criminals graciously reveal their plan to the police, who set out, lickety-split, to stop the clock before it can strike the hour. Though the clock is in view for much of the film, it does not, in fact, mark real time, and the amount of time advanced on the clock from shot to shot does not correspond to the actual time taken up by the action in the parallel shots. It is fairly obvious, in any case, that to be at all useful on the set, where the filming would have taken several hours, the clock could not have been operational. So the notion promoted in Gunning's account, that in this film "each shot finds its place in an irreversible temporal logic," must already be qualified just a bit.[68] More fundamentally, the process of crosscutting between two simultaneous actions, that of the clock and the detective and that of the police racing to rescue her, sets up a complex temporal order. As Gunning puts it, "the order of shots no longer indicates a simple succession in time, but the staggered process of simultaneity."[69] Though the clock on the wall tells the viewer that time marches on ineluctably, the cuts to the racing police in their carriage indicate a slip backward in time, to show something happening simultaneously elsewhere. This is an early and crude example of a technique that would later, Gunning says, be perfected, but it does show in a simple form what would later become a temporal convention in classic Hollywood cinema. As Metz's formula puts it, two scenes succeeding one another would be understood to be happening simultaneously.

This is probably the most basic rule by which the disorderly set of instants delivered by the cinema of attractions is turned into a coherent time-scape. But the order it imposes is incomplete, for the nonsuccessive present of the attraction is not really hammered into orderly succession, one thing logically following and replacing another. Instead, simultaneity and succession are shown to coexist within a very uneasy portrayal of the present. In the time-line represented by the clock, the present is fleeting, each tick of it replaced by another in linear progression. In the simultaneity of montage, however, it is flexible in size and not limited to a purely linear progress. With the switch from one line of action to another, the same present, in fact, succeeds itself, and the testimony of the clock on the wall makes this twist in time all the more shocking. It is not so much that the pure present of the attraction remains as a residual presence within the narrative as that the incomplete imposition of narrative reveals some of the intrinsic peculiarities of the actual present of ordinary experience.

These are all the more obvious in the early Griffith films in which parallel editing has a logical or ideological purpose rather than a temporally dramatic one.[70] In most of these cases, the *ne plus ultra* of which is of course *Intolerance* itself, shots of high and low life are alternated to create what Gunning calls a "moral dualism."[71] One of the best examples is *A Corner in Wheat* (1909), based on material from Frank Norris. In one series of shots, farmers struggle against the elements, and the urban poor line up for handouts, while in another a financial wizard exults and celebrates as he corners the wheat market. There are no dramatic connections between the two sequences, and yet it is clear that they are supposed to be causally related and in some large sense simultaneous. But what sort of simultaneity links these sequences, and in what sense can it correspond to what Griffith announced as the triumphant "now" of film? The farmers seem to live and work in a static time frame, while the financier's machinations seem to take only seconds. In one way, it might seem as if these divergent time-lines are unified by reference to the present of the viewer, but that viewer is elevated, by the freedom granted through film editing, to a time and space not apprehensible by any actual human being. If there is a present here, it is the eternal present traditionally available only to God.

At one point, in fact, time stops still as a breadline of haggard beggars freezes into a kind of tableau vivant. The implication is that those in the breadline are immobilized by their poverty but also that their situation is timeless and eternal.[72] But the frozen tableau, which looks like but is not a freeze-frame, is also a reminder of the photogram that is the static base of even the most dynamic film. In another way, though, the strange immobility of the breadline seems to be an inadvertent revelation of the odd syncopation of screen time that often marks parallel editing, especially the situation of the off-screen character, the Lonedale operator, for example, who seems to wait in exactly the same pose for some seconds, as the train approaching to save her eats up the miles. In this case, it looks as if the camera filming *A Corner in Wheat* has switched back to the second storyline too soon and caught the protagonists, waiting patiently as the primary storyline develops. Of course, there is no reason for these characters to wait, for the relation between them and the financier is not a temporal one in the first place. So what appears on-screen is actually the static present within which logical comparisons are made, the odd, invisible simultaneity at the heart of parallel editing, the necessary moment in which two successive things are made simultaneous so that we can tell they are successive.[73] This is the present, not by any means an ordinary now, in which *Intolerance* takes place.

V

For many years, *Intolerance* was considered to be not just Griffith's masterwork but also the pinnacle of American filmmaking. It has also been compared with some frequency to those hugely ambitious, historically encyclopedic works in literature: *The Waste Land*, *The Cantos*, *Ulysses*.[74] Unfortunately, many such comparisons tend to find these works similar in their failure, especially their failure to cohere. The most extensive of these is Miriam Hansen's, which begins with a sharp judgment of the film as "a gigantic ruin of modernity."[75] She thinks of *Intolerance* in the way literary scholars frequently think of an unfinishable project like *The Cantos*, as a work ruined by its commitment to modernity. To some extent, though, the commitment to modernity is also a commitment to the present in formal terms, to local, immediate, intensive effects rather than articulated narrative or logical design. The relation of the present to the past thus becomes a structural problem.

At its base, *Intolerance* is actually a good deal simpler than *The Cantos* or *The Waste Land*. There are four distinct storylines, taken to represent ancient, sacred, medieval, and modern times. These focus on four events: the fall of Babylon in 539 BCE; the crucifixion of Christ; the massacre of the Huguenots on Saint Bartholomew's Day, 1572; and a modern story, datable by car license plates as occurring not later than 1914.[76] In very general terms, the four stories are meant to be the same story: the eternal conflict Griffith stages between love and intolerance, a concept that is very largely and loosely construed throughout the film. This general ideological matrix is supposed to hold the film together as Griffith intercuts the four time-lines with one another: the betrayal of Babylon to the Persians by jealous, sectarian priests; the crucifixion of the Man of Peace, which Griffith had wanted to ascribe to some narrow-minded Pharisees until he was forcibly reminded of the crucial role of the Romans; the religious animosity between Catholic France and the Huguenots; and a rather tortured and strained sequence of events in the modern period, in which an industrial magnate spends so much money on the charities of his spinster sister that he must cut wages at his factories, throwing people out of work and into poverty, where one of them falls in with bad companions, is falsely blamed for the death of their chief, and is almost hanged. Just how the last few stages in this drama are supposed to be caused by the sexual frustration of the spinster sister is one of the greater logical mysteries of the film.[77]

The stories, then, are meant to be typical examples, moments chosen from a continuing conflict between elemental forces, and thus there are a number of parallels between them. But there are also differences. In one way, the overall story seems to be one of decline, since the Babylon of Belshazzar is portrayed as a model of tolerant authoritarianism, in which the people are left to their innocent pleasures, while the modern period is ruled by puritanical capitalists, who begrudge their underlings even a moment's enjoyment. On the other hand, though, only the modern story ends happily, since the innocent worker is not hanged, and this seems to suggest that a modern justice system is worth something after all. As Hansen suggests, parallelism as a technique tends to slide between comparison and contrast, and even comparisons can be tricky when they are made across time.[78] Are the similarities between Leopold Bloom and Odysseus meant to show how far humanity has fallen since classical times or that classical times weren't necessarily as grand as they have been said to be?

In any case, parallelism between the four storylines has a tendency not to reinforce but rather to undermine narrative coherence. At the most basic level, as Hansen puts it, "*Intolerance*, like few other American films, exemplifies the truism that linking requires cutting: for every connection between periods, one narrative is necessarily disrupted at the expense of another."[79] Even when actual cutting does not occur, the implicit presence of three other time-lines has the tendency to call into question the solidity of the one currently on-screen. As Hansen explains it, this "transhistorical, *temporal* omnipresence" has a tendency to weaken the "*spatial* coherence and closure" on which the fiction effect depends.[80] But this might also be put in purely temporal terms. Having four different historical presents alternate on-screen vastly magnifies the disorienting effect of ordinary parallel editing, for there is no time to which all four might be referred, within which they might be composed. This has an especially attenuating effect on the modern story, which should seem to be happening more or less now, in a time the ultimate conclusion of which has still to be determined, but which ends up in the temporal distance with the Persians and the Huguenots, whose fates were settled long ago.

Even within the individual stories, Griffith's rather casual attitude toward the norms of continuity editing and his devotion to décor and spectacle mean that narrative continuity is often overwhelmed by detail. Many scenes, especially in the Babylonian sequences, are so crowded it is hard to know where to look. Close-ups have a distressing tendency to seem like insertions into rather than selections from the larger canvas. Joyce Jeseniowski picks out the camel that ambles through the opening shot of the Judean sequence, whose qualifications for particular emphasis are not immediately clear.[81] To take another example, the toothless old man vignetted into the marriage market scene in the Babylonian story has little spatial relationship to the shots he interrupts, and thus he seems the tool of a timeless comment about male appreciation of female beauty and not a dramatic elaboration. In short, Griffith's devotion to immediate visual impact and to ideological comment tend to set up a static undertow that impedes the development of a coherent narrative line.

The thrilling conclusion, the final chase scene that should tie all these loose narrative threads into a single satisfying bundle, actually leaves them even more obviously frayed. The chase, at this point in Griffith's career, is obligatory, and this one must have seemed an opportunity to raise the ante, to have four chases in one. But there are problems with some of the older narratives that make this unfeasible. Surely it would be indecorous, even sacrilegious, to figure Christ's passion as a race to the cross, so the Judean story essentially disappears from the last two reels of the film, except for one shot of the Crucifixion that punctuates the tension of the modern execution scene. The Huguenot story becomes a variation on the pattern established with *The Lonely Villa*, but without vehicles, as Prosper works his way across Paris in the vain hope of saving Brown Eyes from the slaughter. So the pure chase scene is concentrated on the Babylonian narrative, in which the plucky Mountain Girl speeds her stolen chariot toward Babylon to warn Belshazzar of the invasion, while a small group in the modern story tries to catch the Governor's train, to secure a stay of execution for the falsely convicted Boy.

The special oddity of this chase scene is that in some weird way the two stories seem to be racing one another. The message of the editing that created such scenes in the past is that two parallel, successive shots are, in fact, happening simultaneously. This was always a seriously strained fiction, but when the two time-lines are 2,500 years apart, the simultaneity acquires a fantastic aspect. Of course, the viewer knows quite well that the stories are separate, but the speeding chariot of the Mountain Girl and the speeding motor car can easily seem to be speeding to the same place, in the same time, as they are apparently speeding to the same purpose. This misimpression may be underscored for the few viewers who notice the tire tracks left by the camera car in the path of the Mountain Girl. The Persian army is also racing toward Babylon on a back road heavily traveled by motorcars. For these viewers, the sense that the two stories are being superimposed on one another may become actual and not just notional. But the comparison may well remind the viewers that, in a real sense, the modern story is in the past as well, and that whatever passes for the present on the screen is, in fact, something done and finished some time ago.

There is a very real tension, then, between the linear narrative of the chase as such and the implications implanted by the parallel editing. On one hand, there is a continuously unrolling present, kept open to the future by the devices of suspense, while on the other hand, there is the vague, amorphous, and curiously static present implied by the parallels. Even the narrative by itself evokes a decidedly nonnarrative pleasure, the pure thrill of the racing elements, which pound away, scene after scene, exciting even when they make no discernible progress. But the grand narrative of *Intolerance* encloses this relatively simple nonnarrative experience, the pleasure of the image as such, within another, more complex experience, located in a different kind of present. This present, external to the four narratives and independent even of the time of viewing, is the focus of a number of specific elements within *Intolerance*.

The inter-titles, for example, though they were composed by the very funny Anita Loos, adopt an "omniscient scriptural voice" that speaks from a position above and beyond all the narratives.[82] The narrator editorializes throughout, making it clear that 16th-century France is a "hotbed of intolerance" and that Monsieur La France is "effeminate."[83] The narrator also quotes, sometimes with and sometimes without actual quotation marks. And there seems to be another level even beyond the narrator, a level that is the source of numerous notes appended to the inter-titles themselves. Some of these are little self-advertisements, like the oddly distancing news that the Babylonian set is a "replica of Babylon's encircling walls, 300 feet in height and broad enough for the passing of chariots."[84] Some are protectively informational, like the news that the harridans grouped around the edges of the Babylonian marriage market are "women corresponding to our street outcasts, for life, the wards of Church and State."[85] And some are frankly tendentious, such as the note claiming that the code of Hammurabi protects the weak from the strong.[86] In any case, these impersonal addresses from a position beyond even the narration of the inter-titles establish a time frame that is as external to the baffled viewers as it is to the characters in the film.

A more visual element with the same effect is the transitional device that Griffith adapted from Whitman. "Out of the cradle endlessly rocking" is a sort of motto for the film as a whole, a common inter-title, and a visual vignette marking transitions from one time to another. The vignette is composed of a long-haired girl, played by Lillian Gish, seated at a huge cradle, with three ghostly women in the background, representing the Fates. It puts birth in the foreground but also matches it with the death dealt out by the Fates, so that there is a full circle of life in one self-contained picture. The endless rocking of the cradle, as well as the repeated appearance of the vignette without any apparent variation, suggest a circular, repetitious time scheme, and there is nothing in the scene itself to place it in a particular time, though the whole thing has a vaguely archaic look. On its first appearance, the cradle scene is accompanied by an additional inter-title that reads: "Today as yesterday, endlessly rocking, ever bringing the same joys and sorrows."[87]

It is fairly obvious, then, that the cradle scene is Griffith's attempt to provide a temporal matrix for the four storylines of his film, to link together what otherwise would look too various. But, as Hansen says in her long, detailed analysis of the cradle motif, what is supposed to link has always had the tendency to divide, so that the cradle has always stood out as just the sort of old-fashioned, nonnarrative element that prevents the film from cohering.[88] This also means, though, that the cradle best represents the peculiar sort of time in which *Intolerance* takes place. William Drew's notion that it represents "the eternal present" makes the paradox clear, for the cradle scene never advances or changes, and thus it occupies the same moment of time for all time.[89] If the contiguity of birth and death is meant to suggest that both take place in an instant, this is still an instant that takes forever, or at least the length of the film. For the eternal present of the cradle scene is also the most appropriate time frame for *Intolerance* as a whole, which should take place in a present distended to the size of all history. The ultimate frame in which the elements of *Intolerance* are supposed to be contained is the instantaneous one of logical comparison, a present that is inherently nonnarrative, though it pretends to contain all of time.

Griffith's gamble in *Intolerance* is that film can transform the ordinary, immediate present of human experience, with its problematic relationship to past and future, into the eternal present traditionally afforded only to God. This is what Ramsaye claims it accomplishes when it satisfies "the human wish to live in the Past, Present and Future all at once."[90] The phrase "all at once" makes the paradox clear, for there is finally no difference between expanding time to the size of eternity and collapsing it into the present moment. In either case, everything happens all at once. This is, more or less, the conclusion of Deleuze's analysis of *Intolerance*: "Time as interval is the accelerated variable present, and time as a whole is the spiral open at both ends, the immensity of past and future. Infinitely dilated, the present would become the whole itself; infinitely contracted, the whole would happen in the interval."[91] What Deleuze calls "the continually diminishing interval between two movements or two actions," the infinitesimal present of the cut itself, also tends inevitably to encompass the full immensity of time.

In somewhat more practical terms, this devotion to the eternal present means that there is no very satisfactory way to end the film. The chase requires a conclusion, and the Boy is finally saved from hanging, but the cradle goes on rocking nonetheless. If the back-and-forth tug of war between love and intolerance is, in fact, timeless, "the same today as yesterday," as the sign proclaims when the workers in the modern sequence are shot down by the police, then the salvation of the Boy is just an episode. The eternal present established above and beyond the chase scenes can be concluded only by apocalypse or, as it happens, by double exposure. *Intolerance* switches for its last few moments to an apocalyptic battle scene, intercut with shots of crowds behind prison walls. These are dissolved by a double exposure, so the prisoners can run through walls suddenly become transparent, and then angels are superimposed over the battle scene. Finally, a cross comes to be superimposed over the entire scene. As a technique, the superimpositions suggest a resolution of the back-and-forth cradle rocking of the parallel editing, which can finally come to an end when two things can actually be seen at once. Only with this end is it possible literally to see what is implied throughout the film, that everything in it should ideally be visible in one instant of revelation.

For Griffith, then, there is a present within film, retarding its attempts to mount a narrative, and another present outside it, containing all the narrative lines and allowing them to be compared. The trick is somehow to seize the local present so fiercely that it reveals itself as that larger present, as if the eternal time outside the film had penetrated into it as a kind of epiphany. This is apparently the sort of thing that Deleuze sees in *Intolerance*, but which is achieved much more successfully in the later films featured in *The Time-Image*.

If Griffith's own time images, his random shots of camels and grinning beggars, were more compelling, then presumably he would have achieved the kind of thing Tarkovsky aims at, when he claims that each single frame contains the whole time of the film.

VI

Almost a hundred years after *Intolerance*, another Hollywood blockbuster combined four different plotlines in a simultaneous race against time. For David Bordwell, the similarities between this film and its distant precursor are strong enough for him to call Christopher Nolan's *Inception* "something like the *Intolerance* of the twenty-first century."[92] *Inception's* plotlines are situated in a descending set of dreamscapes, not in widely separated historical ages, but it depends just as heavily as *Intolerance*, according to Bordwell, on old-fashioned commonplaces of crosscutting. The principle that may still have seemed a little new in 1916, that parallel lines of action crosscut with one another should be understood to be progressing simultaneously, structures the final act of *Inception* as it does that of *Intolerance*. However, both films also expose the artificiality of this apparent simultaneity, Griffith's by stretching it across 2,500 years of history, Nolan's by inserting each subjective dream time within another. The same question is raised by both films: in relation to what time can the four different plotlines be considered simultaneous? For Bordwell, the answer is the same in both cases. *Inception*, he claims, brings us back "once more, to that sort of God's eye view of an eternal present created in *Intolerance*."[93] What made some sense for a conservative believer in 1916, though, can hardly have the same relevance for an apparently secular filmmaker in the 21st century. Perhaps that century has its own ways of moving from the limited present always visible on-screen to the eternal present situated somewhere beyond it.

The published screenplay of *Inception* constantly illustrates the complexity of these issues as it tries to guide the reader up and down the layers of time included in the film. At one point, in the course of a long retrospective monologue by Dominick Cobb (Leonardo DiCaprio), the script helpfully notes that we are "back in the present."[94] But this dramatically simplifies the actual situation, which involves a voice-over from one time, describing on-screen events from another time, which depend for their exposition on long, interpolated scenes from a more distant past, all of which is inserted into the lowest of four levels of nested dreams. Even in the simplest possible version of this arrangement, the "present" to which the script returns us is actually a dream in which time is moving several magnitudes more slowly than it does four levels up, where the ostensibly real present awaits our eventual return. In a more conventional film, with ordinary flashbacks, the present remains a constant from which the deviations can be seen to depart, but in a situation as complex as this one, where what counts as the "actual" present is off-screen for more than half the film and the deviations from it have deviations of their own with deviations of *their* own, the present loses its temporal authority and its capacity as a touchstone.

Nolan has made a particular specialty of negotiating through such complex temporal structures, from his first film, *Following* (1998), to his most recent, *Interstellar* (2014). But he is also considered a leading exponent of a new genre, the atemporal or anachronic film, which itself might be considered a subset of the more general category of puzzle films.[95] Suffice it to say that *Inception* stood out less prominently from the general run of contemporary films than did *Intolerance*. This general turn to more complex temporal structures has been traced to a number of causes, the most obvious of which is the advent of recording technologies beginning with VHS tape.[96] Where a film critic such as Cavell had once to rely on a fairly faulty memory, now his successors could watch and re-watch at will, stopping the action whenever necessary. As Nolan puts it, tape allowed the viewer "to control the time-line."[97] It is hardly a surprise, then, that films came to be constructed as if they had already been rewound, stopped, and replayed. Such films are hardly atemporal, since they contain more time, or at least more times, than their more conventional counterparts. What they lack is a secure present, an absolute moment in screen time against which the others might be calibrated. In films like *Following* or *Memento*, everything appears on-screen as if it had already been watched at least once, so that even the present tense of the viewer is made to seem belated and out of sync. In other words, the celebrated cinematic time machine has been inserted into another time machine, with different powers and different rules, and the result is a new take on the nature of the present.

In Nolan's first two films, the formal disorder of the time-line is linked thematically to some pathology in the main character. This is most overt in *Memento*, where Leonard Shelby (Guy Pearce) has apparently lost his ability to form new memories, though he retains quite vivid recollections, true or not, of the rape and murder of his wife. Without the ability to remember what he has done, Leonard is prone to repetition. Appropriately enough, the action he repeats most is telling others that he cannot remember. More seriously, he also repeats the action that has become the goal of his life: wreaking revenge on the killer of his wife. For all we know, Leonard may have done this several times, with different suspects, by the time the film begins with the murder of Teddy (Joe Pantoliano), which is, in fact, its last scene chronologically. Since he cannot remember and the film is restricted to his point of view, we have no idea.[98]

In narrative terms, Leonard lives a purely anecdotal life.[99] But his temporal stasis has a peculiarly restless quality because he is driven by a goal, in the future, that he can never know himself to have attained. As Leonard puts it, he is stuck in the present: "I want time to pass, but it won't. How can I heal if I can't feel time?"[100] It is common within the film and in the criticism of it to consider this condition fatal to Leonard's humanity, since the formation of basic emotions, such as fear or anger, seems to depend on temporal relations that he cannot construct.[101] But Leonard does actually feel these emotions, particularly anger, and he is far more aggressively goal-oriented than anyone else in the film. The problem for him is that he can never actually discharge the future, and so his present remains perpetually open, as if with a wound that cannot heal.

Viewers and critics generally consider this to be an abnormal condition, but Nolan has identified his film so closely with its main character as to make it difficult to judge. *Memento* alternates between black-and-white scenes that tell the fairly limited story of Leonard getting ready to leave his motel room and color scenes, moving steadily backward in time, that tell the story, in reverse order, of how he came to murder Teddy. Presented in reverse order, the color scenes put the viewers in the same position as Leonard, as each scene erases the memory of the one before. Though the black-and-white scenes move forward in what would seem to be normal time, they all occur before any of the color scenes, and so they do not establish a norm from which the color scenes could be seen to deviate, which would be the usual effect of crosscutting. The usual format for crosscutting of this kind would be an alternation between present and past, such that the past sequences could explain those in the present and the present could serve as an anchor in time, so that the past can be seen *as* past. Nolan's very different method, Bordwell maintains, sacrifices "the omniscience that usually comes with crosscutting."[102] In other words, there is no time-line in *Memento* within which the two different sets of scenes could be included and so compared. Leonard's inconclusive present is all there is.

Nolan has also packed *Memento* with reminders that this sort of wounded present is basic to film itself. The most obvious of these are the Polaroids that Leonard tries to use to document his activities. The general failure of these bits of visual evidence may be indicated in the first scene of the film, the only one to be shot in reverse, which shows a Polaroid being sucked back into the camera. A mnemonic method that erases rather than preserves evidence is a good visual metaphor for the film to follow. The Polaroids are also generally considered to be a good metaphor for Leonard's condition, a life lived as a series of disconnected snapshots.[103] But what is a film, if not a series of disconnected snapshots? The Polaroids, like the still photos studied by Garrett Stewart, are reminders of the photogram, made invisible within the smooth course of filmed movement. But the photogram itself is just the smallest in a whole series of filmic discontinuities, including the cuts between scenes that Nolan makes more painfully obvious by presenting the scenes out of order.

This, finally, is the most interesting discontinuity in *Memento* itself, since Nolan has taken great pains to extract and exaggerate those aspects of film that most painfully represent his character's pathology. What reads as mental illness at the level of content, however, appears at the level of form as aesthetic achievement. Nolan's great distinction as a director is founded on his insistence that conventional narrative chronology is dispensable in film, as it has been for many decades in literature.[104] The same disconnected, anecdotal quality that makes Leonard's life a hell on earth is taken as an index of freedom for the filmmaker. Of course, Leonard is a sort of filmmaker himself, with his storyboards on Polaroids, his casting calls and endless rehearsals, his campaign to get the script executed and recorded once and for all. In his obsession, he reaches a kind of stillness, an incessant interruption, at the very heart of film. Is this what Nolan is aiming at in structuring *Memento* as he does, or is there another reason for presenting his film as if it were a still photo disappearing before our eyes?

At the very least, Nolan turns out to be consistently interested in Leonard's situation, which he reproduces with Cobb in *Inception*. He, too, is obsessed with a dead wife, trapped by guilt about the past in a present that cannot advance. In literal terms, Cobb cannot return to his former life in the United States because he is suspected of having caused his wife's death. His situation in this respect is represented by a repeated scene of his children, locked in a tiny loop of action, with their faces turned away. This loop is, in a sense, what remains of the true movie of Cobb's life, interrupted by his wife's death and prevented from progressing by his unresolved legal situation. Cobb's only hope is to use his professional skills as a kind of hacker, invented by Nolan for this film, whose specialty is breaking into other people's dreams. Since this is exactly the kind of thing that implicated him in his wife's suicide in the first place, Cobb is doubling down on the most dangerous bet of his life.

On one level, *Inception* is a version of the "one last job" variety of heist film. In return for a resolution of his legal situation, Cobb will use his professional skills to implant a potentially self-destructive idea deep within the dreams of the heir to a great industrial empire. The only way to do this, as it turns out in Nolan's very intricate plot, is to nest this idea three levels deep in the subject's dreaming mind, not in a dream, where it would be detected instantly, but rather in a dream within a dream within a dream. Nolan's version of the dream world turns out to be quite rational in at least one respect, that time within the descending dream levels runs in precise ratios, slower and slower the deeper you go. Cobb's plot thus requires very careful synchronization of three and, as it turns out, four time-lines running at different rates. Abstracted a bit from all this folderol about dream levels, Cobb's task is fairly clear. In order to earn his release from the time loop he is caught in, to get out of its own subjective present, he must reestablish an objective time within which the four dream levels could be synchronized. If this synchronization fails, then Cobb himself and all his associates will be marooned within the dream, perhaps forever.

In general terms, then, the stakes could hardly be more obvious, for Cobb and for the film itself. The subjective time of dreams, as Nolan calculates it, is always slower than waking time, exactly twenty times slower, in fact.[105] At the very bottom, lower than Cobb hopes to penetrate, lies Limbo, where time hardly advances at all. To save themselves from being pitched into this endless present, Cobb and his team must carry out a precisely timed plan on three dream levels simultaneously, though time runs at drastically different rates on the three different levels. On one hand, then, there is the chaotic, endless present of pure subjectivity, and on the other, the supremely objective present within which three subjective times can become one. Nolan's gamble as a filmmaker is roughly parallel to this one, since he is asking his audience to construct and maintain a temporal point of view that hardly exists at all in the film itself. This is much trickier than ordinary crosscutting, where the different scenes can be assumed to progress at the same rate, though it is roughly similar to what Griffith does in *Intolerance*, where the plotlines are so far from one another in historical time.[106] In both cases, the same question arises, what sort of present could accommodate such drastically different temporalities? Bordwell suggests that there must be an omniscient level of narration in order to convey the dramatically different time-lines of the different levels.[107] On what is that omniscience to be founded? What is the opposite of Limbo?

These abstract difficulties appear as concrete effects in the film itself. The conceit, at this point, is that in order to extract themselves from the dream—to wake up, that is—the team must synchronize a set of "jumps" or shocks, on the model of the odd start that sometimes awakens a sleeper just on the edge of consciousness. And yet how are four different times, running at different rates, to be synchronized? What would synchronization mean in such a case? What is more or less punctual at level one would be twenty times longer at the next and so on. How could an alarm sounded at level one be synchronized with its counterparts twenty or four hundred times longer at the other levels? Nolan more or less advertises this problem by making the dream levels selectively permeable, especially to sound. Thus an Edith Piaf tune played at the top level sounds like some kind of deep sub-bass on the next level down and like distant wind on the next below that.[108] If, as it seems, the first note of the song takes a good twenty minutes to register at the deepest level, how is the timing to work? Any short action performed at the last level will be of infinitesimal duration at the top, making the timing all the more crucial.

The characters' necessary concentration on timing, along with their very frequent references to clock-time, make it all the more obvious that screen time does not equal elapsed time within any level. At one point, Cobb calculates that the team at his level has another sixty minutes to complete their task, which may be a bit of a shock to the audience. Even his recalculated time of twenty minutes turns out to be much more than the screen time left for this scene.[109] Cobb cannot be making this calculation using his watch because watches in the film seem to keep something like "real time," so that they can be seen to move with unnatural slowness at the lower levels. Of course, if this were carried out with real consistency, watches at the lowest level would move so slowly that their hands could not be used to calculate at all, for they would tend to look completely still.[110] Selective use of slow motion raises some of the same questions about screen time. It is fairly clear that action at the highest level must be slowed down somehow so that there will be enough time to show the necessary action at the lower levels. Nolan moves to slow motion at one point, virtually suspending the action at the top level, but he mostly uses selective cutting to eke out the second level, until close to the end when it too shifts to slow motion. This means that the first level must go to "extreme slow motion" to stay more or less in sync. But then he also uses slow motion at the lowest level, apparently just for dramatic emphasis.[111]

In other words, there is no time, most certainly not screen time, within which the dream levels might be compared and thus measured against one another. Of course, Cobb does ostensibly complete his task, even after a series of fantastic complications, and he is reunited with his children in something more or less like real time. But the end of the film, which cuts away from the spinning top that is supposed to tell Cobb whether he is in a dream or not, puts even this in question. This cut to black is, according to Nolan, the final kick, imposed from "outside the film," as if there were another temporal level yet.[112] This seems to admit that everything within the film is finally relative, even what passes for experience outside the dream. And though this admission might occasion all sorts of speculations about the essential subjectivity of human experience, what it makes clear in relation to film is that the ordinary mechanisms of screen editing have already qualified out of existence the kind of absolute simultaneity on which Cobb's plan depends. As was obvious from the first in simple examples like *The Fatal Hour*, the temporal matrix within which shots are composed is infinitely elastic. The clock may stop when the camera looks away, or it may race ahead. The present tense of film, the tense installed deep within it by the gaps between the frames, which appears again in the cuts and shifts of editing, is finally indistinguishable from Limbo.

The gravity of this problem is evinced by the cosmic methods necessary to resolve it in *Interstellar*. In several ways, this film represents a massive inflation of the basic situation of Nolan's earlier works. In this case, the Earth itself suffers from the pathological condition that afflicted Leonard Shelby and Dominick Cobb. Infected with a rather vague blight, the Earth can no longer support the human population, which then languishes, without a future, in a reduced version of the recent past. Stylistically, the first act of the film also lives in the past, as Nolan consciously evokes the Dust Bowl and the films and photographs that immortalized it. The only way out of this terminal condition of temporal stasis is to leave the Earth itself, an apparent impossibility that has been made marginally possible by the convenient appearance of a wormhole out past Saturn. The rest of the film then becomes a conventional race against time, a structure old at the time of *Intolerance*, but in this case the race really is against time and not just against the clock. The distances from this planet to any other likely to support life are so vast that in order to make the trip feasible, time itself must be defeated, first by means of the wormhole and then by the agency of a massive black hole on the far side of it.

These cosmic structures also set up a narrative situation reminiscent of Nolan's earlier films, especially *Inception*. In this case, the massive gravitational pull of the black hole asserts a drag against time, so that every hour spent exploring a planet in its vicinity might equal seven years back on Earth.[113] Thus the astronauts, on their expedition beyond the wormhole, do not age perceptibly at all, while their relatives back on Earth grow up, grow old, and, in some cases, die. On-screen, of course, everything runs at the usual pace, and the storyline back on Earth has to be severely edited and truncated so that it can stay more or less in sync with the much slower time-line beyond the stars. Crosscutting in this situation is like hitting a moving target, the difficulties of which are advertised whenever the two time-lines communicate. In one such scene, Murphy Cooper (Jessica Chastain), now a grown woman, sends a message into the wormhole for her father, who has hardly aged at all, though he left Earth when she was a little girl. Her message continues in voice-over as the scene cuts from her lab to the spacecraft *Endurance*, now empty, as its crew drops to the planet below.[114] A single sentence thus extends over three different time-lines, moving at three dramatically different rates. The implication is that Murph is speaking as the crew leaves the *Endurance*, and some of the poignancy of the scene depends on this dramatic convergence of events. But this is, of course, a mere effect, covering the practical reality that Murph's entire message, in its original form on Earth, would only have taken the merest millisecond on board the spacecraft.

In what sort of space are we, the audience, situated, such that we can experience these convergences between subplots that are not even time-lines any longer but completely different times? Nolan's ambition in this film is to answer this question, posed but not resolved in his earlier work. The answer lies on the other side of the black hole into which Cooper plunges when the expedition seems to have failed. What he finds there is the modern version of God's eternal present, an extradimensional space within which all times are simultaneous and equally available. A certain amount of explanation has already grown up around this device, which is more or less an expansion of a tesseract, or four-dimensional cube.[115] For better or worse, little of this is available in the film itself, where it appears that Cooper has fallen into a cross between the New York Public Library and a laundry chute. Suffice it to say that he has found himself in a kind of space that affords access to any time-line, including the ones we have already seen earlier in the film. In fact, we now re-watch these scenes from the other side of the screen, as it were, and realize, along with Murph herself, that the mysterious gravitational effects that made her childhood bedroom seem so uncanny were, in fact, messages from her father, communicating via gravity, which strings a line of communication between different times and spaces.

There is no God in this film, but there are godlike beings, who are apparently responsible for the wormhole and for vaulting Cooper across dimensions and back into his own past. But these gods turn out to be us, evolved beyond the confines of time and space.[116] Cooper's expedition through the wormhole is apparently the first step in this process, one result of which is the placing of the wormhole itself. This sort of logical nonsense has an accepted place in time-travel fiction of the 21st century, where it is sometimes assumed that the relativity of time is such that it could loop back on itself so that an effect could become its own cause.[117] Here, though, it may seem a little desperate, as if the awful recursiveness of human influence on our planet could somehow turn out to be not a trap at all but rather an escape. In any case, this cosmic loop back through time is a vast, massively redemptive version of the time loops suffered by Nolan's earlier characters. The vicious circle of lives like Leonard's or Cobb's now becomes a virtuous one, and the recurrent present in which they were trapped reappears as a quasi-scientific version of eternity.

In short, relativity plays in *Interstellar* the role that God plays in *Intolerance*. The very fact that so worried Einstein, that in relativistic terms there is no Now and therefore no one standard by which to synchronize different times, turns out to be the escape hatch for a humanity trapped in a dead end of its own making. The positive turn that Nolan gives this fact is exemplified by the use of watches as communicators. Initially, Cooper gives his daughter a watch to match his own, as if this were a symbol of faithfulness, though she immediately realizes that the two watches mean exactly the opposite, since they cannot remain in sync once her father leaves Earth.[118] This classic exposition of the facts of relativity is then reprised at the end of the film, when Cooper uses gravity to manipulate the second hand of Murph's watch, sending her data from a distant future that will allow her to achieve that future.[119] From the point of view offered by the tesseract, the watches *are* in sync, not because they keep the same time but rather because time has ceased to matter in this extradimensional space.

Nolan thus extracts a double happy ending, for his characters and for humanity at large, from what might otherwise seem the rather dire notion that time is not a constant. Though it might be said that the only way he escapes the unhappy ending that seems so certain at the beginning of the film is to avoid ending altogether, by turning the human story into a loop. Avoiding the apocalyptic, as it turns out, was one of Nolan's basic ambitions for *Interstellar*. In an interview published with the screenplay of the film, he congratulates his brother for transcending "the negative aspects of the continuing human story." Such is our pessimism right now about the human condition that there is always "this apocalyptic mode to storytelling."[120] Though Nolan must mean this in fairly practical terms, his words also have some bearing on the formal shape of his film. To avoid the apocalyptic, in this sense, is to avoid ending at all, which can only be achieved if time can somehow be made to stop. For all his storytelling verve, then, Nolan is constitutionally biased against the demands of narrative, particularly its inevitable allegiance to the end. The cure for a pathological isolation in the present, for an individual or a planet, is not narrative but rather a larger, more perfect present, preferably an eternal one. God's eternal present, the expedient that Griffith uses to wrap up his multi-story film, has this disadvantage, that it appears on Earth in the form of apocalypse. The eternal present that Nolan adapts from relativistic physics has this fundamental advantage, that it does not require the end of anything.

Here and Now

AT THIS POINT, it may seem easier to say what the present is not than what it is. In fact, it may seem easiest of all to say simply that the present is not. If many physicists, neurobiologists, and linguists contend that the respective versions of the present that have been so important in their disciplines do not stand up to scrutiny, then perhaps the present as such could be dispensed with. It would be interesting to see if ordinary standards of punctuality could be sustained without the concept of now. Would simply knowing that one has to be there at noon be enough without adding to one's arrival at noon the additional notion of now? But this is to suppose that a category of thought has arisen and sustained itself without playing any necessary role in human life, which is a lot to swallow, no matter what logic seems to dictate.

Clearly the present is necessary in some way, or it would not have persisted as one of the longest-running puzzles of human thought. As contemporary artist Harry Dodge puts it in a pamphlet released as part of the Hammer Biennial, "humans need an architecture that pushes later away from now,"[1] or to put it more comprehensively, humans seem to need a device to keep the past and the future away. The alternative, as Dodge puts it—that "everything is next to itself. And is happening at once"—is a little hard to take in, much less accept. And yet that does seem to be the implication of much recent art history, which sees art as essentially anachronic, as it is also the assumption of many recent films, like those of Christopher Nolan, and perhaps of the present-tense novels of writers like David Mitchell. One of the surefire devices of contemporary narrative of all kinds is time-travel, a trope that seems to thrive by defying the ordinary restrictions of the present, though it may simply be expressing a principled disbelief in them. What is a time-travel movie but a literalization of Kubler's metaphor for the present as a screen on which all of time is projected?[2]

If these contemporary artists, scholars, and writers are confined to the present, then, it is a much different, much larger present than the traditional instant, longer even than the present that James managed to extend, by philosophical might and main, to about a minute. At the very least, there does not seem to be any particular reason to fear the brevity of this present, if it is different from other presents in the past. If anything, the present seems to be getting longer, more capacious, the more we think about it. It is the oldest authoritative version of the present, Aristotle's, that makes it out to be nothing at all, and one of the most recent, Nolan's, that expands it to include all time.

It may be, though, that to expand the present is to redefine it out of existence. If it is at all long, it can no longer be the present. This seems to mean that the present is, in its essential brevity, a metaphor for our sense of the passage of time. If we think of time as movement, then there must be some part of it that moves, and this must be distinct from past and future, since these may grow or shrink but do not seem to move. But this sense of the present as sheer movement clashes with another apparently necessary attribute of the present, which is the stillness implied by its constant presence. Perhaps these difficulties arise from the entrenched habit of thinking of the present as a part of something else. Perhaps the present is really something more like the way we encompass within ourselves the whole of time. In this sense, the present would not be the actual part of time but rather the actuality of time. This is perhaps what Dodge has in mind with the idea that "everything is next to itself. And is happening at once," a notion that sounds a lot like Kubler and the generally anachronic approach to the visual arts in general.

A philosophical work that offers a more systematic explanation of this approach to time is Paolo Virno's *Déjà Vu and the End of History*, originally published in 1999 and recently translated into English. Virno's analysis depends on two different "readings of time." On one hand, there is the time of past and present, related as cause to effect: "The most immediate of presences always appears to be a *consequence*, standing out from a now-faded 'back then.'"[3] On the other hand, time can be considered a matter of potential and act. As Virno explains it, the relation between cause and effect obtains "between two different 'nows', one succeeding the other," whereas the relation between potential and act is "between not-now and a single 'now', between the never-actual and the present."[4] Cause and effect, for Virno, determine a time-line of strict succession. Since a cause gives way to its effect in giving rise to it, cause and effect inhabit fundamentally separate times, the time of a past now gone and the time of a present in isolation. Potential and act, however, are related to one another

simultaneously, since potential does not cease to exist whenever it is actualized. Therefore, according to Virno, "when they assume the features of potential and act, the past and present no longer designate successive moments, but
concomitant dimensions."[5] Virno's best example in this respect is language,
since the potential of a language to generate utterances does not diminish in
any way as people speak, nor does it reside somehow in the past but coexists
with the time of every statement.[6]

It is not too much of an exaggeration to say that, as Virno describes potential, it gradually comes to be a name for time itself. Potential, as he puts it, is
"the *non-chronological past* of the act."[7] Potential must always come before the
act, but not in a strictly temporal sense, since its *before* is more logical than
chronological. For the same reason, there are no temporal distinctions within
the past-as-potential: it is all there all the time. At one point, Virno calls it "a
not-now devoid of any date."[8] Though it must change, the past-as-potential is
also always complete and total, though in a rather paradoxical sense. A particular act never reduces in any way the compass of the potential from which it
comes. Potential of the kind Virno describes, which is not a physical quantity,
is not converted or used up and so it always remains full and complete. In this
sense, then, the past-as-potential is also permanent: "Potential is neither transitory nor retractable: its temporal prerogative is that of *permanence*."[9]

Despite some terminological differences, Virno's description of the past-
as-potential bears a significant resemblance to Bergson's idea that "the whole
of the past goes into the making of the living being's present moment" and to
similar ideas in the phenomenological tradition that follows from Heidegger.[10]
The basic distinction between a time of chronological succession and one of
constant coexistence is fairly clear, though it is hard to tell in Virno, as it is in
Bergson, whether these times are ontological or phenomenological. Potential
as Virno describes it must be outside the individual mind as it is outside the
present, but if so, what is its basis? Virno's most useful example, language, suggests that potential may be social, though he sometimes speaks of "a general
disposition towards articulated discourse" that sounds like an innate capacity.[11] In any case, language as "the past-in-general of acts of speaking" is Virno's
model for the past-in-general-in-general, for he maintains that all human acts
realize a prior potentiality that never diminishes and never ceases to exist.

The relation between past and present that Virno describes does not itself
occur in any measurable time, for the relation between an utterance and the
rules that make it possible is not a temporal relation. Figuring the present on
this model means that it may imply a vast tract of time, all the time it took to

make the speaker as well as the utterance, without distending itself toward either past or future. It does not need to include these because it *is* these, as the throw of a ball to first base *is* the act of putting the runner out. The relation of the present to everything else is, appropriately, a present-tense relation, and thus relations need not take the present out of itself at all. Virno speaks quite eloquently about a higher form of déjà vu he calls a "memory of the present," by which he means a kind of self-reference by which the mind recalls itself to itself. But he might as easily have adapted his phrase to suggest something else, not that we can remember the present but rather that the present has a memory. As the result of all that has happened, the present retains a memory of it, but only *as* the present. Even if the present is all there is, that doesn't stop it from being everything.

For a concrete actualization of this version of the present, we might look to a recent graphic novel by Richard McGuire. *Here* first appeared as a short strip in the comic magazine *Raw* in 1989, and it immediately asserted an influence so profound that Chris Ware, who is constantly quoted in this respect, has said, "I don't think there's another strip that's had a greater effect on me or my comics."[12] But that original version was quite short, and the new version, expanded to about 290 pages, raises much more complex questions about time and narrative. As the title implies, *Here* is the story of a place, in particular the house in Perth Amboy, New Jersey, in which McGuire grew up. As an all-purpose deictic, though, the title also implies that it is the story of *the* place, the place we always are whether we are at home or not. Every two-page spread is focused on the same spot, one corner of the living room of the Perth Amboy house, and different times flit past this fixed optic, rather as if McGuire were illustrating the "Time Passes" section of Virginia Woolf's *To the Lighthouse*. As in that novel, the point of view seems to be that of the house itself, independent of all its human inhabitants. But the view straight into the corner of the room also seems designed to remind us of our own binocular vision, the always centered, always symmetrical view of things we carry with us everywhere, the view that, for all sighted people at least, is the sensory substrate that supports the grammatical notion of *here*.

The inevitable partner of that personal *here* is, of course, *now*. As *here* is the name of the place we always occupy, *now* is what we call the corresponding time. And this turns out to be one of the basic concerns that drove McGuire to expand his original strip. "If you stop to think about this, the 'now' becomes heightened," he told the *Atlantic*. "We are so rarely 'in the moment,' we spend most of our time thinking of the past or worrying about the future. The 'now'

is the only thing that really exists."[13] *Here*, therefore, is just as much about time as it is about space, and though it covers a vast tract of time, the way it pictures this time makes it seem a collection of mutually exclusive presents. Joel Smith has referred to the "perpetual present tense" in which *Here* takes place, and this may seem inappropriate for a book that stretches from 3 billion BCE to 22175 CE, but it is apt in the sense that each time is shown to exist in its own limited present tense.[14] Time-travel, in this case at least, just takes us to another now, as spatial travel simply lands us in another here.

Where most graphic novels struggle mightily to justify the form by connecting the adjective to its noun, *Here* tries to separate them, posing the pictorial against the narrative and vice versa. Apparently on purpose, McGuire breaks most of the rules that Will Eisner set out, when the term graphic novel was still new, for what he defined as "sequential art." Eisner's very influential treatise states as a given that visual images operate as a language, so that their order can be superimposed on that of the dialogue and narration to produce what he calls a "visual narrative" that can be read like a book.[15] For Eisner, getting this narrative right depends on a sense of timing in which punctuation can exist only against a background of continuity. The major task of the comics artist, therefore, "is to arrange the sequence of events (or pictures) so as to bridge the gaps in action."[16] This is just what McGuire does not do. In *Here*, the panels float above or below one another, widely separated by date, discontinuous and out of order, connected only by their shared relationship to the same point in space. As it is, that space seems to separate more than it connects. A typical two-page spread suspends two to five different presents in a spatial matrix provided by another present, so that the space between times is not a neutral medium connecting them, the box made by the two pages not a solid backdrop, but just another box.

Here is therefore structured by a tension between these still images and the traces of narration that they seem to contain. The basic model for the book is clearly that of the snapshot. Many pages were, in fact, generated by distributing pictures from the family photo album and then, in a process a bit like rotoscoping, transforming these into loose drawings or watercolors.[17] The resulting images retain much of the instantaneous temporality of the snapshot, as indicated by its classic subject matter: the off-balance; the unposed; the casual. McGuire confuses the situation a bit by dating these images only by year, perhaps a purposely anachronistic gesture in a time when every picture taken by phone can be dated to the second. But this gesture does raise an interesting question: how much time is each picture supposed to cover? What does it mean when a moment that can have lasted only a second, like a ladder tipping over, is labeled 2014?[18] Is this the typical or the climactic moment of the year? The weirdly related image next to it, of a paint can toppling over in 1990, shows rather vividly how the arbitrarily restricted spatial boundaries of the snapshot have always helped to indicate its similarly arbitrary excision from the flow of time. But if a moment like this is such a tiny piece of time, then why is it named for an entire year? On one hand, this practice gives these ephemeral moments an odd kind of stability, the stability of photographs, in which the moment does indeed last much, much longer than it can have in reality. On the other hand, labeling these instants with the year alone implies an exceedingly long view, far from the time in question, from which a whole year is reduced to "the year Dad fell off the stepladder," as if 365 days of experience has dwindled to a pinprick. In other words, these inset images raise the question first raised quite self-consciously by instantaneous photography: how long is an instant?

The toppling stepladder, lined up as it is with the falling paint can from 24 years before and the fallen mirror from 65 years before and the ungracious

insult from 162 years before, also poses the other major question about snapshots: how do they fit together? In this respect, *Here* leaves unresolved some
fairly major puzzles. It is clear enough that the wallpaper going up in 1949 (56)
is the wallpaper coming down in 1960 (55), though it is not the same stepladder (in fact, the house does not seem to be able to hang onto stepladders,
since it has a different one in 1998 and yet another in 2014). But is it the same
person in both cases? The man who takes down the wallpaper in 1960 seems
to be the same man taking the family photo in 1957 (31–32), but the woman in
that picture does not seem to be the one who wanders through 1957 just a few
pages earlier (7–8). One wears glasses and the other does not, though she is
searching for her book. In other words, the compositional fact that the pictures
are cut up and scattered unchronologically through the book is matched by
a deeper anachronism, in that the stories told in the pictures do not seem to
add up. One two-page spread featuring babies in their mothers' arms seems to
imply a series of families, moving into and out of the house, from 1924 to 1945
to 1949 to 1957 to 1988, but the mothers do not seem to belong to the families
otherwise identified with those years. In fact, it is hard to tell whether the

mothers from 1945, 1949, and 1957 are supposed to be the same or different. Sadly, the wallpaper seems more durable than the people.

Still, there are quite a few segments in the book that suggest some sort of long-term continuity, such as the two-page spread in which a man in 1954 seems to complain about a dog barking in 1986 (59–60). The man fusses about the dog's barking at the mailman "every day," and, in fact, this seems to go on for another thirty years, though it can hardly be the same dog. There is another two-page spread in which a game of Twister seems to go on for almost fifty years (209–210). Such instances are apparently meant to depict the timelessness of routine, but they also show the odd paradox of routine, which is just as apt to make time feel long as short. When every morning shower is the same morning shower, time may collapse on itself or suddenly come to seem endless.

Perhaps the most appropriate icon for this whole situation is the arrow, shot in 1402, that takes three pages to advance about two inches from its initial position, and which never does reach its destination. This is very obviously time's arrow, but it is also a direct reference to one of Zeno's famous paradoxes. Here McGuire seems to illustrate Zeno's contention that an arrow cannot advance from any one point in its flight, that it is, in fact, motionless at that point. This is a paradox that pictures are especially good at exploring, for it is impossible to tell from this, or any other picture, whether the arrow is at rest or in flight. McGuire applies some graphical motion blur to the background of his drawing, as if to reassure us that the arrow is actually in motion, but it is the same motion blur in the first and third frames in the sequence, so McGuire is either being a little lazy as a draftsman or he wants to suggest that the arrow is somehow arrested in flight. The frames advance across the page, though not very rapidly, but the arrow remains in the same position in each frame. Even if time does advance, these pictures seem to suggest, we still experience it as a series of present moments, each one essentially static, each with the same basic quality of being now. This is perhaps the most obvious image of time that pictures are meant deliver.

On the other hand, Here is not a single image but a book of images, and it often seems to take pains to remind us of that fact. The basic visual unit of this work is the two-page spread, with the gutter in the middle aligned to and thus standing for the corner of the room. The easy way in which the book becomes a room suggests that the room was always in some sense a book. This is one of many reasons why the e-book version is almost a different work. There are a number of instances in which the materiality of the page is both used and confused, as in those few sequences of superimposition in which a full-page image becomes an inset image on the next page, making it look for a second as if that page had a hole cut in it (7–9). Though the same effect is achieved in the e-book, it is achieved so naturally and instantaneously that the ironic sense of interference is lost, when the page seems to be there and not there at the same time.

Perhaps it is not an accident that there is a book lying on the table in this particular picture. There are, in any case, a number of books in this book, some on the shelves that appear in later years on the wall by the fireplace, some actually being read. *This* book is probably the most important, though, because it appears at the beginning and the end of *Here*, as if to establish a frame for everything that happens in between. This book is the focal point of a narrative that encloses all these various images within a story, one that starts as the woman at the beginning wanders into the living room, having forgotten what she is looking for, and which ends almost 290 pages later when she remembers and picks up her book. "Now I remember," she says, and she seems to mean merely that she has remembered wanting her book, but McGuire may also mean that books are particularly good at reinforcing memory, better even perhaps than pictures, precisely because they can create narratives like this one, about the book. Or he may mean something even broader, that people in general have forgotten books, that they tend now to think of books in a context established by pictures, so that when we see a book we remember, "oh, right, that thing with pages." Where photography once seemed at odds with the established flow of narrative, narrative, in a weirdly inverted way, now seems to interrupt the stasis of photographs.

This frame story, this two-part narrative about forgetting and then remembering, establishes a theme that runs throughout the book. The passage of time, the loss of it, is often signified in these pages by the loss of objects. One sequence starts with the loss of a wallet, an umbrella, then a mind and self-control, as if to explain all this forgetfulness; first the car keys and then the car itself, a dog, eyesight, hearing, and then in a visual and aural rhyme, an earring (134–142). At the end of this sequence, the reader is plunged back into 1 million BCE, where it seems everything is lost but an empty featureless ocean, and then even further back to 3 billion BCE, where there is nothing but gas. The general loss behind all these particular losses is identified in a small box from 2014: "Where did the time go?" (41).

Against this sense, expressed by someone in 1986, that "the older I get the less I know," many of the figures in the book attempt to tell stories. There is a very long sequence from 1989 involving a joke about a doctor, the point of which is apparently the grim brevity of life, and which is so funny it nearly ends the life of one of the listeners (11–27). There is the courtship story told on the same couch in 1988, which ends with the triumphant punch line "and the rest is history" (79–87). And there is the Native American vignette from 1609, in which the plea "tell me a story" may just be a ploy of the woman to hold off the advances of the man (154). In any case, it is a plea that is so basic it can be expressed, in her language, in a single word.

Together, these vignettes suggest a basic human desire for narrative, of which the physical book is just one manifestation. And yet McGuire himself has offered another interpretation of the climax of his narrative. According to this interpretation, when the woman finally remembers and reaches down for her book, she does not complete a narrative arc but rather finds herself truly in the present for the first time. As he puts it, "the book ends with a moment of recognition of the 'now.'"[19] Scattered and abstracted as she wanders through the room, the woman finally comes to herself when she sees the book. "Now I remember" thus means something like "I remember *now*," or "I have recaptured the present from which I had been displaced." Thus it is not necessary to read the book, but just to find it, and the moment in which the character picks up her book coincides, not so ironically, with the moment in which we put ours down. The purpose of *this* narrative, in other words, is not to overcome or extend the present but rather to place us more firmly in it. It is, as Virno might put it, to remember the present.

McGuire thus upends the traditional relationship between narrative and the present, one that has been a fixture from Lukács to Jameson, and he also adopts an uncommon position in a more general argument about the present. For it is a fixture of much current lamentation about the contemporary world that it has lost its grip on the past and the future and spends too much time in the present. But it must also be the case that our present is much larger than any in the past, simply because it includes that past. By now, that inclusion is largely literal, since the recording technologies of the past two centuries have surrounded us with images and sounds from other times. The structure of *Here* implies that this has turned the present into a vast screen onto which the past and the future are projected, not in sequences, by and large, but rather in bursts and fits of reverie. The whole of time is always available, always present, and equally present, since we don't have to go through the intervening years to get to any particular point in time.

By organizing his book as he has, McGuire implies a basic commonality between the punctual moment in which the woman, finding her book, says "now" and the vast stretch of time extending from 3 billion BCE to 22175 CE. For the way that *Here* is organized suggests that all these times are equally present within or around the house in Perth Amboy. Time is a vast, potential fund of moments, any of which can be actualized in any order, since we do not have to go through recent times to arrive at ones farther past. All the nows are still here. What links them together is that elementary sense of presence we get by looking at where we are now, which is where we will always be, as long as we are.

And yet McGuire's book also raises uncomfortable questions about how long that may be. The point of view on which the pages depend is extended in both directions beyond the time of human habitation, so that technically speaking, there is no one to see the gas clouds in which the planet begins and ends. What sense do the dates make at these extremes? What would the present mean then, before and after there is anyone to experience it? McGuire's book, like Mitchell's novel and Nolan's movies, thus seems to participate in a contemporary vogue for the postapocalyptic that may be quite closely related to a general uneasiness about the category of the present. The timelessness so frequently evoked by books and movies beyond the end of history seems the inverse of the inextensive moment of time in which we are said to live. Or is it the fatally ironic fulfillment of that time, the emptiness of that brief instant extended into infinity as a kind of fairy-tale punishment? For some contemporary writers, filmmakers, and artists, such prefigurations are also refigurations, alternate metaphors for time and the present. Extending the present beyond the end may be a way of suggesting that it is already extensive, as long as we avoid the traditional metaphors that pin it down.

NOTES

Introduction

1. Helen Molesworth, response to Questionnaire on "The Contemporary," *October* 130 (Fall 2009), 112.

2. Richard Meyer, *What Was Contemporary Art?* (Cambridge, MA: MIT Press, 2013), 11.

3. Pamela Lee, *New Games: Postmodernism After Contemporary Art* (New York: Routledge, 2012), xxviii.

4. Keith Moxey, *Visual Time: The Image in History* (Durham, NC: Duke University Press, 2013), 37.

5. Harry Harootunian, "Remembering the Historical Present," *Critical Inquiry* 3 (Spring 2007), 480.

6. Stephen Kern, *The Culture of Time and Space 1880–1918* (Cambridge, MA: Harvard University Press, 1983), 88.

7. David Harvey, *The Condition of Post-Modernity* (Oxford: Basil Blackwell, 1989), 240.

8. Fredric Jameson, "The End of Temporality," *Critical Inquiry* 29 (2003): 708.

9. Paul Virilio, *The Futurism of the Instant: Stop-Eject*, tr. Julie Rose (Cambridge, UK: Polity Press, 2010), 71.

10. Bernard Stiegler, *Technics and Time: Cinematic Time and the Question of Malaise*, tr. Stephen Barker (Stanford, CA: Stanford University Press, 2011), 75.

11. Virilio, *Futurism of the Instant*, 59.

12. François Hartog, *Regimes of Historicity: Presentism and Experiences of Time*, tr. Saskia Brown (New York: Columbia University Press, 2015), 114.

13. See the discussion in David Couzens Hoy, *The Time of Our Lives* (Cambridge, MA: MIT Press, 2009), 57.

14. For a discussion with many examples, see Leo Charney, "In a Moment: Film and the Philosophy of Modernity," in *Cinema and the Invention of Modern Life* (Berkeley: University of California Press, 1995), 279–95. See also Karl Heinz Bohrer, *Suddenness: On the Moment of Aesthetic Appearance* (New York: Columbia University Press, 1994).

15. John Locke, *An Essay Concerning Human Understanding*, ed. Peter H. Nidditch (Oxford: Clarendon Press, 1975), 190.

16. G. W. Leibniz, *New Essays on Human Understanding*, tr. and ed. Peter Remnant and Jonathan Bennett (Cambridge, UK: Cambridge University Press, 1996), 153.

17. See, for example Ben Singer, *Melodrama and Modernity* (New York: Columbia University Press, 2001).

18. This is the argument of Jonathan Crary, *Techniques of the Observer* (Cambridge, MA: MIT Press, 1990).

19. David Bordwell, *On the History of Film Style* (Cambridge, MA: Harvard University Press, 1997), 141–46.

20. Meyer, *What Was Contemporary Art?*, 31; Marc Augé, *The Future*, tr. John Howe (London: Verso, 2014).

21. Peter Osborne, *Anywhere or Not at All: Philosophy of Contemporary Art* (London: Verso, 2013), 175, 24.

22. Marcus Aurelius, *Meditations, Books 1–6*, tr. Christopher Gill (Oxford: Oxford University Press, 2013), 18. See Pierre Hadot, *Philosophy as a Way of Life* (Malden, MA: Blackwell, 1995), 227.

23. Quoted in Hadot, *Philosophy*, 228.

24. Goethe, "The Book of the Cup-Bearer," quoted in ibid., 220. Note that Hartog does cite Hadot's discussion, *Regimes*, 228, n26.

25. Osborne, *Anywhere or Not at All*, 176.

26. Paul Ricoeur, *Time and Narrative*, tr. Kathleen Blamey and David Pellauer (Chicago: University of Chicago Press, 1988), 3:253.

27. Saint Augustine, *Confessions*, tr. R. S. Pine-Coffin (New York: Penguin, 1961), 264.

28. Henri Poincaré, "The Measure of Time," in *Time & the Instant*, ed. Robin Durie (Manchester, UK: Clinamen Press, 2000), 30.

29. "Carnap's Intellectual Biography," in *The Philosophy of Rudolf Carnap*, ed., P. A. Schilpp (La Salle, IL: Open Court, 1963), 37–38.

30. John G. Cramer, "The Plane of the Present and the New Transactional Paradigm of Time," in Durie, ed., *Time & the Instant*, 187.

31. Aristotle, *Complete Works*, ed. Jonathan Barnes (Princeton, NJ: Princeton University Press, 1984), 678–79, 710–12; Daniel Heller-Roazen, *The Inner Touch: Archaeology of a Sensation* (New York: Zone Books, 2009), 51–52.

32. Alex O. Holcombe, "Are There Cracks in the Façade of Continuous Visual Experience?" in *Subjective Time: The Philosophy, Psychology, and Neuroscience of Temporality*, ed. Valtteri Arstila and Dan Lloyd (Cambridge, MA: MIT Press, 2014), 193.

33. Arstila and Lloyd, untitled chapter introduction in ibid., 200.

34. Ian Phillips, "The Temporal Structure of Experience," in ibid., 139.

35. Immanuel Kant, *Critique of Pure Reason*, tr. Norman Kemp Smith (New York: Palgrave Macmillan, 2007), 76–77.

36. David Cockburn, *Other Times: Philosophical Perspectives on Past, Present and Future* (Cambridge, UK: Cambridge University Press, 1997), 11.

37. Edmund Husserl, *On the Phenomenology of the Consciousness of Internal Time*, tr. John Barnett Brough (Dordrecht, Netherlands: Kluwer, 1991), 37.

38. William James, *Principles of Psychology* (1890; rpt., New York: Dover, 1950), 1:613.

39. Ibid., 1:406.

40. Augustine, *Confessions*, 276.

41. Hollis Frampton, *On the Camera Arts and Consecutive Matters*, ed. Bruce Jenkins (Cambridge, MA: MIT Press, 2009), 26, 45.

42. Augustine, *Confessions*, 220.

43. For a detailed example of the latter, see Tyler Burge, "Memory and Persons," *Philosophical Review* 112 (2003): 289–337. For a statement of the same case from a phenomenological point of view, see Paul Ricoeur, *Memory, History, Forgetting* (Chicago: University of Chicago Press, 2007), 101.

44. Maurice Merleau-Ponty, *Phenomenology of Perception*, ed. Donald A. Landes (Abingdon, Oxon./New York: Routledge, 2012), 360.

45. Jacques Derrida, *Voice and Phenomenon*, tr. Leonard Lawlor (Evanston, IL: Northwestern University Press, 2011), 53.

46. Robin Le Poidevin, *The Images of Time: An Essay on Temporal Representation* (New York: Oxford University Press, 2009), 46.

47. Emmanuel Levinas, *Time and the Other*, tr. Richard A. Cohen (Pittsburgh, PA: Duquesne University Press, 1987), 52.

48. Ibid., 39.

49. E. H. Gombrich, "Moment and Movement in Art," *Journal of the Warburg and Courtauld Institutes* 27 (1964): 297.

50. Ibid.

51. Michel Foucault, "Kant on Enlightenment and Revolution," tr. Colin Gordon, *Economy and Society* 15: 88. See also "What Is Enlightenment?" in *The Foucault Reader*, ed. Paul Rabinow (New York: Vintage, 2010), 32–50.

52. Foucault, "Kant on Enlightenment," 90.

53. Ibid., 96.

54. Vincent Descombes, *The Barometer of Modern Reason: On the Philosophies of Current Events*, tr. Stephen Adam Schwartz (New York: Oxford University Press, 1993), 18.

55. Joel Burges and Amy J. Elias, eds., *Time: A Vocabulary of the Present* (New York: New York University Press, 2016).

Chapter 1: This Point in Time

1. Immanuel Kant, *Critique of Pure Reason*, tr. Norman Kemp Smith (New York: Palgrave Macmillan, 2007), 77.

2. *Aristotle, Complete Works*, ed. Jonathan Barnes (Princeton, NJ: Princeton University Press, 1984), 440–41 (VIII.8.263b 10, 264a 1, 264b 8, etc.).

3. Eric Schliesser, "Newton's Philosophy of Time," in *A Companion to the Philosophy of Time*, ed. Heather Dyke and Adrian Bardon (New York: Wiley, 2013), 94.

4. Lorne Falkenstein, "Classical Empiricism," in *Companion to the Philosophy of Time*, 104.

5. Ibid., 106.

6. Ibid., 109–11.

7. Gaston Bachelard, *Intuition of the Instant*, tr. Eileen Rizo-Patron (Evanston: University of Illinois Press, 2013), 11.

8. Aristotle, *Complete Works*, 395 (*Physics* VI.3 234a 17).

9. Saint Augustine, *Confessions*, tr. R. S. Pine-Coffin (London/New York: Penguin, 1961), 266.

10. Immanuel Kant, *Kant's Inaugural Dissertation and Early Writings on Space*, tr. John Handyside (La Salle, IL: Open Court, 1929), as reprinted in Charles Sherover, ed., *The Human*

Experience of Time (Evanston, IL: Northwestern University Press, 2001), 146. According to Kant, moments are not parts of time, but divisions within it.

11. Aristotle, *Complete Works*, 711 (*Sense and Sensibilia*, 7 448a 25–27).

12. Ibid., 317 (*Physics*, I.2 185b 10).

13. Ibid., 395 (*Physics*, VI.3). For discussions, see Richard Sorabji, *Time, Creation and the Continuum* (Chicago: University of Chicago Press, 1983), 10–11; Tony Roark, *Aristotle on Time* (Cambridge, UK: Cambridge University Press, 2011), 98; Andrea Falcon, "Aristotle on Time and Change," in *Companion to the Philosophy of Time*, 49.

14. Aristotle, *Complete Works*, 404 (*Physics*, VI.9 239b 8–9).

15. Sarah Waterlow remarks that Aristotle seems to place the now "outside any temporal order." "Aristotle's Now," *Philosophical Quarterly* 34 (1984): 125.

16. See Sorabji, 49.

17. Aristotle, *Complete Works*, 400 (*Physics* VI.6 237a 15).

18. Ibid., 375. (*Physics* IV.13 222a 14).

19. Ibid (*Physics* IV.13 222a 15).

20. W. von Leyden, "Time, Number, and Eternity in Plato and Aristotle," *Philosophical Quarterly* 14 (1964): 49.

21. Sorabji, 49. See also Roark, 199.

22. Aristotle, *Complete Works*, 372 (*Physics* IV.11 219a 1).

23. Waterlow, 127; von Leyden, 52; Roark, 213.

24. Waterlow, 112.

25. Paul Ricoeur, *Time and Narrative*, tr. Katherine Blamey and David Pellauer (Chicago: University of Chicago Press, 1988), III.19.

26. J. E. McTaggart, "The Unreality of Time," *Mind* 17 (1908): 457–74.

27. This is particularly true of Ricoeur, who uses the terms "cosmological instant" and "lived present." See, for example, *Time and Narrative*, III.19.

28. Aristotle, *Complete Works*, 377 (*Physics* 4.14 223a 23); Sorabji, 90; Roark, 116, 217.

29. Aristotle, 711 (*Sense and Sensibilia*, 7 448a 25–27). Roark argues from an analysis of *De Anima* and *Parva Naturalia* that Aristotle affirms the possibility of instantaneous perception. See 106–9.

30. Plato, *Complete Works*, ed. John M. Cooper (Indianapolis, IN: Hackett, 1997), 328.

31. Von Leyden, 41–42.

32. John R. Wilson, "Kairos as 'Due Measure,'" *Glotta* 58 (1980); 200–201.

33. Hans Ruin, *Enigmatic Origins: Tracing the Theme of Historicity through Heidegger's Works* (Stockholm: Almquist & Wiksell International, 1994), 180–81.

34. Barbara Cassin, ed., *Dictionary of Untranslatables: A Philosophical Lexicon*, tr. Steven Rendall et al. (Princeton, NJ: Princeton University Press, 2014), 685; Wilson, 180.

35. Wilson, 186.

36. Koral Ward, *Augenblick: The Concept of the 'Decisive Moment' in 19th- and 20th-Century Western Philosophy* (Burlington, VT: Ashgate, 2008), 144.

37. Wilson, 193, 197.

38. Ibid., 191.

39. Von Leyden, 42.

40. James Barr, *Biblical Words for Time* (Napervile, IL: Allenson Inc., 1969), 50–51.

41. Cassin, *Dictionary*, 24.

42. Frank Kermode, *The Sense of an Ending*, 1966, rpt., (Oxford: Oxford University Press, 2000), 46–49.

43. Ibid., 47–49; see Barr, pp. 21–49. For another discussion of the distinction between these two terms in classical literature, see Giorgio Agamben, *The Time That Remains*, tr. Patricia Dailey (Stanford, CA: Stanford University Press, 2005), 68–69.

44. Cassin, *Dictionary*, 685.

45. Barr, 129.

46. Acts 9:3–4, 17–18. King James Version.

47. As quoted in Geoffrey Bennington, "Is It Time?" in *The Moment: Time and Rupture in Modern Thought*, ed. Heidrun Friese (Liverpool: Liverpool University Press, 2001), 20. According to Agamben, the *ho nyn kairos*, the time of the now, is the time between the birth of Christ and the return of the Messiah (63–64).

48. Søren Kierkegaard, *The Concept of Anxiety*, tr. Alastair Hannay (New York: Liveright, 2014), 102.

49. Ibid., 103.

50. Ibid., 128.

51. Karl Marx, *The Poverty of Philosophy* (New York: International Publishers, 1973), 54.

52. Georg Lukács, *History and Class Consciousness*, tr. Rodney Livingstone (Cambridge, MA: MIT Press, 1971), 89–90.

53. Kierkegaard, 107.

54. Ibid., 106. See Ward, 8.

55. Thomas Wägenbauer, *The Moment: A History, Typology and Theory of the Moment in Philosophy and Literature* (Frankfurt: Peter Lang, 1993), 110. See also Cassin, 688.

56. Kierkegaard, 184, 113. See Ward, 22–23.

57. Martin Heidegger, *The Basic Problems of Phenomenology*, tr. Albert Hofstadter (Bloomington: Indiana University Press, 1982), 257.

58. Heidegger, *Basic Problems*, 271.

59. Martin Heidegger, *Being and Time*, tr. Joan Stambaugh (Albany: State University of New York Press, 2010), 405–6.

60. Heidegger, *Basic Problems*, 288. Heidegger also quarrels with Kierkegaard in this passage, though his reasoning seems particularly close to that of his predecessor.

61. Ward, 112–13.

62. Ibid., 99. See also Peter Poellner, "Existential Moments," in *The Moment: Time and Rupture in Modern Thought*, ed. Heidrun Friese (Liverpool: Liverpool University Press, 2001), 53–72.

63. Walter Benjamin, *Selected Writings*, tr. Edmund Jephcott et al. (Cambridge, MA: Belknap Press of Harvard University Press, 2003), 4: 395. See Cassin *Dictionary*, 529. Agamben points out that *Jetztzeit* had previously been used in German philosophy in a negative sense to mean ordinary, everyday time (143).

64. See, for example, Karl Heinz Bohrer, *Suddenness: On the Moment of Aesthetic Appearance*, tr. Ruth Crowley (New York: Columbia University Press, 1994), 196–99.

65. M. H. Abrams, *Natural Supernaturalism* (New York: Norton, 1971), 386. For Abrams, the relevant background to these moments is provided not by Plato or even Paul but Augustine, and there is nothing in his analysis about the normative content of such moments.

66. Ibid., 387–88.

67. Ibid., 424–25.

68. Walter Pater, *The Renaissance: Studies in Art and Poetry*, ed. Donald L. Hill (Berkeley: University of California Press, 1980), 188. See Abrams, 419; Bohrer, 53–54; and Sue Zemka, *Time and the Moment in Victorian Literature and Society* (Cambridge, UK: Cambridge University Press, 2012), 222.

69. Isaiah Berlin, *The Roots of Romanticism*, ed. Henry Hardy (Princeton, NJ: Princeton University Press, 1999), 56.

70. Virginia Woolf, *The Moment and Other Essays* (San Diego, CA: Harcourt Brace Jovanovich, 1948), 3.

71. Ibid., 8.

72. Virginia Woolf, *Moments of Being: Unpublished Autobiographical Writings*, ed. Jeanne Schulkind (New York: Harcourt Brace Jovanovich, 1976), 71–73.

73. Kierkegaard, 108.

74. Karl Jaspers, *Psychologie der Weltanschauungen*, as quoted in Cassin, 689.

75. See Adorno's extensive complaint against the mere juxtaposition of time and eternity in Kierkegaard in Theodor Adorno, *Kierkegaard: Construction of the Aesthetic*, tr. Robert Hullot-Kentor (Minneapolis: University of Minnesota Press, 1989), 97–103. Note that he also charges that "the point serves as the model of every Kierkegaardian paradox" (114). See also 117.

76. Kierkegaard, 75; see Wagenbauer, 106. For a critique of the leap in Kierkegaard, see Adorno, 89–90.

77. Ward, 83; Poellner in Friese, 65.

78. Benjamin, 395.

79. Woolf, *Moments of Being*, 71.

80. Bachelard, 21.

81. Poellner in Friese, 59; Bohrer, 200–201.

82. Friese, 2.

83. Ward, 3; Zemka, 46.

84. Ward, 76.

85. Benjamin, 395, 396.

86. Ibid., 40. See also Wägenbauer, 104.

87. Kierkegaard, 106. See Friese, 5.

88. Heidegger, *Fundamental Concepts of Metaphysics*, 148, as quoted in Ward, 115.

89. Kierkegaard, 106. See Wägenbauer, 14, for a discussion and a slightly different translation.

90. Ward, 94.

91. Quoted in Agamben, 145.

92. See the discussion of Aristotle in Éric Alliez, *Capital Times: Tales from the Conquest of Time*, tr. Georges Van Den Abbeele (Minneapolis: University of Minnesota Press, 1996), especially 22–23.

93. Quoted in Bohrer, 50.

94. Quoted in Adorno, 52.

95. Fredric Jameson, *A Singular Modernity* (London: Verso, 2002), 195. See Zemka, 12.

96. Benjamin, 391.

Chapter 2: The Search for the Experiential Present

1. Aristotle, *Complete Works*, ed. Jonathan Barnes (Princeton, NJ: Princeton University Press, 1984), 376 (*Physics*, 222b 9).

2. Ibid., 712 (*Sense and Sensibilia*, 448b 17).

3. Ibid., 711 (*Sense and Sensibilia*, 448a 26).

4. Ibid. (*Sense and Sensibilia*, 448b 13).

5. Plutarch, paraphrasing Poseidonius, quoted in Richard Sorabji, *Time, Creation and the Continuum* (Chicago: University of Chicago Press, 1983), 22.

6. Quoted in ibid., 275.

7. Saint Augustine, *Confessions*, tr. R. S. Pine-Coffin (London/New York: Penguin, 1961), 265. Andrea Nightingale points out that he makes the same point in a sermon. *Once Out of Nature: Augustine on Time and the Body* (Chicago: University of Chicago Press, 2011), 53.

8. Augustine, 268. See Nightingale, 99.

9. Augustine, 277–78.

10. These impressions have come in for a good deal of criticism. For example, see Paul Ricoeur, *Time and Narrative*, tr. Kathleen Blamey and David Pellauer (Chicago: University of Chicago Press, 1988), III:14, and Shaun Gallagher, *The Inordinance of Time* (Evanston, IL: Northwestern University Press, 1998), 7.

11. Augustine, 277.

12. Ibid.

13. John Locke, *An Essay Concerning Human Understanding*, ed. Peter H. Nidditch (Oxford: Clarendon Press, 1975), 203.

14. Ibid., 147.

15. Ibid.

16. Ibid., 185.

17. Ibid., 184.

18. For a discussion of the relation of "time itself" to experiential time in Locke, see Lorne Falkenstein, "Classical Empiricism," in *A Companion to the Philosophy of Time*, ed. Heather Dyke and Adrian Bardon (Malden, MA: Wiley, 2013), 105–7.

19. Dugald Stewart, *Elements of the Philosophy of the Human Mind* (London, 1792): I:116. See Holly Andersen, "The Development of the 'Specious Present' and James's Views on Temporal Experience," in *Subjective Time*, ed. Valtteri Arstila and Dan Lloyd (Cambridge: MIT Press, 2014), 32.

20. Stewart, I:116.

21. Ibid.

22. Karl M. Figlio, "Theories of Perception and the Physiology of Mind in the Late 18th Century," *History of Science* 13 (1975): 192–93. For a discussion of Locke, see 193–95.

23. René Descartes, *Meditations on First Philosophy*, tr. John Cottingham (Cambridge, UK: Cambridge University Press, 2013), 121. In the *Passions of the Soul*, Descartes describes the animal spirits that power the nerves as moving "very quickly." *Descartes: Selected Philosophical Writings*, tr. John Cottingham et al. (Cambridge, UK: Cambridge University Press, 1988), 222.

24. Aristotle, 710–11 (*Sense and Sensibilia*, 447b, 10–448a, 31).

25. See Daniel Heller-Roazen, *The Inner Touch: Archaeology of a Sensation* (New York: Zone Books, 2009), 52.

26. Descartes, *Meditations*, 121.

27. Thomas Reid, *Essays on the Intellectual Powers of Man* (Edinburgh: John Bell, 1785), 106. See also Theo C. Meyering, *Historical Roots of Cognitive Science* (Dordrecht, Netherlands: Kluwer, 1989), 86–87, and Edwin G. Boring, *Sensation and Perception in the History of Experimental Psychology* (New York: Appleton-Century, 1942), 13–14.

28. Reid, 304.

29. Ibid., 326.

30. Ibid.

31. Holly K. Andersen and Rick Grush, "A Brief History of Time-Consciousness: Historical Precursors to James and Husserl," *Journal of the History of Philosophy* 47 (2009): 277–307. See also Andersen, "Development of the 'Specious Present,'" in *Subjective Time*.

32. Herbert Nichols, "The Psychology of Time," *American Journal of Psychology* 3 (1891): 502.

33. G. E. Müller, "On the Psychophysical Axioms," in *A Source Book in the History of Psychology*, ed. Richard J. Herrnstein and Edwin G. Boring (Cambridge, UK: Harvard University Press, 1966), 257–59. See also Boring, *Sensation and Perception*, 89.

34. Michael Heidelberger, *Nature from Within: Gustav Theodor Fechner and His Psychophysical Worldview*, tr. Cynthia Klohr (Pittsburgh, PA: University of Pittsburgh Press, 2004), 6–7, 168–69.

35. Arthur L. Blumenthal, "A Wundt Primer: The Operating Characteristics of Consciousness," in *Wilhelm Wundt in History: The Making of a Scientific Psychology*, ed. Robert W. Rieber and David K. Robinson (New York: Kluwer, 2001), 128. See also Heidelberger, *Nature from Within*, 162–64, 175–77.

36. David K. Robinson, "Reaction-Time Experiments in Wundt's Institute and Beyond," in Rieber and Robinson, eds., *Wundt in History*, 169. For a history of the term *apperception*, as a synonym for consciousness, see Heller-Roazen, 201–9.

37. Alan Kim, "Wilhelm Wundt," *Stanford Encyclopedia of Philosophy*, 22, http://plato .stanford.edu/archives/spr2009/entries/wilhelm-wundt/.

38. Edwin G. Boring, *A History of Experimental Psychology*, 2nd ed. (Englewood Cliffs, NJ: Prentice-Hall, 1950), 41.

39. Kathryn M. Olesko and Frederic L. Holmes, "Experiment, Quantification, and Discovery," in *Hermann von Helmholtz and the Foundations of 19th-century Science*, ed. David Cahan (Berkeley: University of California Press, 1993), 79; Henning Schmidgen, "Of Frogs and Men: The Origins of Psychophysiological Time Experiments, 1850–1865," *Endeavour* 26 (2002): 142–44.

40. Henning Schmidgen, "The Donders Machine: Matter, Signs, and Time in a Physiological Experiment, ca. 1865," *Configurations* 13 (2005): 232–33.

41. F. C. Donders, "On the Speed of Mental Processes," *Acta Psychologica* 30 (1969): 416.

42. Edward J. Haupt, "Laboratories for Experimental Psychology," in Rieber and Robinson, eds., *Wundt in History*, 230.

43. David K. Robinson, "Reaction-Time Experiments in Wundt's Institute and Beyond," in Rieber and Robinson, eds., *Wundt in History*, 163.

44. Ibid., 164.

45. Ibid., 169.

46. Ibid.; Ruth Benschop and Douwe Draaisma, "In Pursuit of Precision: The Calibration of Minds and Machines in Late-19th-century Psychology," *Annals of Science* 57 (2000): 5–6.

47. Donders, "On the Speed of Mental Processes," 418–19; Schmidgen, "The Donders Machine," 219.

48. Donders, "On the Speed of Mental Processes," 414.

49. Donders, "On the Speed of Mental Processes," 414; Schmidgen, "The Donders Machine," 224.

50. Robinson, "Reaction-Time Experiments," 174.

51. Donders, "On the Speed of Mental Processes," 413.

52. Benschop and Draaisma, "In Pursuit of Precision," 22.

53. Ruth Benschop, *Unassuming Instruments: Tracing the Tachistoscope in Experimental Psychology* (Groningen, Netherlands: ADNP, 2001), 51.

54. Quoted in Olesko and Holmes, "Experiment, Quantification, and Discovery," 84.

55. Francesca Bordogna, *William James at the Boundaries: Philosophy, Science, and the Geography of Knowledge* (Chicago: University of Chicago Press, 2008), 96.

56. Ibid., 46–47.

57. Claude Debru, "Helmholtz and the Psychophysiology of Time," *Science in Context* 14 (2001): 478.

58. Bordogna, *William James*, 97.

59. William Boring, "Human Nature vs. Sensation: William James and the Psychology of the Present," *American Journal of Psychology* 55 (1942): 310.

60. Bordogna, *William James*, 254; Stephanie L. Hawkins, "William James, Gustav Fechner, and Early Psychophysics," *Frontiers in Physiology* 2 (2011): 1–10.

61. Andersen and Grush, "Brief History of Time Consciousness," 290.

62. Ibid., 294–95.

63. Ibid., 295–96.

64. Quoted in Barry Dainton, *Stream of Consciousness: Unity and Continuity in Conscious Experience* (London: Routledge, 2006), 120.

65. Charles Sherover, ed., *The Human Experience of Time* (Evanston, IL: Northwestern University Press, 2001), 349.

66. Quoted in Andersen and Grush, "Brief History of Time Consciousness," 292.

67. Boring, *Sensation and Perception*, 86.

68. William James, *Principles of Psychology* (1890; rpt., New York: Dover, 1950), 1:687.

69. That is to say, he renounced the idea that consciousness is some sort of entity, like the common sense of Aristotle, to which all experience is submitted. See the essay "Does Consciousness Exist?" William James, *Writings: 1902–1910*, ed. Bruce Kuklick (New York: Library of America, 1987), 1141–58.

70. James, *Principles of Psychology* 2:453.

71. See the account of James as an interactionist in Owen Flanagan, "Consciousness as a Pragmatist Views It," in *The Cambridge Companion to William James*, ed. Ruth Anna Putnam (Cambridge, UK: Cambridge University Press, 1997), 25–48.

72. James, *Principles of Psychology* 1:242.

73. Ibid., 2:104.

74. Ibid., 1:405.

75. Ibid.

76. Ibid., 1:407.

77. Ibid., 1:430.

78. Ibid., 1:406.

79. Ibid., 1:407.

80. Ibid., 1:606.

81. Ibid., 1:613.

82. Ibid.

83. Ibid., 1:635.

84. For a critical account of the bases of the specious present, see Richard M. Gale, "From the Specious to the Suspicious Present: The Jack Horner Phenomenology of William James," *Journal of Speculative Philosophy* 11 (1997): 163–87.

85. James, *Principles of Psychology* 1:420.

86. Ibid., 1:421. Quoting from Volkmann, whose account James says is admirable.

87. Ibid., 2:633.

88. J. E. McTaggart, "The Unreality of Time," *Mind* 17 (1908): 472.

89. C.W.K. Mundle, "How Specious Is the 'Specious Present'?" *Mind* 63 (1954): 26.

90. For a recent discussion, see Barry Dainton, "Temporal Consciousness," *Stanford Encyclopedia of Philosophy*, 147–52, http://plato.stanford.edu/archives/fall2010/entries/consciousness-temporal.

91. Jacques Derrida, *Voice and Phenomenon: Introduction to the Problem of the Sign in Husserl's Phenomenology*, tr. Leonard Lawlor (Evanston, IL: Northwestern University Press, 2011), 85.

92. See Holly Andersen, "The Development of the 'Specious Present' and James's Views on Temporal Experience," in *Subjective Time*, 36.

93. John Barnett Brough, "Translator's Introduction," *On the Phenomenology of the Consciousness of Internal Time*, by Edmund Husserl (Dordrecht, Netherlands: Kluwer, 1991), xxxvi–xxxvii.

94. Husserl, *Consciousness of Internal Time*, 42.

95. Ibid., 37.

96. Ibid., 30.

97. Ibid., 28.

98. Brough, "Translator's Introduction," xxxix.

99. Husserl, *Consciousness of Internal Time*, 41.

100. Tim van Gelder, "Wooden Iron? Husserlian Phenomenology Meets Cognitive Science," in *Naturalizing Phenomenology: Issues in Contemporary Phenomenology and Cognitive Science*, ed. Jean Petitot (Stanford, CA: Stanford University Press, 1999), 249–50.

101. Derrida, *Voice and Phenomenon*, 55–56.

102. Gallagher, *Inordinance of Time*, 7.

103. David Couzens Hoy, *The Time of Our Lives* (Cambridge, MA: MIT Press, 2012), 52.

104. Husserl, *Consciousness of Internal Time*, 61. See Susan Pockett, "How Long Is 'Now'?: Phenomenology and the Specious Present," *Phenomenology and the Cognitive Sciences* 2 (2003): 56.

105. An objection registered some time ago by Wilfrid Sellars. See Andersen, *Subjective Time*, 26.

106. Jean-Paul Sartre, *Being and Nothingness: A Phenomenological Essay on Ontology*, tr. Hazel E. Barnes (New York: Washington Square Press, 1956), 152. See also 599.

107. See the references to Stern's critique of Brentano in Barry Dainton, "The Perception of Time," in Dyke and Bardon, *Companion to the Philosophy of Time*, 395.

108. Dainton, "The Perception of Time," 402.

109. A question posed about the retentional model in general by Barry Dainton, "The Phenomenal Continuum," in *Subjective Time*, 104. For a critique of this kind more directly aimed at Husserl, see Marc Wittmann, "Embodied Time: The Experience of Time, the Body, and the Self," in *Subjective Time*, 517.

110. Eric R. Kandel, James H. Schwartz, and Thomas M. Jessell, *Principles of Neural Science* (New York: McGraw-Hill, 2000), 313.

111. R. Epstein, "The Neuro-Cognitive Basis of the Jamesian Stream of Thought," *Consciousness and Cognition* (2000); S. Pockett, "How Long Is 'Now'?"

112. Alex O. Holcombe, "Are There Cracks in the Façade of Continuous Visual Experience?" in *Subjective Time*, 179–98.

113. Wittmann, 513.

114. Valtteri Arstila and Dan Lloyd, "Subjective Time: From Past to Future," in *Subjective Time*, 309–22.

115. Bruno Mölder, "Constructing Time: Dennett and Grush on Temporal Representation," in *Subjective Time*, 217.

116. Konstantin Moutoussis, "Perceptual Asynchrony in Vision," in *Subjective Time*, 203–5.

117. Mölder, 222–23.

118. Holcombe, 193.

119. Dean V. Buonomano, "The Neural Mechanisms of Timing on Short Timescales," in *Subjective Time*, 335.

120. Ibid., 330.

121. Arstila and Lloyd, *Subjective Time*, 199.

122. Moutoussis, 205.

123. Wittmann, 513.

124. Locke,163.

125. Phillip Prodger, *Time Stands Still: Muybridge and the Instantaneous Photography Movement* (New York: Oxford University Press, 2003), 55.

126. E. H. Gombrich, "Standards of Truth: The Arrested Image and the Moving Eye," *Critical Inquiry* 7 (1980): 244, 260.

127. James, *Principles of Psychology*, 1:421.

128. William James, *A Pluralistic Universe* (London: Longmans, Green, 1909), 235.

129. Quoted in Ian Phillips, "The Temporal Structure of Experience," in *Subjective Time*, 141.

130. Niko A. Busch and Rufin van Rullen, "Is Visual Perception like a Continuous Flow or a Series of Snapshots?" in *Subjective Time*, 165.

Chapter 3: The Longest Now

1. Norbert Elias, *An Essay on Time* (Dublin: University College Press, 1992), 63.

2. Peter Osborne, *Anywhere or Not at All* (London: Verso, 2013), 17.

3. See, for example, Peter Fritzsche, *Stranded in the Present: Modern Time and the Melancholy of History* (Cambridge, MA: Harvard University Press, 2004).

4. François Hartog, *Regimes of Historicity: Presentism and Experiences of Time*, tr. Saskia Brown (New York: Columbia University Press, 2015), 203.

5. Reinhart Koselleck, *Futures Past: On the Semantics of Historical Time*, tr. Keith Tribe (New York: Columbia University Press, 2004), 149. The influence of Koselleck is clear, for example, in Hartog, who quotes from his work dozens of times.

6. Ibid., 39.

7. Ibid., 259.

8. Ibid., 310, n 4.

9. Ibid. Augustine does claim that what is true of the action of singing a psalm is "true of a man's whole life, of which all his actions are parts. It is true of the whole history of mankind, of which each man's life is a part." Saint Augustine, *Confessions*, tr. R. S. Pine-Coffin (London: Penguin, 1961), 277.

10. Harry Harootunian, "Remembering the Historical Present," *Critical Inquiry* 33 (2007): 471–94. Harootunian engages Koselleck critically and at length.

11. Osborne, 176.

12. Ibid., 175.

13. Helga Nowotny, *Time: The Modern and Postmodern Experience*, tr. Neville Plaice (New York: Polity, 1994), 41.

14. Paul Ricoeur, *Time and Narrative*, tr. Kathleen Blamey and David Pellauer (Chicago: University of Chicago Press, 1988), III. 253.

15. Hartog, 106.

16. Hartog, 33.

17. Elias, 34, 40.

18. Ibid., 75.

19. For a discussion in a modern context, see Roland Boer, "Revolution in the Event: The Problem of Kairos," *Theory, Culture & Society* 30 (2013): 116–34.

20. Georges Gurvitch, *The Spectrum of Social Time*, tr. Myrtle Korenbaum (Dordrecht, Netherlands: Reidel, 1964), 106.

21. Jack Goody, "The Time of Telling and the Telling of Time in Written and Oral Cultures," in *Chronotypes: The Construction of Time*, ed. John Bender and David E. Wellbery (Stanford, CA: Stanford University Press, 1991), 94.

22. Gerhard Dohrn-van Rossum, *History of the Hour: Clocks and Modern Temporal Orders*, tr. Thomas Dunlap (Chicago: University of Chicago Press, 1996), 18–19.

23. Ibid., 42.

24. Ibid., 282.

25. Ibid., 350. For evidence about earlier periods, see 220, 224.

26. Ibid., 37, 56.

27. David Landes, *Revolution in Time*, rev. ed. (Cambridge, MA: Belknap Press, 2000), 22.

28. Elias, 64.

29. Ibid.

30. J. E. McTaggart, "The Unreality of Time," *Mind* 17 (1908): 457–74.

31. Hartog, 34.

32. Ibid., 42.

33. Ibid., 45.

34. Gurvitch, 115.

35. Ibid., 116.

36. Ibid., 15.

37. Ibid., 20–21. Or, as Nowotny puts it, simultaneity is always a normative aspiration and an illusion (42).

38. Denis Feeney, *Caesar's Calendar: Ancient Time and the Beginnings of History* (Berkeley: University of California Press, 2007), 3.

39. Ibid., 9, 17.

40. Ibid., 15–16. See also John Burrow, *A History of Histories* (New York: Knopf, 2008), 7–8.

41. Ibid., 18.

42. Ibid., 48.

43. Polybius, III.1, quoted in Burrow, 66. See also Feeney, 54.

44. Paul Ricoeur, *Time and Narrative*, tr. Kathleen McLaughlin and David Pellauer (Chicago: University of Chicago Press, 1984), I.38.

45. Feeney, 48.

46. Ibid., 146–48.

47. Ibid., 188.

48. Ibid., 192–93.

49. See, for example, Nowotny, 94.

50. Dohrn-van Rossum, 37, 56.

51. Ibid., 79. This was also the dogma, if not the practice, of the early Reformation. See 212.

52. Feeney, 2–3.

53. Hannah Arendt, *Between Past and Future* (New York: Penguin, 2006), 65–67.

54. Giorgio Agamben, *The Time That Remains*, tr. Patricia Dailey (Stanford, CA: Stanford University Press, 2005), 67–78.

55. Philippians, 3:13; Agamben, 78.

56. Gurvitch, 120. See also *Dictionary of Untranslatables: A Philosophical Lexicon*, ed. Barbara Cassin, tr. Emily Apter, Jacques Lezra, and Michael Wood (Princeton, NJ: Princeton University Press, 2014), 26–27.

57. Daniel Rosenberg and Anthony Grafton, *Cartographies of Time* (New York: Princeton Architectural Press, 2010), 26–27.

58. Ibid., 28.

59. Ibid., 36, 42, 69.

60. John Locke, *An Essay Concerning Human Understanding*, ed. Peter H. Nidditch (Oxford: Clarendon Press, 1975), 203.

61. Immanuel Kant, *Political Writings*, ed. H. S. Reiss (Cambridge, UK: Cambridge University Press, 1991), 51.

62. Ibid.

63. Koselleck, 195. See also 104 for comments on Kant.

64. Rosenberg and Grafton, 126.

65. Ibid., 20, 140.

66. Ibid., 134–35.

67. Peter Sloterdijk, *In the World Interior of Capital*, tr. Wieland Hoban (Cambridge, UK: Polity Press, 2013), 141.

68. Walter Benjamin, *The Arcades Project*, tr. Howard Eiland and Kevin McLaughlin (Cambridge, MA: Belknap Press, 1999), 394.

69. In addition to the discussion provided above, see Arendt, 64–66.

70. Koselleck, 266.

71. Ibid., 164.

72. Gurvitch, 73.

73. Ibid., 96.

74. Ibid., 140–41.

75. Nowotny, 9.

76. Fredric Jameson, *A Singular Modernity: Essay on the Ontology of the Present* (London: Verso, 2002), 17.

77. Rosenberg and Grafton, 222.

78. Ibid., 100.

79. For a discussion of modernist proclamations on the present, see Sascha Bru, "Avant-Garde Nows: Presentist Reconfigurations of Public Time," *Modernist Cultures* 8.2 (2013): 272–87.

Chapter 4: The Present in Pictures

1. Henri Bergson, "Memory of the Present and False Recognition," in *Time & the Instant*, ed. Robin Durie (Manchester, UK: Clinamen Press, 2000), 38.

2. Immanuel Kant, *Critique of Pure Reason*, tr. Norman Kemp Smith (New York: Palgrave Macmillan, 2007), 77.

3. Ibid., 131.

4. Ibid., 132.

5. See the explanation in the translator's introduction to Kant's *Critique of Judgment*, tr. Werner S. Pluhar (Indianapolis, IN: Hackett, 1987), xxvi.

6. Kant, *Critique of Pure Reason*, 185. For a discussion of the relationship between the image and the schema, see *Dictionary of Untranslatables: A Philosophical Lexicon*, ed. Barbara Cassin, tr. Emily Apter, Jacques Lezra, and Michael Wood (Princeton, NJ: Princeton University Press, 2014), 108–9.

7. Craig Callender, "The Common Now," *Philosophical Issues* 18 (2008): 341, 342, 345.

8. Ibid., 357–58. For more of such evidence, see chapter 2.

9. Kant, *Critique of Pure Reason*, 77.

10. Richard Sorabji, *Time, Creation and the Continuum* (Chicago: University of Chicago Press, 1983), 67–83.

11. Working from the standpoint of linguistics rather than phenomenology or physiology, Louis Marin also decides that the present is unrepresentable. See *On Representation*, tr. Catherine Porter (Stanford, CA: Stanford University Press, 2001), 133.

12. Jacques Aumont, *The Image*, tr. Claire Pajackowska (London: British Film Institute, 1997), 123.

13. Quoted in James Heffernan, "Space and Time in Literature and the Visual Arts," *Soundings* 70 (1987): 105–6.

14. E. H. Gombrich, "Moment and Movement in Art," *Journal of the Warburg and Courtauld Institutes* 27 (1964): 248.

15. Ibid., 293.

16. Ibid., 294.

17. Gotthold Ephraim Lessing, *Laocoön: An Essay on the Limits of Painting and Poetry*, tr. Edward Allen McCormick (Indianapolis, IN: Bobbs-Merrill, 1962), 19. See also Peter Geimer, "Picturing the Black Box: On Blanks in 19th-Century Paintings and Photography," *Science in Context* 17 (2004): 472–73.

18. Lessing, *Laocoön*, 20.

19. Ibid., 78.

20. Ibid., 92.

21. Robin Le Poidevin, *The Images of Time: An Essay on Temporal Representation* (Oxford: Oxford University Press, 2007), 131.

22. Jean-Paul Sartre, *The Imaginary* (New York: Routledge, 2004), 75.

23. William Cowper, "The Task" (1785), quoted in Geoffrey Batchen, *Burning with Desire: The Conception of Photography* (Cambridge, MA: MIT Press, 1997), 84.

24. William Henry Fox Talbot, "A Brief Historical Sketch of the Invention of the Art" (1844), in *Classic Essays on Photography*, ed. Alan Trachtenberg (New Haven: Leete's Island Books, 1980), 29.

25. Quoted in Batchen, 33.

26. Quoted in ibid., 39.

27. See, for example, ibid., 44.

28. Quoted in ibid., 44.

29. Lady Elizabeth Eastlake, "Photography" (1857), in Trachtenberg, 44.

30. Fox Talbot, in Trachtenberg, 29.

31. Quoted in Jennifer Green-Lewis, "Not Fading Away: Photography in the Age of Oblivion," *19th Century Contexts* 22 (2001): 562.

32. Gombrich, "Moment," 295.

33. Eastlake, "Photography," 52.

34. Quoted in Geimer, 478.

35. Batchen, 93.

36. Le Poidevin, 70.

37. William Henry Fox Talbot, "Some Account of the Art of Photographic Drawing," *London and Edinburgh Philosophical Magazine and Journal of Science* 14 (March 1839): 41.

38. H. F. Talbot, "On the Production of Instantaneous Photographic Images," *Journal of the Franklin Institute* 53 (1852): 137–40.

39. Phillip Prodger, *Time Stands Still: Muybridge and the Instantaneous Photography Movement* (New York: Oxford University Press, 2003), 78, 87.

40. Tom Gunning, "New Thresholds of Vision: Instantaneous Photography and the Early Cinema of Lumiére," in *Impossible Presence: Surface and Screen in the Photogenic Era*, ed. Terry Smith (Chicago: University of Chicago Press, 2001), 95.

41. Prodger, 135.

42. Ibid., 35.

43. Ibid., 41.

44. Ibid., 34.

45. Geimer, 482.

46. Prodger, 50.

47. Rudolf Arnheim, "On the Nature of Photography," *Critical Inquiry* 1 (1974): 150.

48. For discussions, see Thierry de Duve, "Time Exposure and Snapshot: The Photograph as Paradox," *October* 5 (1978): 113–25, and Mary Ann Doane, "Real Time: Instantaneity and the Photographic Imaginary," in *Stillness and Time: Photography and the Moving Image* (Brighton, UK: Photoworks, 2006), 23–28.

49. Prodger, 36.

50. Quoted in François Dagognet, *Etienne-Jules Marey: A Passion for the Trace*, tr. Robert Galeta (New York: Zone Books, 1992), 141.

51. Marta Braun, *Picturing Time: The Work of Etienne-Jules Marey* (Chicago: University of Chicago Press, 1992), 268.

52. Braun, 62, 66, 78, 83.

53. Gombrich, 44.

54. Aumont, 174–75. See also James E. Cutting, "Representing Motion in a Static Image: Constraints and Parallels in Art, Science, and Popular Culture," *Perception* 31 (2002): 1165–93.

55. Plato, *Complete Works*, ed. John M. Cooper (Indianapolis, IN: Hackett, 1997), 419. Quoted in Jay Lampert, *Simultaneity and Delay: A Dialectical Theory of Staggered Time* (London: Continuum, 2012), 58.

56. Aristotle, *Complete Works*, 1856. See Pierre Hadot, *Philosophy as a Way of Life* (Malden, MA: Blackwell, 1995), 224.

57. James I. Porter, *The Origins of Aesthetic Thought in Ancient Greece: Matter, Sensation, and Experience* (Cambridge, UK: Cambridge University Press, 2010), 45–46.

58. Ibid., 64. See also 55 and 246.

59. Aristotle, *Complete Works*, 2322.

60. Edmund Burke, *A Philosophical Enquiry into the Origin of our Ideas of the Sublime and Beautiful*, ed. Adam Phillips (New York: Oxford University Press, 1990), 124.

61. Kant, *Critique of Judgment*, 116–17.

62. Marin, 298.

63. Goethe, "The Book of the Cup-Bearer," quoted in Hadot, 220.

64. Marin, 295.

65. Ibid., 303.

66. Quoted in Jean-Francois Lyotard, *The Inhuman: Reflections on Time*, tr. Geoffrey Bennington and Rachel Bowlby (Cambridge, UK: Polity Press, 1991), 86.

67. Ibid.

68. Ibid., 90.

69. Hans Belting, *An Anthropology of Images*, tr. Thomas Dunlap (Princeton, NJ: Princeton University Press, 2011), 118–19.

70. Ibid., 10. Note also the similar definition offered by W.J.T. Mitchell in *Picture Theory* (Chicago: University of Chicago Press, 1994), 11.

71. Jacques Rancière, *The Future of the Image*, tr. Gregory Elliott (London: Verso, 2007), 15.

72. George Kubler, *The Shape of Time: Remarks on the History of Things* (New Haven, CT: Yale University Press, 1962), 84.

73. *Dictionary of Untranslatables*, 247.

74. Belting, *Anthropology of Images*, 116–17.

75. Alexander Nagel and Christopher S. Wood, *Anachronic Renaissance* (New York: Zone Books, 2010), 30, 32.

76. Georges Didi-Huberman, *Confronting Images*, tr. John Goodman (University Park: Pennsylvania State University Press, 2005), 189.

77. Georges Didi-Huberman, *Fra Angelico: Dissemblance & Figuration*, tr. Jane Marie Todd (Chicago: University of Chicago Press, 1995), 115. See also *Confronting Images*, 22.

78. Jean-Luc Nancy, *The Ground of the Image*, tr. Jeff Fort (New York: Fordham University Press, 2005), 113.

79. Didi-Huberman, *Fra Angelico*, 26.

80. Ibid., 124. See also *Confronting Images*, 185.

81. Rancière, *Future*, 89.

82. Didi-Huberman, *Fra Angelico*, 113.

83. Marin, 288.

84. Ibid.

85. Ibid., 321. See also 352.

86. Ibid., 265–66.

87. Ibid., 139. See also 357–58.

88. Ibid., 369.

89. Alexander Nagel, *Medieval Modern: Art out of Time* (New York: Thames & Hudson, 2012), 18–19.

90. Ibid., 19.

91. Ibid., 20–21.

92. Lutz Koepnick, *On Slowness: Toward an Aesthetic of the Contemporary* (New York: Columbia University Press, 2014), 64.

93. Ibid., 96.

94. Ibid., 261.

95. Laura Hoptman, "The Forever Now: Contemporary Painting in an Atemporal World," in *The Forever Now: Contemporary Painting in an Atemporal World*, ed. Laura Hoptman (New York: Museum of Modern Art, 2014), 16.

96. Kubler, 17.

Chapter 5: Narration and the "Unexplained Instant"

1. Elizabeth Bowen, *The Heat of the Day* (1948; rpt., New York: Penguin, 1976), 15.

2. Dorrit Cohn, *Transparent Minds: Narrative Method for Presenting Consciousness in Fiction* (Princeton, NJ: Princeton University Press, 1978), 209.

3. Willa Cather, *The Professor's House* (New York: Vintage, 2011), 248.

4. Paul Ricoeur, *Time and Narrative*, tr. Kathleen McLaughlin and David Pellauer (Chicago: University of Chicago Press, 1985), 2:98. See also Peter Brooks, *Reading for the Plot* (Cambridge, MA: Harvard University Press, 1992), 23.

5. Käte Hamburger, *The Logic of Literature*, 2nd ed., tr. Marilynn Rose (Bloomington: Indiana University Press, 1973), 81.

6. Robin Le Poidevin, *The Images of Time: An Essay in Temporal Representation* (Oxford: Oxford University Press, 2007), 147. See also Mark Currie, *About Time: Narrative, Fiction and the Philosophy of Time* (Edinburgh: Edinburgh University Press, 2010), 5.

7. For an influential account in sociology, see Andrew Abbott, *Time Matters: On Theory and Method* (Chicago: University of Chicago Press, 2001). For psychology, see Jerome Bruner, *Actual Minds, Possible Worlds* (Cambridge, MA: Harvard University Press, 1986), and *Making Stories: Law, Literature, Life* (New York: Farrar, Straus and Giroux, 2002).

8. Arthur Danto, *Narration and Knowledge* (New York: Columbia University Press, 1985), 355.

9. Ibid., xiii.

10. Ibid., 343.

11. Brooks, 23.

12. Plato, *Complete Works*, ed. John M. Cooper (Indianapolis, IN: Hackett, 1997), 1030.

13. Aristotle, *Complete Works*, ed. Jonathan Barnes (Princeton, NJ: Princeton University Press, 1984), 2321–22.

14. Ricoeur, *Time and Narrative*, 1:38–42.

15. *Correspondence between Goethe and Schiller*, tr. L. Dora Schmitz (London: George Bell, 1877), 451.

16. Ibid., 453.

17. Ibid., 455.

18. Ibid.

19. George Lukács, *Theory of the Novel*, tr. Anna Bostock (Cambridge, MA: MIT Press, 1971), 122.

20. Ibid.

21. Ibid., 126.

22. Mikhail Bakhtin, *The Dialogic Imagination*, tr. Caryl Emerson and Michael Holquist (Austin: University of Texas Press, 1981), 18.

23. Ibid., 107.

24. Ibid., 38.

25. Ricoeur, *Time and Narrative*, 1:60.

26. Ibid., 2:108.

27. Ibid., 1:56.

28. Frank Kermode, *The Sense of an Ending* (Oxford: Oxford University Press, 2000), 46.

29. Ricoeur, *Time and Narrative*, 2:98.

30. Ibid., 3:253.

31. Ibid., 3:243.

32. Fredric Jameson, *The Antinomies of Realism* (London: Verso, 2013), 8.

33. Ibid., 46.

34. Ibid., 21.

35. Jean-Paul Sartre, *Being and Nothingness*, tr. Hazel E. Barnes (New York: Washington Square Press, 1956), 600–601.

36. Jameson, *Antinomies of Realism*, 25, 27. Jameson also uses the term "eternal present" in the more recent treatment of these issues included in *The Ancients and the Postmoderns* (London: Verso, 2015), 20.

37. Jameson, *Antinomies*, 31.

38. Jameson, *Antinomies*, 81. For the notion that affects in general are nameless, see *Ancients and Postmoderns*, 38.

39. Jameson, *Antinomies*, 10.

40. Alexander Kluge, "The Assault of the Present on the Rest of Time," tr. Tamara Evans and Stuart Liebman, *New German Critique* 49 (1990): 18.

41. Sartre, *Being and Nothingness*, 503. See also 429.

42. Brooks, xiv.

43. Jameson also takes up these issues in "The End of Temporality," *Critical Inquiry* 29 (2003): 712.

44. Georg Lukács, *The Historical Novel*, tr. Hannah and Stanley Mitchell (Lincoln: University of Nebraska Press, 1983), 229, 198.

45. Ibid., 183, 235.

46. James Phelan, "Editor's Column: Who's Here? Thoughts on Narrative Identity and Narrative Imperialism," *Narrative* 13 (2005): 206.

47. Bakhtin, 41.

48. *The New Science of Giambattista Vico*, tr. Thomas Goddard Bergin and Max Harold Fisch (Ithaca, NY: Cornell University Press, 1968), 238.

49. G.W.F. Hegel, *Philosophy of History*, tr. J. Sibree (1899; rpt., New York: Dover, 1956), 72.

50. Jack Goody, "From Oral to Written: An Anthropological Breakthrough in Storytelling," in *The Novel*, ed. Franco Moretti (Princeton, NJ: Princeton University Press, 2006), 1:3.

51. Ibid., 1:31.

52. Brooks, xii.

53. Cheryl Nixon, ed., *Novel Definitions: An Anthology of Commentary on the Novel: 1688–1815* (Peterborough, Ont.: Broadview Press, 2009), 87.

54. Quoted in ibid., 94.

55. For a recent example, see Anthony Rudd, "In Defence of Narrative," *European Journal of Philosophy* 17 (2009): 60–75.

56. Alasdair MacIntyre, *After Virtue*, 3rd ed., (Notre Dame, IN: University of Notre Dame Press, 2007), 205.

57. Ibid., 211. Hardy's evidence for the prevalence of narrative is entirely drawn from British novels. See Barbara Hardy, "Towards a Poetics of Fiction," *Novel* 2 (1968): 2–14.

58. MacIntyre, 129.

59. Ibid., 147.

60. Ibid., 178.

61. Ibid., 226.

62. Charles Taylor, *Sources of the Self: The Making of the Modern Identity* (Cambridge, UK: Cambridge University Press, 1989), 47.

63. Ibid., 49.

64. Ibid., 173.

65. Ibid., 52.

66. Louis O. Mink, "History and Fiction as Modes of Comprehension," *New Literary History* 1 (1970): 547.

67. David Carr, *Time, Narrative, and History* (Bloomington: Indiana University Press, 1991).

68. Galen Strawson, *Selves: An Essay in Revisionary Metaphysics* (Oxford: Clarendon Press, 2009), 223.

69. Galen Strawson, "Against Narrativity," *Ratio* 17 (2004): 433.

70. Owen Flanagan, "My Non-narrative, Non-forensic *Dasein*: The First and Second Self," in *Consciousness and the Self: New Essays*, ed. Jeeloo Liu and John Perry (Cambridge, UK: Cambridge University Press, 2012), 215.

71. Ibid., 219.

72. Ibid., 238.

73. Armen Avanessian and Anke Hennig, *Present Tense: A Poetics*, tr. Nils F. Schott with Daniel Hendrickson (London: Bloomsbury Academic, 2015), 44, 141–42.

74. Ibid., 3. For another searching investigation of this truism, see Dorrit Cohn, *The Distinction of Fiction* (Baltimore, MD: Johns Hopkins University Press, 1999), 96–108.

75. Avanessian and Hennig, 19. For another discussion, see Cohn, *Distinction*, 109–31.

76. Avanessian and Hennig, 4. For the classic version of the post-structuralist notion that story is an effect of the discourse, see Jonathan Culler, "Fabula and Sjuzhet in the Analysis of Narrative: Some American Discussions," *Poetics Today* 1 (1980): 27–37. For a rejoinder, see Dan Shen, "Defense and Challenge: Reflections on the Relation between Story and Discourse," *Narrative* 10 (2002): 222–43.

77. Avanessian and Hennig, 2.

78. Ibid., 7, 20.

79. Ibid., 197.

80. Ibid., 49.

81. Ibid., 185.

82. Ibid., 7.

83. Currie, 138–39. Currie cites the linguist David Crystal in support.

84. Craig Callender, "The Common Now," *Philosophical Issues* 2008: 358.

85. Bastian Van Fraassen, "Time in Physical and Narrative Structure," in *Chronotypes: The Construction of Time*, ed. John Bender and David E. Wellbery (Stanford, CA: Stanford University Press, 1991), 29.

86. Ibid., 26.

87. Avanessian and Hennig, 205.

88. Philip Pullman, "Philip Pullman Calls Time on the Present Tense," *Guardian*, September 17, 2010.

89. Ibid.

90. Charles Dickens, *A Christmas Carol* (1843; rpt., London: Penguin, 1984), 42.

91. Pullman.

92. Richard Lea, "Make It Now: The Rise of the Present Tense in Fiction," *Guardian*, November 21, 2015.

93. Ibid.

94. David Mitchell, *Cloud Atlas* (New York: Random House, 2004), 393.

95. Jameson, *Antinomies of Realism*, 305.

96. Mitchell, *Cloud Atlas*, 224.

97. Ibid., 211.

98. Ibid., 503.

99. Ibid., 272.

100. Ibid., 309.

Chapter 6: The Cinematic Present from *Intolerance* to *Interstellar*

1. D. W. Griffith, "Five Dollar 'Movies' Prophesied," in *Focus on D. W. Griffith*, ed. Harry M. Geduld (Englewood Cliffs, NJ: Prentice-Hall, 1971), 34.

2. Ibid.

3. Hugo Münsterberg, *The Photoplay: A Psychological Study and Other Writings*, ed. Allan Langdale (New York: Routledge, 2002), 133.

4. Terry Ramsaye, *A Million and One Nights: A History of the Motion Picture* (New York: Simon and Schuster, 1926), 157.

5. Seymour Chatman, *Story and Discourse: Narrative Structure in Fiction and Film* (Ithaca, NY: Cornell University Press, 1978), 84.

6. Stanley Cavell, *Cavell on Film*, ed. William Rothman (Albany: State University of New York Press, 2005), 4.

7. Gilles Deleuze, *Cinema 2: The Time-Image*, tr. Hugh Tomlinson and Robert Galeta (Minneapolis: University of Minnesota Press, 1989), 39.

8. Stanley Cavell, *The World Viewed*, enlarged ed. (Cambridge, MA: Harvard University Press, 1979), 42.

9. Ibid., 23.

10. Ibid., 79.

11. Andrey Tarkovsky, *Sculpting in Time: Reflections on the Cinema*, tr. Kitty Hunter-Blair (Austin: University of Texas Press, 1987), 68.

12. Münsterberg, *The Photoplay*, 95.

13. Deleuze, *Cinema 2*, xii.

14. Ibid., 104.

15. Tarkovksy, *Sculpting in Time*, 194.

16. Deleuze, *Cinema 2*, 101.

17. Raymond Bellour, *Between-the-Images*, tr. Allyn Hardyck (Zurich; Dijon: JRP/Ringier Kunstverlag AG; Les presses du réel, 2012), 130.

18. Ibid., 131.

19. Ibid., 136.

20. Joseph Anderson and Barbara Anderson, "The Myth of Persistence of Vision Revisited," *Journal of Film and Video* 45 (1993): 3–4; Yves Galifret, "Visual Persistence and Cinema?" *C. R. Biologies* 329 (2006): 370.

21. Münsterberg, *The Photoplay*, 75.

22. Ibid., 77.

23. Galifret, "Visual Persistence," 371.

24. Anderson and Anderson, "Myth of Persistence," 9–10.

25. Münsterberg, *The Photoplay*, 98.

26. Rosalind Krauss, *Under Blue Cup* (Cambridge, MA: MIT Press, 2011), 86.

27. See Tom Gunning, "The Play between Still and Moving Images: Nineteenth-Century 'Philosophical Toys' and Their Discourse," in *Between Stillness and Motion: Film, Photography,*

Algorithms, ed. Eivind Røssaak (Amsterdam: Amsterdam University Press, 2011), 27–43 for a somewhat different explanation of the influence of persistence of vision.

28. Plato, *Complete Works*, ed. John M. Cooper (Indianapolis, IN: Hackett, 1997), 212. For one of many discussions, see Kurt Danziger, *Marking the Mind: A History of Memory* (Cambridge, UK: Cambridge University Press, 2008), 31–34.

29. Douewa Draaisma, *Metaphors of Memory* (Cambridge, UK: Cambridge University Press, 2000), 35.

30. Ibid., 92.

31. Giorgio Agamben, "Nymphs," tr. Amanda Minervini, in *Releasing the Image: From Literature to New Media*, ed. James Khalip and Robert Mitchell (Stanford, CA: Stanford University Press, 2011), 67.

32. Münsterberg, *The Photoplay*, 91.

33. Annette Michelson, "Toward Snow," in *The Avant-Garde Film: A Reader of Theory and Criticism*, ed. P. Adams Sitney (New York: New York University Press, 1978), 172.

34. Deleuze, *Cinema 2*, 38.

35. Münsterberg, *The Photoplay*, 98.

36. Rudolf Arnheim, *Film as Art* (Berkeley: University of California Press, 1971), 100.

37. David Carr, *Time, Narrative, and History* (Cambridge, UK: Cambridge University Press, 1986).

38. Roland Barthes, *Camera Lucida*, tr. Richard Howard (New York: Hill and Wang, 1982), 89–90. He is quoting from Husserl here.

39. Ibid., 92.

40. Laurent Guido, "Between Deadly Trace and Memorial Scansion," in Laurent Guido and Olivier Lugon, eds., *Between Still and Moving Images* (London: John Libbey, 2012), 227; Christian Metz, "Photography and Fetish," in David Campany, ed., *The Cinematic* (Cambridge: MIT Press, 2007), 126–27.

41. Metz, "Photography and Fetish," 128.

42. André Bazin, *What Is Cinema?*, tr. Hugh Gray (Berkeley: University of California Press, 1967), 14–15.

43. Laurent Guido, "The Paradoxical Fits and Starts of the New 'Optical Unconscious,'" *Between Still and Moving Images*, 11–12; Metz, "Photography and Fetish," 128.

44. Garrett Stewart, *Between Film and Screen: Modernism's Photo Synthesis* (Chicago: University of Chicago Press, 1999).

45. Bazin, *What Is Cinema?*, 14.

46. David Campany, *Photography and Cinema* (London: Reaktion, 2008), 11.

47. Olivier Lugon, "Cinema Flipped Through: Film in the Press and in Illustrated Books," *Between Still and Moving Images*, 137–46.

48. Peter Wollen, "Fire and Ice," in Campany, *The Cinematic*, 109.

49. Bellour, *Between-the-Images*, 33; Thomas Elsaesser, "Stop/Motion," *Between Stillness and Motion*, 118.

50. Lugon, *Between Still and Moving Images*, 145–46.

51. Roland Barthes, *Image-Music-Text*, tr. Stephen Heath (New York: Hill and Wang, 1977), 67.

52. Pier Paolo Pasolini, "Observations on the Long Take," in Campany, *The Cinematic*, 84, 86.

53. A very useful essay that argues something like this is Mark B. N. Hansen's "Digital Technics Beyond the 'Last Machine': Thinking Digital Media with Hollis Frampton," in *Between Stillness and Motion*, 45–72.

54. Gunning, "The 'Arrested' Instant," in *Between Still and Moving Images*, 25.

55. Olivier Lugon, Laurent Guido, "Sequence, Looping," in *Between Still and Moving Images*, 324.

56. Bellour, *Between-the-Images*, 103.

57. See Sean Cubitt, *The Cinema Effect* (Cambridge: MIT Press, 2004), 32–33.

58. Tom Gunning, "'Now You See it, Now You Don't': The Temporality of the Cinema of Attractions," in *Silent Film*, ed. Richard Abel (New Brunswick, NJ: Rutgers University Press, 1996), 77.

59. Ibid., 73–74.

60. See, for example, Charles Musser, "Rethinking Early Cinema: Cinema of Attractions and Narrativity," in *The Cinema of Attractions Reloaded* (Amsterdam: Amsterdam University Press, 2006), 389–416.

61. David Forgacs, "Photography and the Denarrativization of Cinematic Practice in Italy, 1935–55," in Guido and Lugon, *Between Still and Moving Images*, 245–60. See also Bellour, *Between-the-Images*, 136–42.

62. D. W. Griffith, "Working for the Biograph Company," in Geduld, *Focus*, 36.

63. Jacques Aumont, *The Image*, tr. Claire Pajackowska (London: British Film Institute, 1997), 105.

64. Ibid., 179–81.

65. David Bordwell, Janet Staiger, and Kristen Thompson, *The Classical Hollywood Cinema* (London: Routledge, 1985), 220.

66. Arnheim, *Film as Art*, 22.

67. Christian Metz, quoted in André Gaudreault and Philippe Gauthier, "Crosscutting: A Programmed Language," in *The Griffith Project*, vol. 12, ed. Paolo Cherchi Usai (London: British Film Institute, 2008), 31.

68. Gunning, *D. W. Griffith and the Origins of American Narrative Film* (Urbana and Chicago: University of Illinois Press, 1993), 99.

69. Ibid., 103.

70. Gaudreault and Gauthier, in fact, reserve the term "parallel editing" for this situation, in which the temporal relation of the motifs to each other is not pertinent (Gaudreault and Gauthier, "Crosscutting," 31).

71. Gunning, *D. W. Griffith*, 134.

72. See Richard J. Meyer, "The Films of David Wark Griffith: The Development of Themes and Techniques in Forty-two of His Films," in Geduld, *Focus*, 111.

73. Max Jammer, *Concepts of Simultaneity: From Antiquity to Einstein and Beyond* (Baltimore, MD: Johns Hopkins University Press, 2006), 7.

74. Tom Gunning, *The Griffith Project*, vol. 9, ed. Paolo Cherchi Usai and Eileen Bowser (London: British Film Institute, 2005), 99.

75. Miriam Hansen, *Babel to Babylon: Spectatorship in American Silent Film* (Cambridge, MA: Harvard University Press, 1991), 132. For a comparison to Pound's anxieties about the coherence of *The Cantos*, see 136.

76. William M. Drew, *D. W. Griffith's Intolerance: Its Genesis and Its Vision* (Jefferson, NC: McFarland, 1986), 34.

77. The case for this part of the film is made best by Drew (ibid., 20–22). His suggestion is that the lack of explicit causal connection between the beginning and the end of this storyline shows the power of distant forces over the working class.

78. Hansen, *Babel*, 223.

79. Ibid., 211.

80. Ibid., 148. This is her way of putting what is probably the oldest and most consistent objection to *Intolerance*, that the four stories are not really integrated. See, for example, Sergei Eisenstein, *Film and Form: Essays in Film Theory*, tr. Jay Leyda (San Diego, CA: Harcourt, 1977), 243. Interestingly, Deleuze feels that the four achieve an "organic unity." See Gilles Deleuze, *Cinema 1: The Movement Image*, tr. Hugh Tomlinson and Barbara Habberjam (Minneapolis: University of Minnesota Press, 1986), 31.

81. Joyce Jeseniowski, "Style and Technique," *Griffith Project*, vol. 9, 60.

82. Claire Dupré de la Tour, "Intertitles," *Griffith Project*, vol. 9, 81.

83. Theodore Huff, *Intolerance: The Film by David Wark Griffith, Shot-by-Shot Analysis* (New York: Museum of Modern Art, 1966), 9. It should be noted that Huff's "analysis" is actually a shot-by-shot description and that the print on which he relies is not universally considered the most authoritative. See Russell Merritt, "D. W. Griffith's *Intolerance*: Reconstructing an Unattainable Text," *Film History* 4 (1990); 337–75.

84. Huff, *Intolerance*, 18.

85. Ibid., 28.

86. Ibid., 20.

87. Ibid., 2.

88. Hansen, *Babel*, 211.

89. Drew, *Griffith's Intolerance*, 20.

90. Ramsaye, *A Million and One Nights*, 157.

91. Deleuze, *Cinema I*, 32.

92. David Bordwell with Kristin Thompson, *Christopher Nolan: A Labyrinth of Linkages* (Madison, WI: Irvington Way Institute Press, 2013), 48.

93. Ibid., 51.

94. Christopher Nolan, *Inception: The Shooting Script* (San Rafael, CA: Insight, 2010), 200.

95. Todd McGowan, *Out of Time: Desire in Atemporal Cinema* (Minneapolis: University of Minnesota Press, 2011), 31; David Bordwell, *The Way Hollywood Tells It* (Berkeley: University of California Press, 2006), 73.

96. McGowan, *Out of Time*, 33.

97. Christopher Nolan, *Memento & Following* (London: Faber and Faber, 2001), 98.

98. For a useful diagram and discussion, see Andrew Kania, "Introduction," in *Memento*, ed. Andrew Kania (London: Routledge, 2009), 1–21.

99. See Nolan's statement to this effect in *Memento & Following*.

100. Ibid., 147.

101. See Natalie's taunts in ibid., 186. See also John Sutton, "The Feel of the World: Exograms, Habits, and the Confusion of Types of Memory," in Kania, *Memento*, 79.

102. Bordwell, *Christopher Nolan*, 31.

103. Sutton, "Feel of the World," 80; Jacqueline Furby, "About Time Too: From *Interstellar* to *Following*, Christopher Nolan's Continuing Preoccupation with Time-Travel," in *The Cinema of Christopher Nolan: Imagining the Impossible*, ed. Jacqueline Furby and Stuart Joy (London: Wallflower Press, 2015), 262.

104. Nolan, *Memento*, 97–98.

105. Nolan, *Inception*, 103.

106. Andrew Kania, "*Inception*'s Singular Lack of Unity among Christopher Nolan's Puzzle Films," in Furby and Joy, *Cinema of Christopher Nolan*, 179.

107. Bordwell, *Christopher Nolan*, 43.

108. Nolan, *Inception*, 179.

109. Nolan, *Inception*, 180, 184.

110. Note the early scene in which this actually happens. Ibid., 26.

111. Ibid., 192.

112. Jonathan R. Olson, "Nolan's Immersive Allegories of Filmmaking in *Inception* and *The Prestige*," in Furby and Joy, eds., *Cinema of Christopher Nolan*, 54.

113. Jonathan Nolan and Christopher Nolan, *Interstellar: The Complete Screenplay* (New York: Opus, 2014), 59.

114. Nolan and Nolan, *Interstellar*, 89.

115. Kip Thorne, *The Science of Interstellar* (New York: Norton, 2014), 252–75.

116. Nolan and Nolan, *Interstellar*, 144.

117. David Wittenberg, *Time Travel: The Popular Philosophy of Narrative* (New York: Fordham University Press, 2013).

118. Nolan and Nolan, *Interstellar*, 39.

119. Ibid., 142–43.

120. Ibid., xvi.

Conclusion: *Here* and Now

1. Harry Dodge, *The River of the Mother of God* (Los Angeles: Hammer Museum, 2014), 26.

2. See David Wittenberg, *Time Travel: The Popular Philosophy of Narrative* (New York: Fordham University Press, 2013).

3. Paolo Virno, *Déjà Vu and the End of History*, tr. David Broder (London: Verso, 2015), 111.

4. Ibid., 75.

5. Ibid., 135.

6. See also Paolo Virno, *When the Word Becomes Flesh: Language and Human Nature*, tr. Giuseppina Mecchia (South Pasadena, CA: Semiotext(e), 2015).

7. Virno, *Déjà Vu*, 110.

8. Ibid., 93.

9. Ibid., 87.

10. Henri Bergson, *Key Writings*, ed. Keith Ansell Pearson and John Mullarkey (London: Bloomsbury, 2002), 223.

11. Virno, *Déjà Vu*, 24.

12. Ibid.

13. Steven Heller, "The One-Room Time Machine," *Atlantic*, September 25, 2014.

14. Joel Smith, "Richard McGuire Makes a Book," *Five Dials* 35 (2014): 55.

15. Will Eisner, *Comics and Sequential Art* (Tamarac, FL: Poorhouse Press, 1985), 8–10.

16. Eisner, *Comics*, 38.

17. See the mockups displayed at the New York Public Library, some of which were published in *Five Dials* 35 (2014).

18. Richard McGuire, *Here* (New York: Pantheon, 2014), 129. Specific references to *Here* are made difficult by the absence of page numbers. Page numbers included parenthetically in the text were arrived at by counting.

19. Quoted in Heller, "One-Room Time Machine."

INDEX

aion, 27

Abrams, M. H., 32–33

Agamben, Giorgio, 78, 142

Aquinas, Thomas, 77

Arendt, Hannah, 78

Aristotle, 36, 37, 46, 54, 102, 117, 121, 122–23; definition of the instant, 28, 29, 34–35, 55, 168; on the common sense, 7, 45, 50, 62, 80, 100–101; on the experiential present, 40–41, 66; on the present as a point, 21, 22, 23–25, 27, 31, 32, 70; *Physics*, 21, 23, 26, 31, 40–41; *Poetics*, 113, 114; *Sense and Sensibilia*, 40–41, 45

Arnheim, Rudolf, 143, 148–49

Arsham, Daniel, 1

Arstila, Valtteri, 61–62

attraction, the, 147

Auerbach, Erich, 74; *Mimesis*, 74

Augé, Marc, 4

Augustine, 6, 9, 10, 28, 108, 117, 120; *Civitas Dei*, 78; *Confessions*, 41–42; on the present as an instant, 22, 41–42; threefold present of, 64, 68–69, 70–71, 116

Aumont, Jacques, 92

Avanessian, Armen, 126–30; *Present Tense: A Poetics*, 126–30

Bachelard, Gaston, 22, 35, 36

Bakhtin, Mikhail, 114–15

Barr, Alfred, 84

Barr, James, 27

Barthes, Roland, 143–44, 145; *Camera Lucida*, 144

Batchen, Geoffrey, 96

Baudelaire, Charles, 83

Bazin, André, 144

Beaumont, George, 92

Bellour, Raymond, 139, 145, 146, 147

Belting, Hans, 104, 105

Benjamin, Walter, 32, 35, 36, 37, 38, 81, 103; *Arcades Project*, 81; "On the Philosophy of History," 32

Benschop, Ruth, 49

Bergson, Henri, 8, 22, 89, 138, 142, 169

Berlin, Isaiah, 82

binding problem, 7, 62, 100; *See also* common sense

Blake, William, 33

Bloch, Ernst, 36

Bordwell, David, 157

Boring, Edwin, 53

Bowen, Elizabeth, 109–10, 126, 128; *The Heat of the Day*, 109–10

Brand, Stewart, 67

Braun, Marta, 99

Broad, C. D., 56

Brontë, Charlotte, 130; *Jane Eyre*, 111, 126, 130

Brooks, Peter, 111, 119, 121

Brown, Thomas, 52

Buonomano, Dean V., 61

Burke, Edmund, 101–2

Caillebotte, Gustave, 106

Callender, Craig, 90–91

camera obscura, 63

Carnap, Rudolph, 7

A NOTE ON THE TYPE

This book has been composed in Arno, an Old-style serif font in the classic Venetian tradition, designed by Robert Slimbach at Adobe.